FIELD GUIDES

THE NIGHT SKY

Kathryn Hulick

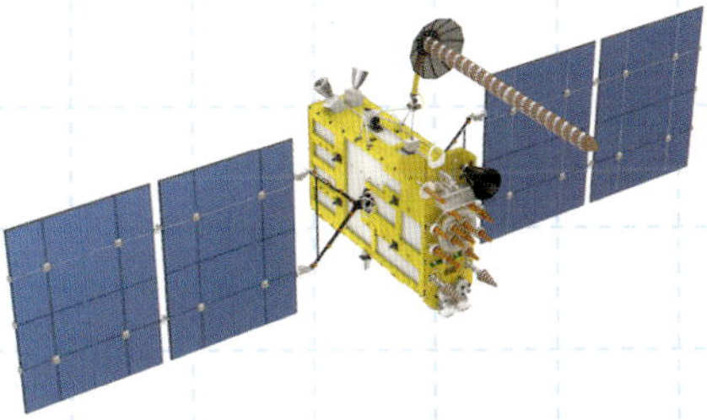

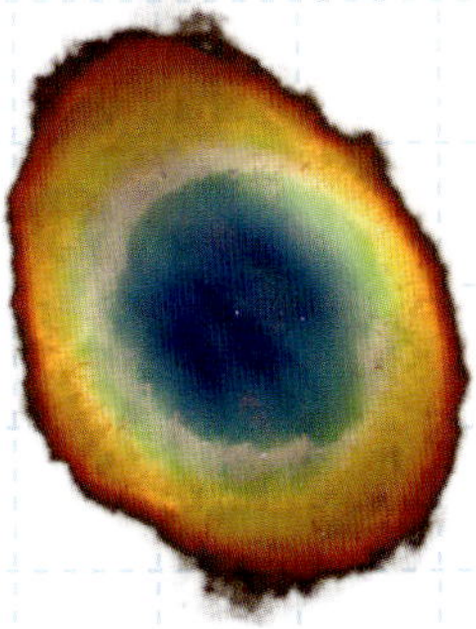

Abdo Reference

An Imprint of Abdo Publishing | abdobooks.com

CONTENTS

Stars

Star Clusters

Nebulae

Galaxies

Comets

Meteor Showers

Atmospheric Phenomena

Human Objects

WHAT IS THE NIGHT SKY?

The night sky inspires wonder and amazement in people of all ages. All major world cultures have told stories about the stars, planets, and Milky Way. Most grouped the stars together into shapes called constellations. Different cultures saw different shapes resembling people, animals, and objects. Astronomers today recognize 88 separate constellations in the night sky.

THE MOVING SKY

- During the course of a night, constellations appear to rotate around the sky. The timing of this rotation changes over the course of a year. New constellations become visible just after sunset, and other ones disappear beyond the horizon.
- The stars themselves aren't moving like this. Earth spins on its axis and orbits the sun. These motions change our view of the stars. Some constellations and night sky objects are visible only from the Northern Hemisphere. Others are visible only from the Southern Hemisphere.
- All of the objects in our solar system orbit around the sun. Most of them move along a nearly flat plane called the ecliptic. The sun follows the line of the ecliptic during the daytime. Planets move along this same path but are easiest to see at night.

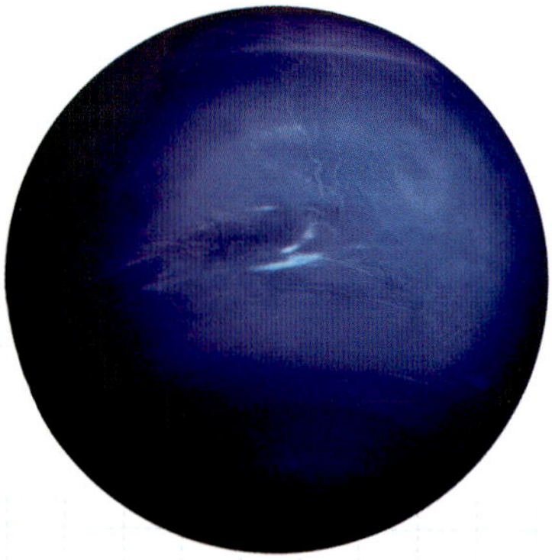

SEEING IN THE DARK

In the past, the night sky was clear and bright everywhere. But today artificial lights shining from homes, buildings, vehicles, and more cause light pollution. In cities and suburbs, light pollution washes out everything except the very brightest stars and planets. The best night sky viewing experiences are in dark rural areas. Most of the sights in this book are visible to the naked eye in a very dark sky. Binoculars or telescopes can provide more detail and bring dim objects into view.

Astronomers use a measurement called magnitude to tell how bright something appears in the sky. The scale goes from negative to positive. The lower the number, the brighter an object is. For example, the moon is the brightest thing in the night sky. Its magnitude is about -12.6. In a completely dark sky, most people can see things as dim as magnitude +6.0. Light pollution may limit visibility to magnitude +2.0 and brighter.

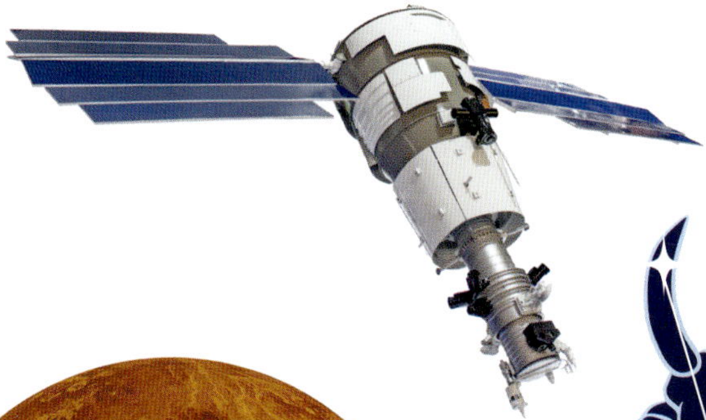

HOW TO USE THIS BOOK

Tab shows the night sky object category.

The night sky object's name appears here.

MOONS

IO

In 1610, Italian astronom... ...piter through one of the world's first telesc... ...is tool, he saw four moons. Astronomers still call them the Galilean satellites. They are the largest of Jupiter's many moons. Io is one of these moons. It is the closest one to Jupiter. Volcanoes are scattered on Io's surface. Some spew lava as far as 250 miles (402 km) into space.

HOW TO SPOT

Where: Lined up with Jupiter

When: Whenever Jupiter is visible

...'l telescope

...e: +5.0

...eter of ...s (3,643 km)

The *Voyager 2* spacecraft took photos of volcanoes erupting on Io.

FUN FACT

Io is the only world other than Earth known to have active volcanoes.

How to Spot boxes explain where to find the night sky object and what it looks like.

Fun Facts give interesting information about night sky objects.

EUROPA

Europa is one of Jupiter's moons. It has a very smooth, shiny surface of ice that is several miles thick, crisscrossed with cracks and streaks. This icy world reflects lots of light, but binoculars or a telescope are required to see Europa because it is so close to Jupiter in the sky. Scientists have found evidence that a vast liquid ocean flows beneath Europa's surface. This moon has an atmosphere that contains oxygen, though not very much of it.

HOW TO SPOT

Where: Lined up with Jupiter
When: Whenever Jupiter is visible
How: Binoculars or a small telescope
Magnitude: +5.3
Size: Diameter of 1,940 miles (3,120 km)

LIFE BENEATH THE ICE?

Life thrives beneath ice in Earth's oceans. Some scientists think the subsurface ocean on Europa could be home to alien microbes. Searching for life there is one of NASA's top goals. It planned to launch the *Europa Clipper* spacecraft to study Europa's ocean.

21

This paragraph gives information about the night sky object.

Images show the night sky object.

Sidebars provide additional information about the topic.

MERCURY

Mercury, the closest planet to the sun, is named after the Roman god of messages and speed. It is the fastest planet in the solar system, zipping along at 29 miles per second (47 km/s). The sun's light usually hides this planet from view. But at certain times of the year, the planet is visible near the horizon just after sunset or just before sunrise. At its brightest, Mercury shines with a yellow-orange hue, more brightly than any star.

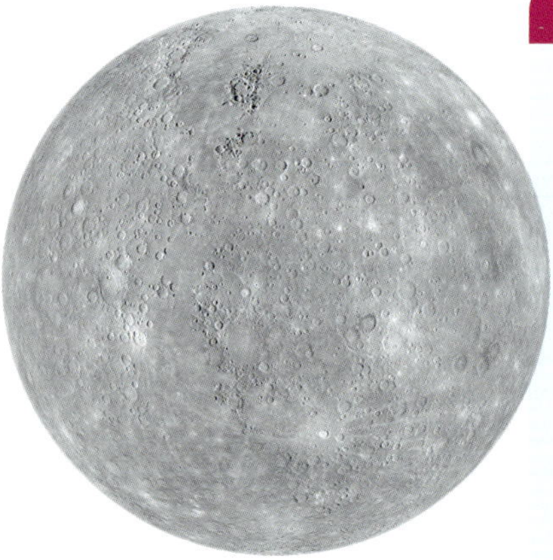

HOW TO SPOT

Where: Northern or Southern Hemisphere

When: Varies; use a sky chart to check

How: Naked eyes

Location: Very close to the horizon, near where the sun sets or rises

Distance from the Sun: 36 million miles (58 million km)

Magnitude: As bright as -1.9

Size: Diameter of 3,032 miles (4,880 km)

Special telescopes can be used to safely watch Mercury pass in front of the sun.

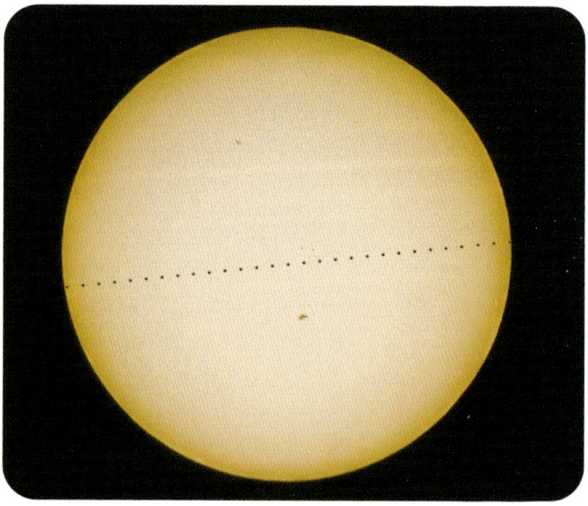

VENUS

Venus is the brightest planet in the night sky and the closest planet to Earth. It is often called the morning star or the evening star, since it rises and sets each day, just like the sun. This planet would not be pleasant to visit. It has a thick, heavy atmosphere filled with clouds of sulfuric acid, a chemical that burns skin and smells like rotten eggs. The temperature near the surface is hot enough to melt lead, and the air pressure would crush a submarine. The ancient Maya associated Venus with their most powerful god.

FUN FACT
Venus spins very slowly. Its day is longer than its year.

HOW TO SPOT

Where: Northern or Southern Hemisphere
When: For a few hours after sunset or before sunrise
How: Naked eyes
Location: Near the horizon where the sun sets or rises
Distance from the Sun: 67 million miles (108 million km)
Magnitude: As bright as -4.5
Size: Diameter of 7,520 miles (12,100 km)

MARS

Mars is often called the red planet. It looks orange or reddish from far away, but from the surface its sky is pink and the ground is mostly dark yellow. Mars is the only planet where humans have landed robotic rovers. In 2021, the NASA rovers *Curiosity* and *Perseverance* and the Chinese rover *Zhurong* were all studying the planet. Researchers have learned that billions of years ago, liquid water flowed on Mars. Now the planet is cold, dusty, and rocky, with almost no atmosphere.

HOW TO SPOT

Where: Northern or Southern Hemisphere
When: Varies; use a sky chart to check
How: Naked eyes
Location: Following the sun after it sets
Distance from the Sun: 142 million miles (229 million km)
Magnitude: As bright as -2.9
Size: Diameter of 4,212 miles (6,779 km)

FUN FACT

The largest volcano in the solar system, Olympus Mons, is located on Mars.

HUMANS ON MARS

Elon Musk, founder of the company SpaceX, plans to send humans to Mars. NASA, the US government space agency, has plans to get people there too. The trip will take six to nine months in each direction. It will be a risky journey. Mars has no breathable air, and it is colder than Antarctica.

CERES

Millions of rocky chunks called asteroids orbit in a band between Mars and Jupiter. This is called the asteroid belt. The asteroids here range in size from large boulders to miniature worlds. The largest of them is Ceres. In 2006, astronomers promoted it from an asteroid to a dwarf planet. Ceres contains lots of water, but most likely all of it is frozen. Viewing Ceres is very tricky since it moves from night to night and can be viewed only through binoculars or a telescope. Use online resources to locate it.

HOW TO SPOT

Where: Northern or Southern Hemisphere
When: Varies; use a sky chart to check
How: Binoculars or a telescope
Location: Varies; use online resources
Distance from the Sun: 257 million miles (414 million km)
Magnitude: As bright as +7.0
Size: Diameter of 592 miles (952 km)

The *Dawn* spacecraft arrived at Ceres in 2015.

VESTA

Vesta is the second-largest body in the asteroid belt between Mars and Jupiter. But it is the brightest because its shiny surface reflects more light than Ceres does. When Vesta travels closest to Earth, it may be visible to the naked eye in a very dark sky. Vesta doesn't qualify as a dwarf planet because it isn't quite large enough and its shape isn't quite spherical. However, scientists believe it has a planet-like structure with a core and crust. In Roman mythology, Vesta is the goddess of home and the hearth.

FUN FACT

Asteroids and comets sometimes smash into planets. In case astronomers spot one that could collide with Earth, engineers are thinking of ways they could knock it off course.

A close-up view of Vesta from the *Dawn* spacecraft

HOW TO SPOT

Where: Northern or Southern Hemisphere

When: Varies; use a sky chart to check

How: Binoculars

Location: Varies; use a sky chart to check

Distance from the Sun: 219 million miles (352 million km)

Magnitude: As bright as +5.1

Size: Diameter of 326 miles (525 km)

JUPITER

Jupiter, named for the king of the Roman gods, is the largest planet in the solar system. It has twice the mass of all the other planets combined. Seventy-nine moons orbit around the giant planet, and more will likely be discovered. Jupiter is made of layers of swirling gases surrounding a molten metal core. Jupiter's most famous feature is the Great Red Spot. This is a storm that is almost twice the size of Earth. The *Juno* spacecraft has been studying Jupiter and its moons since 2016.

HOW TO SPOT

Where: Northern or Southern Hemisphere

When: Varies; use a sky chart to check

How: Naked eyes

Location: In any one of the 12 zodiac constellations

Distance from the Sun: 484 million miles (779 million km)

Magnitude: -1.6 to -2.6

Size: Diameter of 88,846 miles (142,984 km)

FINDING THE PLANETS

The planets in our solar system are much closer to us than the stars we see in the night sky. This means that while the stars appear in consistent patterns, the planets move around throughout the year. There is no single place to find Jupiter or other planets in the night sky. However, the planets can be found near the 12 zodiac constellations. Ancient people noted that the planets remained near this line of constellations in the sky. This results from the fact that the objects in our solar system travel around the sun in a flat disc shape.

SATURN

Many people consider Saturn to be the most beautiful planet to observe because of its stunning rings, which are made of swirling pieces of rocks and ice. The rings are thousands of miles wide but just 30 feet (9 m) thick in some places. The spacecraft *Cassini* spent 13 years observing Saturn and its many moons. As a gas giant, Saturn has no solid ground. Its atmosphere is filled with swirling winds that blow harder than the strongest hurricane on Earth.

FUN FACT

Saturn has a very low density. It would float on water—if you could find a lake big enough to hold it.

HOW TO SPOT

Where: Northern or Southern Hemisphere
When: Varies; use a sky chart to check
How: Naked eyes (use a telescope to see the rings)
Location: In any one of the 12 zodiac constellations
Distance from the Sun: 886 million miles (1,426 million km)
Magnitude: +0.6 to +1.5
Size: Diameter of 72,367 miles (116,464 km)

URANUS

Uranus is the only sideways planet. As it travels around the sun, it spins on its side instead of spinning upright, as the other planets do. This means that seasons on Uranus last 20 Earth years or longer. The planet is icy and windy with a unique blue-green color and very faint rings. Ancient people didn't know about Uranus. William Herschel discovered the planet with a telescope in 1781. Most of Uranus's 27 moons are named after characters from William Shakespeare's works.

HOW TO SPOT

Where: Northern or Southern Hemisphere

When: Varies; use a sky chart to check

How: Binoculars

Location: In any one of the 12 zodiac constellations

Distance from the Sun: 1.8 billion miles (2.9 billion km)

Magnitude: +5.3

Size: Diameter of 31,518 miles (50,724 km)

A small telescope or binoculars can be used to see Uranus in the night sky.

NEPTUNE

Neptune is the solar system's farthest planet from the sun. It is bright blue in color and was named after the Roman god of the sea. In fact, Neptune is almost entirely an ocean, but instead of salt water it is made of a thick, slushy mixture of water, ammonia, and methane. Winds swirl in the atmosphere above, reaching speeds of 1,500 miles per hour (2,400 kmh). The planet has reddish rings and 14 moons. Its largest moon is Triton.

HOW TO SPOT

Where: Northern or Southern Hemisphere

When: Varies; use a sky chart to check

How: Small telescope

Location: In any one of the 12 zodiac constellations

Distance from the Sun: 2.8 billion miles (4.5 billion km)

Magnitude: +7.8

Size: Diameter of 30,599 miles (49,244 km)

The *Voyager 2* spacecraft launched from Earth in 1977. It reached Neptune in 1989.

PLUTO

Pluto is a small, rocky, frigid dwarf planet. Seeing this dim, distant world requires a large telescope. Clyde Tombaugh discovered Pluto in 1930. For decades, it was considered the ninth planet in the solar system. But then astronomers discovered that Pluto is just one of many icy objects that form a huge ring called the Kuiper Belt. Instead of adding more planets, in 2006 they decided to call Pluto a dwarf planet. Pluto follows a diagonal, stretched-out orbit. Occasionally, it comes closer to the sun than Neptune.

HOW TO SPOT

Where: Northern or Southern Hemisphere
When: Varies; use a sky chart to check
How: Large telescope
Location: Varies; use a sky chart to check
Distance from the Sun: 3.7 billion miles (5.9 billion km)
Magnitude: +13.6
Size: Diameter of 1,430 miles (2,302 km)

The *New Horizons* probe studied Pluto and Charon in 2015.

FUN FACT

Pluto's moon Charon is half Pluto's size. Together they are sometimes called a double dwarf planet system.

THE MOON

Many cultures have revered the moon as a god or goddess, and it is still a beloved sight in the night sky. It is visible everywhere, even in places with a lot of light pollution. The moon appears to shine brightly, but in fact it is reflecting sunlight. As the moon orbits Earth, it reflects less sunlight and wanes, becoming thinner until it reaches the dark new moon phase. Then it waxes, becoming thicker until it is full again. This cycle takes approximately 29 days.

HOW TO SPOT

Where: Varies

When: Any night except during a new moon

How: Naked eyes

Distance: 238,855 miles (384,400 km) from Earth

Magnitude: -12.6

Size: Diameter of 2,159 miles (3,475 km)

MOON LANDINGS

The moon is the only place beyond Earth that humans have visited. Neil Armstrong and Buzz Aldrin set foot on the moon for the first time on July 20, 1969. On later visits, astronauts hit golf balls on the moon and drove a lunar rover.

LUNAR ECLIPSE

The moon orbits Earth on a tilted path. Usually, when the moon is on the opposite side of Earth from the sun, we see a full moon that shines brightly. But a few times each year, the sun, Earth, and moon line up just right, and Earth's shadow falls across the full moon. This is called a lunar eclipse. Some ancient Inca people believed that a lunar eclipse meant a jaguar was attacking the moon. They would make lots of noise to scare it away.

FUN FACT
The moon doesn't disappear from view during an eclipse. Instead, it appears red or orange.

HOW TO SPOT

Where: Varies; check NASA's website for locations
When: Usually twice each year; check NASA's website for dates
How: Naked eyes
Duration: Typically several hours

IO

In 1610, Italian astronomer Galileo Galilei looked at Jupiter through one of the world's first telescopes. Using this tool, he saw four moons. Astronomers still call them the Galilean satellites. They are the largest of Jupiter's many moons. Io is one of these moons. It is the closest one to Jupiter. Volcanoes are scattered on Io's surface. Some spew lava as far as 250 miles (402 km) into space.

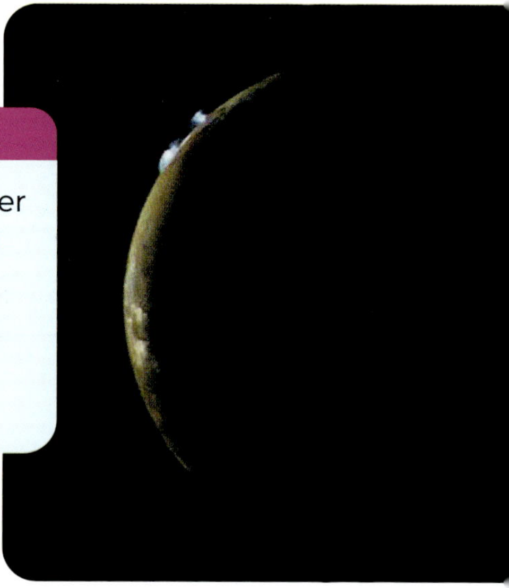

HOW TO SPOT

Where: Lined up with Jupiter
When: Whenever Jupiter is visible
How: Small telescope
Magnitude: +5.0
Size: Diameter of 2,264 miles (3,643 km)

The *Voyager 2* spacecraft took photos of volcanoes erupting on Io.

FUN FACT
Io is the only world other than Earth known to have active volcanoes.

EUROPA

Europa is one of Jupiter's moons. It has a very smooth, shiny surface of ice that is several miles thick, crisscrossed with cracks and streaks. This icy world reflects lots of light, but binoculars or a telescope are required to see Europa because it is so close to Jupiter in the sky. Scientists have found evidence that a vast liquid ocean flows beneath Europa's surface. This moon has an atmosphere that contains oxygen, though not very much of it.

HOW TO SPOT

Where: Lined up with Jupiter

When: Whenever Jupiter is visible

How: Binoculars or a small telescope

Magnitude: +5.3

Size: Diameter of 1,940 miles (3,120 km)

LIFE BENEATH THE ICE?

Life thrives beneath ice in Earth's oceans. Some scientists think the subsurface ocean on Europa could be home to alien microbes. Searching for life there is one of NASA's top goals. It planned to launch the *Europa Clipper* spacecraft to study Europa's ocean.

GANYMEDE

Ganymede, another one of Jupiter's moons, is the largest moon in the solar system. It is bigger than the planet Mercury. Due to its large size, it can be viewed through binoculars. Ganymede is the only moon with a magnetic field. This field traps charged particles, creating glowing auroras at the moon's north and south poles, just like the northern and southern lights on Earth.

HOW TO SPOT

Where: Lined up with Jupiter
When: Whenever Jupiter is visible
How: Binoculars
Magnitude: +4.6
Size: Diameter of 3,270 miles (5,262 km)

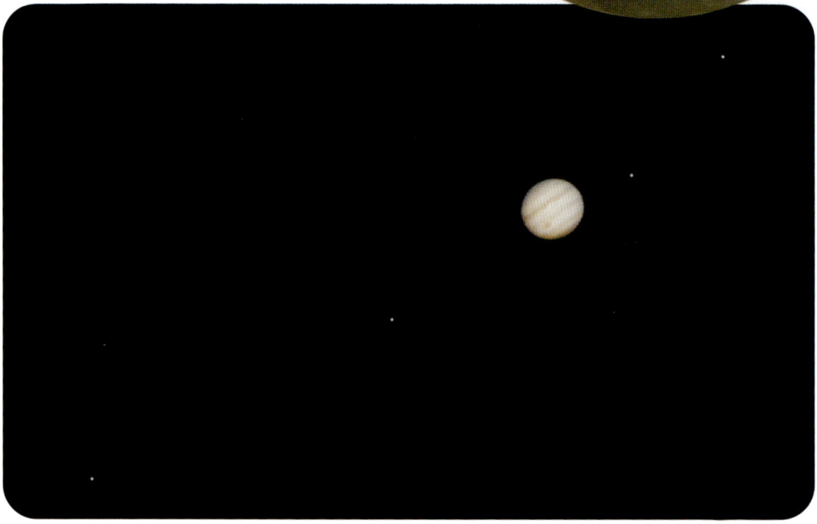

Jupiter's four largest moons, including Ganymede, can be seen through a telescope near the gas giant.

CALLISTO

Of the four Galilean moons, Callisto orbits the farthest from Jupiter. Its surface is speckled with many light spots. All of them are craters left behind after asteroids or comets struck the surface. In fact, this moon has more craters than any other object in the solar system. Its surface may be billions of years old.

HOW TO SPOT

Where: Lined up with Jupiter

When: Whenever Jupiter is visible

How: Binoculars

Magnitude: +5.7

Size: Diameter of 2,996 miles (4,821 km)

FUN FACT

Jupiter has dangerous radiation around it. Callisto's distance from the planet means the radiation is lower there, so experts believe it could be a good place for a future human base near Jupiter.

TITAN

Saturn has 82 known moons, but only seven can be viewed from Earth through a typical telescope. Titan is the largest and easiest to observe. It's also the only moon in the solar system with a significant atmosphere. The yellow, hazy sky is filled with nitrogen and methane. The moon is so cold that methane and ethane, which are gases on Earth, are found in liquid form. The Dutch astronomer Christiaan Huygens discovered Titan in 1655 using a telescope. In 2005, the *Huygens* probe landed on Titan to study this moon.

Titan is larger than our moon but much smaller than Earth.

FUN FACT
Methane and ethane fall as rain and flow as rivers and lakes on Titan.

HOW TO SPOT

Where: Next to Saturn
When: Whenever Saturn is visible
How: Telescope
Magnitude: +8.5
Size: Diameter of 3,200 miles (5,149 km)

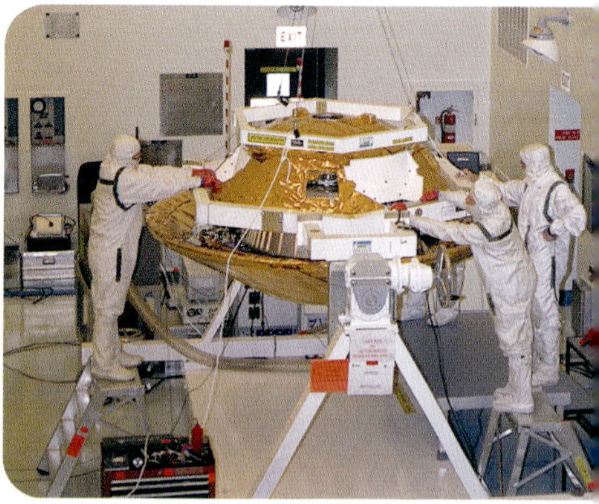

Scientists work on the *Huygens* probe in 1997.

RHEA

A good telescope can reveal six other moons of Saturn in addition to Titan. They are Rhea, Tethys, Enceladus, Iapetus, Dione, and Mimas. NASA describes Rhea, the second largest of Saturn's moons, as a "frozen, dirty snowball" because it is composed of ice and rock mixed together. Rhea is the only moon known to have a ring around it. In Greek mythology, Rhea was the mother of Zeus, king of the gods.

HOW TO SPOT

Where: Next to Saturn
When: Whenever Saturn is visible
How: Telescope
Magnitude: +10
Size: Diameter of 950 miles (1,528 km)

ENCELADUS

Enceladus is among Saturn's most interesting moons. Like several other moons, it most likely has a liquid ocean beneath its frozen surface. What make it unique are huge jets that spray this ocean out into space. The spacecraft *Cassini* grabbed samples of this spray. Scientists learned that this ocean has the chemical ingredients that might make life possible there.

ANDROMEDA *(THE CHAINED MAIDEN)*

Andromeda belongs to a group of constellations that tell a story from Greek mythology. In the story, Andromeda's mother, Cassiopeia, angers the gods. The gods tell Cassiopeia's husband, Cepheus, to sacrifice their daughter to the sea monster Cetus. The hero Perseus arrives just in time on the winged horse Pegasus to save her. All these constellations are located in the same region of the sky. Andromeda can be difficult to see unless the sky is very dark.

HOW TO SPOT

Where: Best viewed from the Northern Hemisphere

When: Evening in October and November

How: Naked eyes

Location: Between Pegasus and Cassiopeia

Size: Medium

AQUARIUS *(THE WATER BEARER)*

Aquarius is a large but faint constellation representing a man pouring water from a jar. It is located in a section of sky known as the Sea, which is home to several other water-themed constellations, including Cetus and Pisces. A very dark sky is required to see Aquarius.

HOW TO SPOT

Where: Northern or Southern Hemisphere

When: Evening in September and October

How: Naked eyes

Location: Between Capricornus and Pisces

Size: Large

FUN FACT

Two stars in Aquarius have names that mean "luck of the king" and "luck of lucks."

THE ZODIAC SIGNS

Aquarius is one of 12 constellations that make up the zodiac. The others are Aries, Taurus, Gemini, Cancer, Leo, Virgo, Libra, Scorpius, Sagittarius, Capricornus, and Pisces. These constellations mark the path through the sky that the sun and the planets appear to follow. Horoscopes based on the zodiac are fun, but they are not at all scientific. The positions of distant stars can't influence people's lives.

AQUILA *(THE EAGLE)*

The head, outstretched wings, and tail of Aquila form a plus sign. The name of Aquila's brightest star, Altair, means "bird" in Arabic. In the mythologies of China, Japan, and Korea, though, the star represents a herdsman who falls in love with a king's daughter. She is represented by the star Vega. The pair ends up banished to either side of the Milky Way, which represents a river. They can see each other only once every year. Tanabata, the Star Festival, is an annual holiday in Japan marking the day when the lovers are allowed to be together.

HOW TO SPOT

Where: Best viewed in the Northern Hemisphere

When: Evening in August and September

How: Naked eyes

Location: Near Cygnus, on the Milky Way

Size: Medium

FUN FACT

In Greek mythology, Aquila is the eagle that carried thunderbolts for Zeus.

ARIES *(THE RAM)*

In Greek mythology, Aries the ram had a fleece made of gold. A dragon guarded the fleece until the hero Jason stole it. Aries is the first of the 12 zodiac constellations, but it can be difficult to see. A dark sky is necessary to find it. The stars of Aries form a straight line that curves at one end.

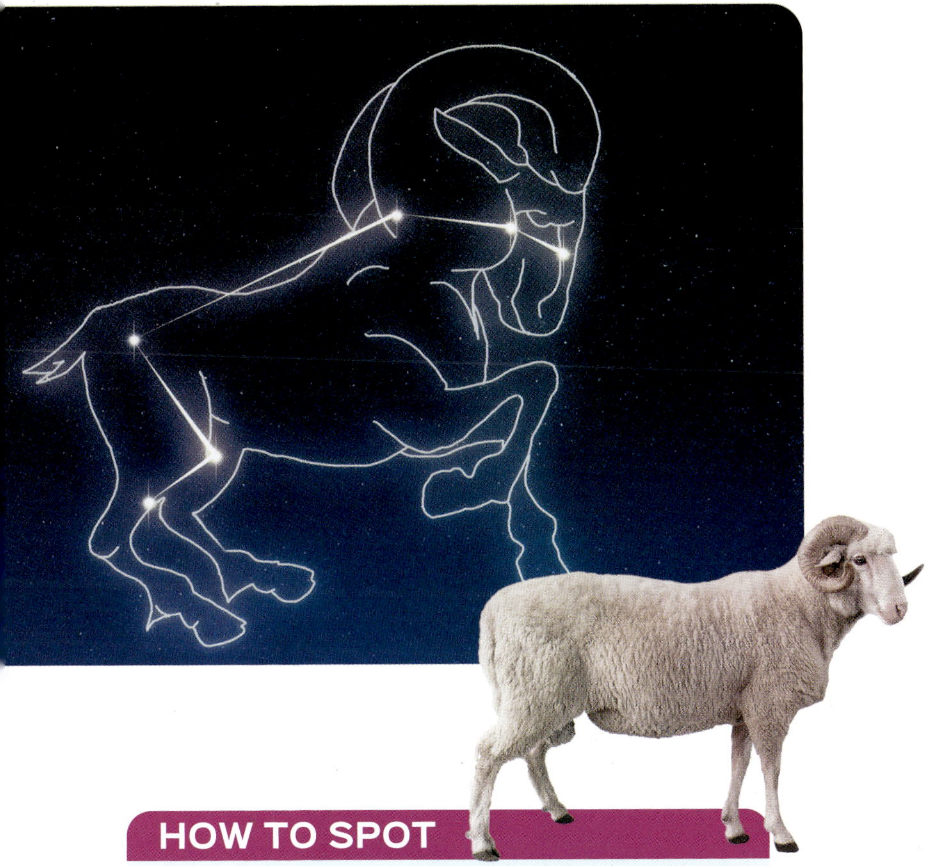

HOW TO SPOT

Where: Northern or Southern Hemisphere
When: Evening in November and December
How: Naked eyes
Location: Between Pisces and Taurus
Size: Small

BOÖTES *(THE HERDSMAN)*

Boötes (pronounced "boo-OH-tees") is visible from the Northern Hemisphere for most of the year. It is an easy constellation to spot because it contains Arcturus, one of the brightest stars. The handle of the Big Dipper points toward this star. The constellation is supposed to represent a person, but it looks more like a kite with Arcturus at its base. The famous ancient Greek story the *Odyssey* mentions Boötes.

HOW TO SPOT

Where: Northern Hemisphere

When: Best viewed in the evening in May and June

How: Naked eyes

Location: Near the Big Dipper

Size: Large

FUN FACT

An area of space near Boötes is almost empty of galaxies. Astronomers call it the Great Void.

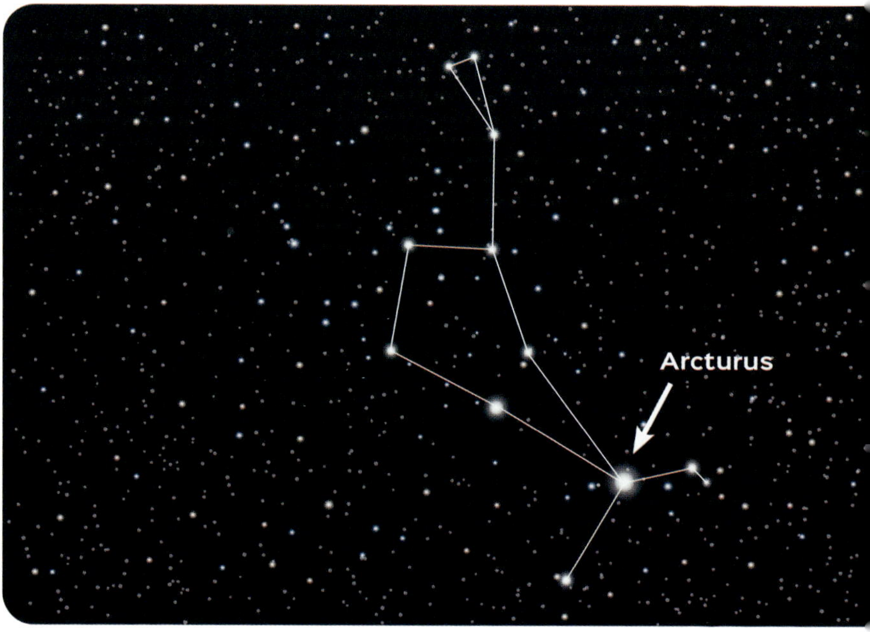

CANCER *(THE CRAB)*

Cancer is the dimmest of all the zodiac constellations, so a dark sky is necessary for viewing it. In the Northern Hemisphere, it looks like an upside-down letter Y. In the Southern Hemisphere, though, it looks right side up. In Greek mythology, the goddess Hera sent this crab to distract Heracles during a battle with the monster Hydra. According to one version of the story, the hero kicked the crab into the sky.

HOW TO SPOT

Where: Northern or Southern Hemisphere

When: Evening in March and April

How: Naked eyes

Location: Between Gemini and Leo

Size: Small

CANIS MAJOR *(THE LARGER DOG)*

Canis Major contains the brightest star in the night sky, Sirius. The constellation is visible from the Northern Hemisphere during the winter just above the southern horizon. From the Southern Hemisphere, it climbs much higher in the sky. Canis Major and a nearby tiny constellation called Canis Minor (the Smaller Dog) seem to follow the constellation of Orion the Hunter across the sky. They represent his hunting dogs.

HOW TO SPOT

Where: Best viewed in the Southern Hemisphere
When: Evening in January and February
How: Naked eyes
Location: Following Orion
Size: Medium

FUN FACT

According to a Greek myth, Canis Major was the dog Laelaps, a hound so fast that no prey could escape it.

CAPRICORNUS *(THE SEA GOAT)*

The name Capricornus means "horned goat" in Latin, but this zodiac constellation is drawn as a mythical beast that is half goat and half fish. The ancient Sumerians and Babylonians called this constellation a goat-fish as far back as 2000 BCE. Capricornus is not very bright, but it forms a distinct triangular shape in a dark enough sky.

HOW TO SPOT

Where: Northern or Southern Hemisphere

When: Evening in August and September

How: Naked eyes

Location: Between Sagittarius and Aquarius

Size: Medium

CASSIOPEIA *(THE QUEEN)*

Cassiopeia is one of the easiest constellations to identify. Its bright stars form a distinctive W shape that represents a seated woman. As it rotates around Polaris, the North Star, it sometimes looks more like an M instead. In Greek mythology, Queen Cassiopeia's boasting angers the gods, leading to her daughter Andromeda getting chained to a rock and Perseus rescuing her. The Sami people of Scandinavia saw this constellation as the antlers of a moose, and the Chukchi of Siberia saw it as a group of reindeer. Cassiopeia is visible all year in the Northern Hemisphere.

HOW TO SPOT

Where: Northern Hemisphere
When: Best viewed in the evening in October and November
How: Naked eyes
Location: Facing the North Star
Size: Medium

FUN FACT

In 1572, a bright new star appeared in Cassiopeia, fading after two years. It was actually a supernova, or an exploding star.

THE FIRST PEOPLE

Cassiopeia and the Big Dipper are located on opposite sides of the North Star. In Navajo tradition, these two constellations are Revolving Woman and Revolving Man. The North Star is their home fire. They represent the first people and lead all the other constellations.

CENTAURUS *(THE CENTAUR)*

Centaurus is a large and bright constellation that can be seen almost all year from the Southern Hemisphere. It is visible in parts of the Northern Hemisphere in May. In Greek mythology, Centaurus represents Chiron the centaur. He was a wise teacher who was half man and half horse. Two of the brightest stars in the sky, Alpha Centauri and Beta Centauri, form the front legs of the centaur.

HOW TO SPOT

Where: Southern Hemisphere

When: Best viewed in the evening in April and May

How: Naked eyes

Location: Wrapping around Crux

Size: Large

CEPHEUS *(THE KING)*

In Greek mythology, Cepheus was Cassiopeia's husband and Andromeda's father. When the gods sent Cetus the sea monster toward Cepheus's kingdom, Cepheus asked an oracle what to do. The oracle told him he had to sacrifice his daughter to save everyone else. This constellation is very easy to spot. Its five bright stars resemble a house with a square bottom and a peaked roof. Cepheus is visible all year in the Northern Hemisphere but not from the Southern Hemisphere.

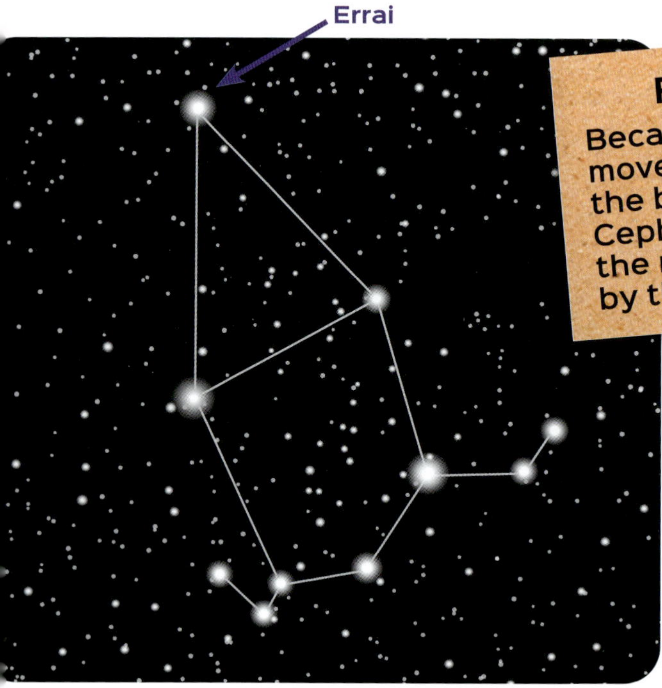

FUN FACT

Because of Earth's movement, Errai, the brightest star in Cepheus, will become the new North Star by the year 4000.

HOW TO SPOT

Where: Northern Hemisphere
When: Best viewed in the evening in September and October
How: Naked eyes
Location: Beside Cassiopeia
Size: Large

CETUS *(THE WHALE)*

Cetus is a very large but faint constellation located in the region of the sky known as the Sea. In Greek mythology, it represents the sea monster sent to devour Andromeda. Early Christians saw it as the whale that swallowed Jonah in a story from the Bible. The constellation looks like a small circle of stars connected to a larger oval-shaped group. The star that connects these two groups, Mira, was the first variable star ever discovered. Over 11 months, it gets quite bright, then fades until it is invisible to the naked eye.

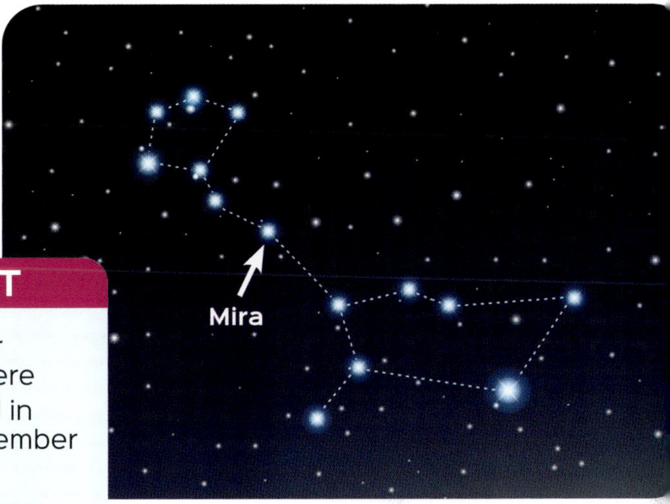

HOW TO SPOT

Where: Northern or Southern Hemisphere

When: Best viewed in the evening in November

How: Naked eyes

Location: Near Pisces and Taurus

Size: Large

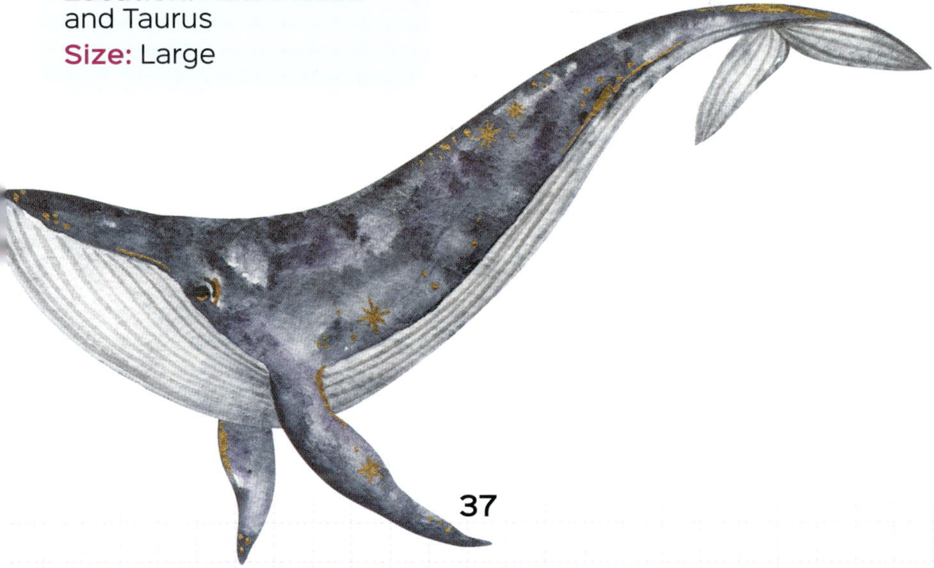

CORONA BOREALIS

(THE NORTHERN CROWN)

Corona Borealis is a very small constellation, but it has a distinctive shape. It resembles a necklace or tiara. Fittingly, it represents a crown. In Greek mythology, this crown belonged to the princess Ariadne. She helped the hero Theseus escape from a labyrinth. In Celtic mythology, this constellation represents a castle called Caer Arianrhod where human souls go after they die. Some Aboriginal cultures in Australia have called this constellation a boomerang.

HOW TO SPOT

Where: Best viewed from the Northern Hemisphere
When: Evening in June and July
How: Naked eyes
Location: Between Boötes and Hercules
Size: Small

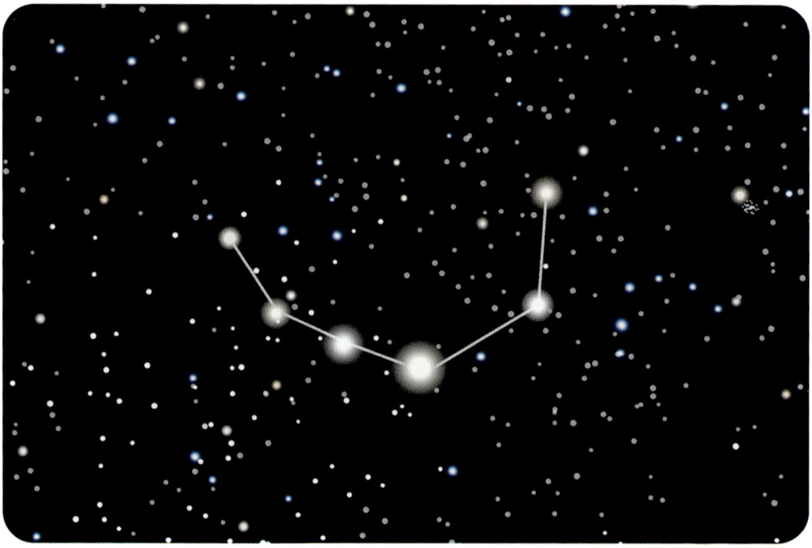

CRUX *(THE SOUTHERN CROSS)*

Crux may be small, but it is the most famous constellation in the Southern Hemisphere and is visible there almost any night of the year. Its four brightest stars form the shape of a cross or kite. Just as Ursa Major and the Big Dipper can be used to find north, this constellation helps a skilled navigator find south. Crux has featured in the mythology of many cultures. The Māori, who live in what is now New Zealand, see it as an anchor. In coastal Australia, it has been seen as a stingray, while inland it is an eagle's footprint.

HOW TO SPOT

Where: Southern Hemisphere
When: Best viewed in the evening in May
How: Naked eyes
Location: Surrounded on three sides by Centaurus
Size: Small

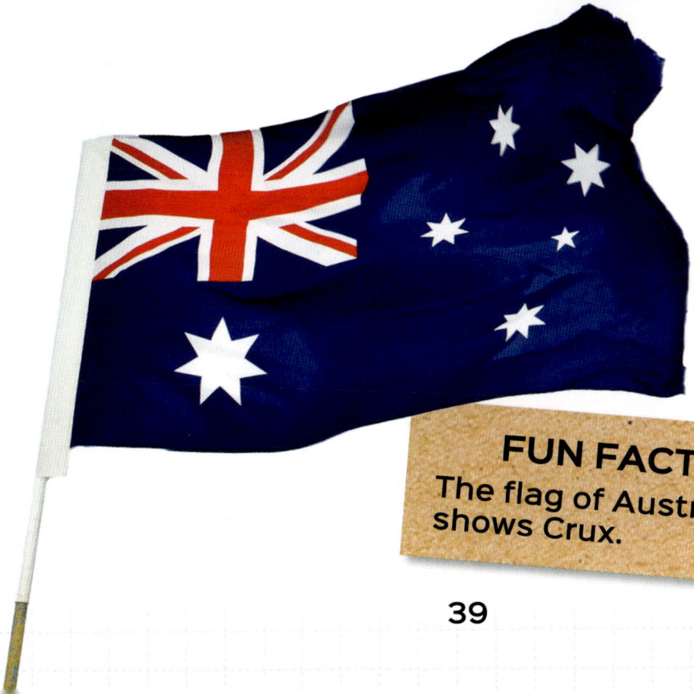

FUN FACT

The flag of Australia shows Crux.

CYGNUS *(THE SWAN)*

The stars of Cygnus form the shape of a cross that represents a bird with outstretched wings. The bird seems to be flying down the Milky Way, so this constellation helps indicate the Milky Way's path through the sky. The brightest star in this constellation is called Deneb. It forms a shape called the Summer Triangle along with Altair and Vega. The central stars of Cygnus are also called the Northern Cross.

HOW TO SPOT

Where: Best viewed in the Northern Hemisphere
When: Evening in August and September
How: Naked eyes
Location: Aligned with the Milky Way, near Pegasus
Size: Large

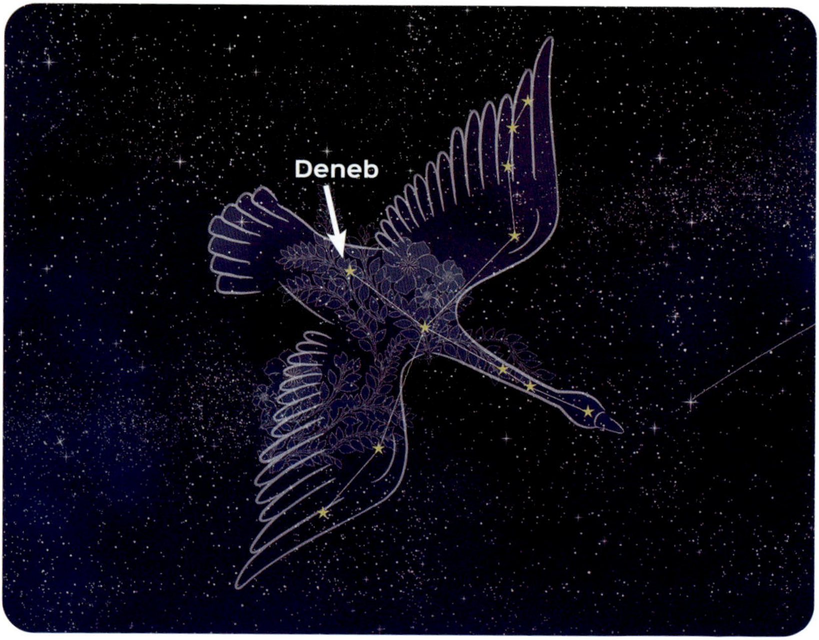

DRACO *(THE DRAGON)*

Draco is a large but not very bright constellation located right next to the North Star. Because of its position, Draco is visible all year from the Northern Hemisphere but never from the Southern Hemisphere. A small group of four stars forms the head of the constellation, which is a dragon. Its tail snakes around, ending between the Big and Little Dippers. Some early Christians identified Draco as the serpent from a story in the Bible.

HOW TO SPOT

Where: Northern Hemisphere

When: Best viewed in the evening in May and June

How: Naked eyes

Location: Beside Ursa Minor

Size: Large

FUN FACT

In Hindu tradition, Draco is an alligator. The ancient Egyptians saw it as a crocodile.

ERIDANUS *(THE RIVER)*

Eridanus is a long but faint constellation that can be seen only in very dark skies. It forms the shape of a winding river. It represented the Euphrates to the Babylonians, the Nile to the ancient Egyptians, and the Ganges to the people of ancient India. The river begins near the hunter Orion's feet. In the Northern Hemisphere, it curves down and disappears behind the horizon. In Southern skies, it extends all the way to the bright star Achernar. This star's name means "the end of the river" in Arabic.

HOW TO SPOT

Where: Best viewed in the Southern Hemisphere
When: Evening in December and January
How: Naked eyes
Location: Beginning near Orion
Size: Large

GEMINI *(THE TWINS)*

Gemini looks like two stick figures holding hands. Their heads are two very bright stars located right next to each other named Castor and Pollux. In Greek mythology, Pollux was immortal, but his twin, Castor, was not. When Castor was killed, Pollux begged the gods to bring him back. Zeus agreed, but the twins had to spend half their time in the heavens. In China, these twin stars likely represented the concept of yin and yang. This is the idea that opposites, such as dark and light or male and female, must rely on each other.

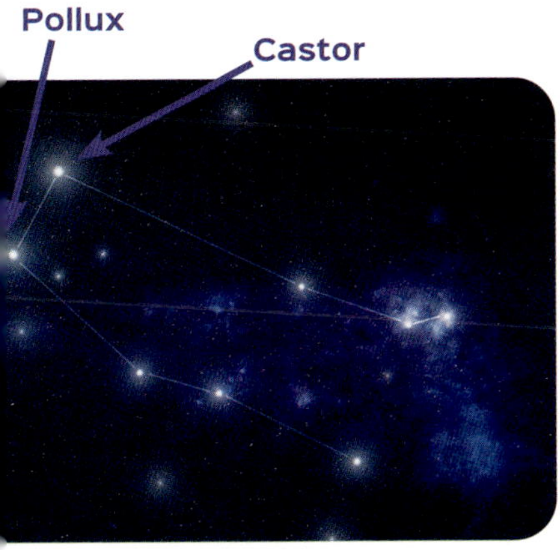

HOW TO SPOT

Where: Northern or Southern Hemisphere

When: Evening in February and March

How: Naked eyes

Location: Between Cancer and Taurus

Size: Medium

FUN FACT

Castor appears to be one star to the naked eye, but it is actually made up of three pairs of binary stars.

HERCULES *(THE STRONGMAN)*

Hercules is the Roman name for Heracles, a hero from Greek mythology who is famous for his strength and cunning. During summertime in the Northern Hemisphere, Hercules is almost directly overhead. The stars of this constellation are not very bright, so a dark sky is best for viewing. A group of four stars forming a square-like shape called the Keystone make up his body. Bent legs and arms extend from the corners of this shape. One arm is sometimes shown holding a club.

HOW TO SPOT

Where: Best viewed in the Northern Hemisphere

When: Evening in July and August

How: Naked eyes

Location: Between the stars Arcturus and Vega

Size: Large

DEFEATING THE DRAGON

In the story of the 12 labors of Hercules, the hero completes seemingly impossible tasks. One task is to pick golden apples guarded by a hundred-headed dragon. Hercules kills the dragon, Draco. In the night sky, the hero seems to be standing on Draco's head.

HYDRA *(THE SEA SERPENT)*

Hydra is the largest constellation in the night sky, but it is not very bright. Representing a long, winding sea serpent, it is a zigzagging line of stars that extends the length of four zodiac constellations. At one end, a small, kite-shaped group of stars forms the monster's head. In Greek mythology, Heracles had to fight Hydra as one of his 12 tasks. Every time he destroyed one head, two more grew in its place.

HOW TO SPOT

Where: Best viewed in the Southern Hemisphere

When: Evening in March and April

How: Naked eyes

Location: Extending from Libra to Cancer

Size: Very Large

LEO *(THE LION)*

Leo is a zodiac constellation that is fairly easy to find. The brightest stars form the shape of a backward question mark, with the bright, blue-white star Regulus at the bottom. This group of stars is also called the Sickle. It represents the head and chest of a lion. More stars extend out behind this shape to form the lion's body. In Greek mythology, Leo was a lion with a hide that no weapon could pierce. Heracles defeated it and placed it in the sky.

FUN FACT

The shape of the Sphinx in Egypt may have been inspired by the constellation Leo.

HOW TO SPOT

Where: Northern or Southern Hemisphere
When: Evening in March and April
How: Naked eyes
Location: Between Virgo and Cancer
Size: Large

LIBRA *(THE SCALES)*

Libra is the only zodiac constellation that doesn't represent a person or animal. Instead, it is an old-fashioned scale that would have been used to weigh goods. It looks like a triangle with two lines extending down. The ancient Greeks combined this constellation with Scorpius, turning it into the scorpion's claws. The Romans named it a scale. They may have done so because the sun passed through Libra during the autumn equinox, when day and night have equal lengths.

HOW TO SPOT

Where: Northern or Southern Hemisphere

When: Evening in June and July

How: Naked eyes

Location: Between Virgo and Scorpius

Size: Medium

LYRA *(THE LYRE)*

Lyra is a small but distinct constellation that is visible for most of the year in the Northern Hemisphere. It represents an ancient Greek stringed instrument called a lyre. It looks like a tilted rectangle stuck to a triangle. One of the saddest stories in Greek mythology involves this constellation. The musician Orpheus's wife dies, so he plays this lyre for the god of death. Orpheus is allowed to have his wife back if he leads her to the land of the living without looking back. At the last minute, the musician turns around and loses his wife forever.

HOW TO SPOT

Where: Best viewed in the Northern Hemisphere

When: Evening in July and August

How: Naked eyes

Location: Between Cygnus and Hercules

Size: Small

OPHIUCHUS AND SERPENS

(THE SERPENT BEARER AND THE SERPENT)

Ophiuchus (pronounced "off-ee-YOO-kiss") and Serpens rotate along the same path as the sun and planets with the 12 zodiac constellations. But Ophiuchus and Serpens are not part of the zodiac constellations. The ancient Babylonians thought 13 was an unlucky number, so they divided the zodiac into just 12 signs to match the 12 months of the year. This faint pair of constellations represents a man carrying a snake. Serpens the snake is a symbol of healing.

FUN FACT

If Ophiuchus were part of the zodiac, it would be the sign for people born between November 29 and December 17.

HOW TO SPOT

Where: Northern or Southern Hemisphere
When: Evening in June and July
How: Naked eyes
Location: Between Sagittarius and Scorpius
Size: Large

ORION *(THE HUNTER)*

Orion is perhaps the most famous and easily recognized constellation. It is visible all over the world, even in places with a lot of light pollution. The easiest part to notice is Orion's belt, a chain of three very bright stars. The brightest star in the constellation, Betelgeuse, marks the hunter's shoulder. Many cultures all around the world have identified this constellation as a heroic figure. In some African cultures, the belt stars represent animals, including zebras, pigs, or tortoises.

HOW TO SPOT

Where: Northern or Southern Hemisphere
When: Evening in January and February
How: Naked eyes
Location: Near Canis Major
Size: Medium

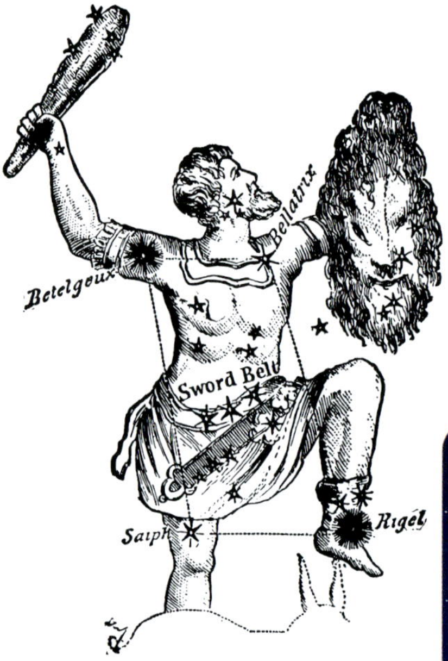

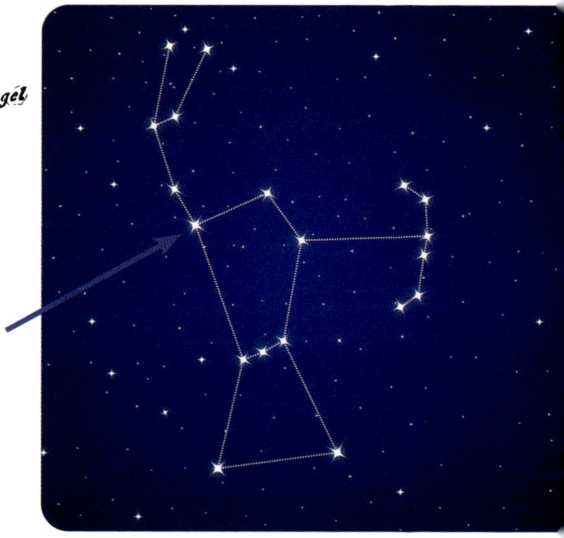

PEGASUS *(THE WINGED HORSE)*

In Greek mythology, Pegasus was a flying horse that played a part in several stories. In one myth, Perseus rode Pegasus to rescue Andromeda. All of these constellations are located together in the sky. The stars of Pegasus are not very bright. However, four of the stars form the shape of a square, so this constellation is easy to recognize in a dark sky. Sky watchers use the square of Pegasus to help find other interesting sights.

HOW TO SPOT

Where: Northern or Southern Hemisphere

When: Evening in September and October

How: Naked eyes

Location: Near Andromeda and Cassiopeia

Size: Large

FUN FACT

The Ojibwa people of North America have called this constellation a moose.

THE SEARCH FOR EXOPLANETS

Planets orbiting other stars are called exoplanets. More than 4,000 have been discovered. Astronomers have found many of them by looking for patterns in the way stars shine. Stars dim slightly when planets pass in front of them. In other cases, astronomers find exoplanets by noticing how the planets' gravity affects stars' motions. In 1995, the first exoplanet orbiting a sun-like star was detected in Pegasus. The scientists who found it earned the Nobel Prize in physics in 2019.

PERSEUS *(THE HERO)*

Perseus is a famous hero from Greek mythology. His constellation lies in the Milky Way. It is in the same section of sky as Cassiopeia, Pegasus, and Andromeda, whom Perseus rescued from Cetus the sea monster. Perseus is a fairly bright constellation that is visible almost all year in the Northern Hemisphere. It represents the hero holding the head of the monster Medusa with his sword raised. The star Algol, also called the demon star, represents the eye of Medusa. It gets dimmer every three days, as if it is winking.

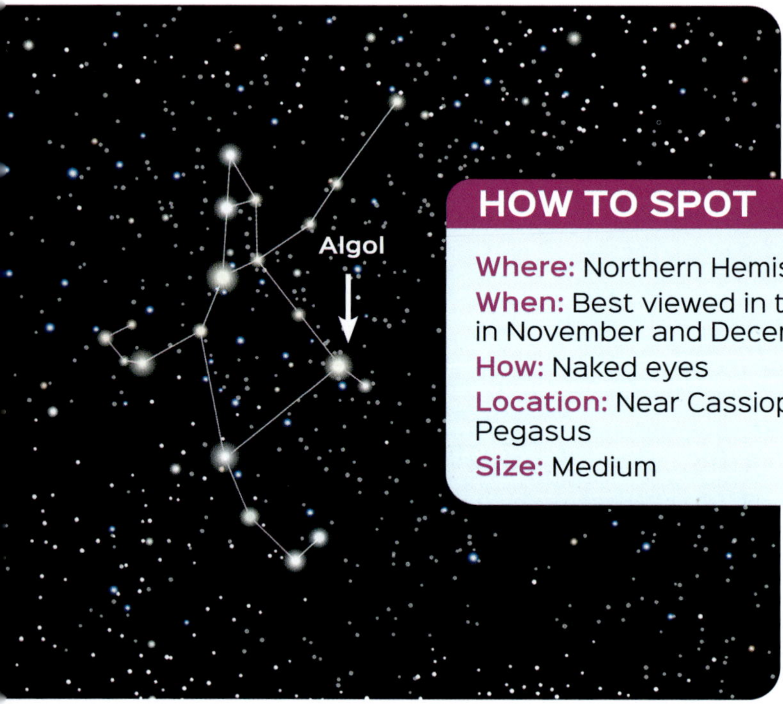

HOW TO SPOT

Where: Northern Hemisphere

When: Best viewed in the evening in November and December

How: Naked eyes

Location: Near Cassiopeia and Pegasus

Size: Medium

PERSEUS AND MEDUSA

In Greek mythology, Medusa was a monster with a woman's body and hair made of snakes. Anyone who saw her turned to stone. Perseus managed to cut off her head by looking only at her reflection in his mirror-like shield. Pegasus was born from Medusa's blood.

PISCES *(THE FISH)*

Pisces represents two fish tied together with string. It resembles a large V shape. A small circle of stars at one end of the V's arms is called the Circlet. The V shape opens toward the square of Pegasus. This zodiac constellation is dim, so a dark sky is required to see it. In Greek and Roman mythology, the two fish are the goddess of love and her son. They transformed into fish and tied themselves together to escape a sea monster.

HOW TO SPOT

Where: Northern or Southern Hemisphere

When: Evening in October and November

How: Naked eyes

Location: Between Aries and Aquarius

Size: Large

SAGITTARIUS *(THE ARCHER)*

Sagittarius is one of the 12 zodiac constellations. It is depicted as a centaur, or a half-man, half-horse creature, holding a bow and arrow. The easiest part of the constellation to see forms a shape that closely resembles a teapot. Sagittarius is bright and visible for most of the year in the Southern Hemisphere. In the Northern Hemisphere, it peeks above the horizon during July and August.

HOW TO SPOT

Where: Best viewed from the Southern Hemisphere

When: Evening in July and August in the Northern Hemisphere

How: Naked eyes

Location: Between Capricornus and Scorpius

Size: Large

FUN FACT

Sagittarius marks the center of the Milky Way galaxy.

SCORPIUS *(THE SCORPION)*

Scorpius is a zodiac constellation that is best viewed from the Southern Hemisphere. In northern skies, it can be seen only near the horizon. Scorpius is one of the easiest constellations to find because its bright stars form the shape of a capital letter J. The bright-orange star Antares marks the heart of the scorpion. In Greek mythology, the hunter Orion died after stepping on this scorpion. Orion and Scorpius never appear together in the sky.

HOW TO SPOT

Where: Best viewed from the Southern Hemisphere
When: Evening in July and August
How: Naked eyes
Location: Between Sagittarius and Libra
Size: Medium

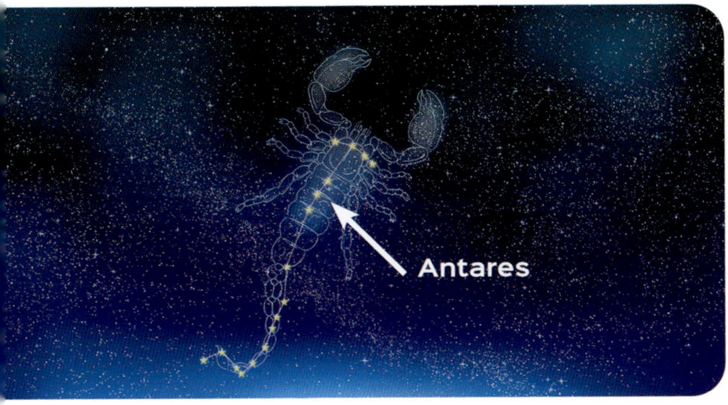

THE FOUR SYMBOLS

Ancient Chinese astronomers divided the sky into four very large constellations. A green dragon in the east included Scorpius, Libra, and Sagittarius. There was also a red bird in the south, a white tiger in the west, and a black tortoise in the north.

TAURUS *(THE BULL)*

Of the 12 zodiac constellations, Taurus is probably the easiest to find. It is visible from all over the world, and its brightest stars outshine light pollution. Orion's belt points toward the brightest star in Taurus, Aldebaran. To the ancient Egyptians, Taurus represented the Apis bull. This was a sacred animal believed to contain the spirit of the god Osiris. The famous star cluster known as the Pleiades forms the bull's shoulder.

HOW TO SPOT

Where: Northern or Southern Hemisphere

When: Evening in January and February

How: Naked eyes

Location: Next to Orion

Size: Large

URSA MAJOR *(THE GREAT BEAR)*

In Greek mythology, the gods transformed a beautiful nymph named Callisto into a bear. The brightest stars of Ursa Major form the Big Dipper, one of the most famous groups of stars in the world. From the Northern Hemisphere, Ursa Major and the Big Dipper stay visible year-round.

HOW TO SPOT

Where: Northern Hemisphere
When: Best viewed in the evening in March and April
How: Naked eyes
Location: Tail and back are formed in part by the Big Dipper
Size: Large

FUN FACT
Ancient Egyptians called this constellation the Hippopotamus.

FINDING NORTH

Harriet Tubman and other people who had been enslaved in the southern United States used the stars to find their way north to freedom. The folk song "Follow the Drinking Gourd" tells of these journeys. The Drinking Gourd is another name for the Big Dipper. The two stars that make up the front side of the Big Dipper form a line that points to the North Star, which always hangs over the North Pole.

URSA MINOR *(THE LITTLE BEAR)*

Ursa Minor is made up in part by the Little Dipper. This collection of stars matches the shape of the larger Big Dipper. The Little Dipper looks as if it is pouring into the larger one. Polaris, the North Star, is at the end of the Little Dipper's handle. The stars of this constellation aren't very bright, so a dark sky offers the best chance to see them.

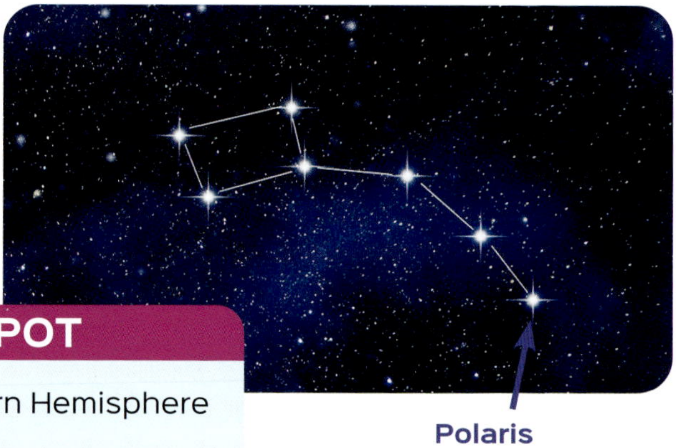

HOW TO SPOT

Where: Northern Hemisphere
When: All year
How: Naked eyes
Location: Near Ursa Major
Size: Small

FUN FACT

The Ojibwa people of North America saw Ursa Minor as a loon.

VIRGO *(THE VIRGIN)*

Virgo is the largest zodiac constellation and the only one that represents a woman. It isn't very bright. In an area with light pollution, only its brightest star, Spica, may be visible. Spica appears blueish white in color. Virgo is usually shown holding wheat and has been associated with many different goddesses. Virgo is also the location of the most distant object visible to a small telescope. It is a bright light source called a quasar that is 3 billion light-years away.

HOW TO SPOT

Where: Northern or Southern Hemisphere
When: Evening in May and June
How: Naked eyes
Location: Between Libra and Leo
Size: Large

THE RETURN OF SPRING

Virgo returns to the sky in spring. This matches the story of Persephone. She was a Greek goddess who had to stay in the underworld for half of the year. During this time, it was winter. When she returned, her mother, the goddess Demeter, let the world grow and bloom again.

ALDEBARAN

Aldebaran is a red giant, a type of star that is nearing the end of its life cycle. These stars are huge, up to hundreds of times larger than the sun. However, they are not as hot. Aldebaran's surface burns at approximately 6,700 degrees Fahrenheit (3,704°C), while the sun's surface is 10,000 degrees Fahrenheit (5,538°C). The name Aldebaran means "the follower" in Arabic. This star appears to follow the Pleiades star cluster, which was the most important night sky object in ancient Arabia.

HOW TO SPOT

Where: Northern or Southern Hemisphere
When: Evening in January and February
How: Naked eyes
Location: Taurus
Distance: 67 light-years from Earth
Magnitude: +0.9
Color: Red-orange

A STAR'S DEATH

When a star runs out of fuel, it expands into a large red giant that slowly drifts apart. The leftover core is called a white dwarf. A very large star becomes a red supergiant, eventually exploding in a massive supernova. This may leave behind a black hole.

ALPHA CENTAURI

Alpha Centauri has two companion stars. Beta Centauri appears nearby in the sky. These two stars form the front hooves of the constellation Centaurus. The third star, Proxima Centauri, is visible only through a telescope. This star system is the sun's nearest neighbor. Alpha Centauri is not visible north of Orlando, Florida.

HOW TO SPOT

Where: Southern Hemisphere
When: Best viewed in the evening in April and May
How: Naked eyes
Location: Centaurus
Distance: 4.4 light-years from Earth
Magnitude: 0.0
Color: Yellow

An artist's vision of the planet Proxima b

PLANETS AT THE ALPHA CENTAURI SYSTEM

Astronomers have found two planets orbiting Proxima Centauri. The planet Proxima b is around the same size as Earth. It is close enough to the star that water could remain liquid on the surface. It may be possible for life to exist there. Studying this planet won't be easy, though. It would take today's spacecraft 80,000 years to get there.

ANTARES

Antares is a red supergiant located in the constellation Scorpius. The Romans called it the heart of the scorpion. Antares is so huge that if it were the width of a basketball court, the sun would be the width of a penny. Antares is visible year-round in the Southern Hemisphere. Every few years, Mars passes near this star. The planet and star are both red, so people regularly confuse the two. This likely happened in ancient times as well; the name Antares means "Not Mars" or "Rival of Mars" in Greek.

HOW TO SPOT

Where: Best viewed from the Southern Hemisphere
When: Evening in July and August
How: Naked eyes
Location: Scorpius
Distance: 554 light-years from Earth
Magnitude: +1.1
Color: Red

In 2017, scientists with the European Southern Observatory created an image of Antares, the most detailed image ever of a star other than the sun.

ARCTURUS

Arcturus is the fourth-brightest star in the entire night sky. It is the brightest one visible in the Northern Hemisphere for most of the year. Extending the curve, or arc, of the handle of the Big Dipper leads to this star. A handy way to remember this is the phrase "arc to Arcturus." The name Arcturus means "guardian of the bear." That's because the star seems to follow the Big Dipper, which is part of Ursa Major (the Great Bear), around the sky. This star is a red giant.

FUN FACT
Most stars rotate through the Milky Way in a flat, spiral shape. Arcturus travels up and down around the galaxy with a small group of other stars.

HOW TO SPOT

Where: Northern Hemisphere
When: Best viewed in the evening in May and June
How: Naked eyes
Location: Boötes
Distance: 36 light-years from Earth
Magnitude: 0.0
Color: Orange-red

BETELGEUSE

One the largest stars visible to the naked eye, Betelgeuse is a red supergiant, a massive star that is nearing the end of its life. At some point in the next 100,000 years, Betelgeuse will explode in a supernova. Some people thought this was starting to happen in 2019 because the star dimmed unexpectedly. Astronomers figured out that Betelgeuse had actually just belched out a cloud of gas that blocked some of the star's light. This star marks one shoulder of the constellation Orion. In some myths, the red star represents a wound on the hero.

FUN FACT

The name Betelgeuse comes from Arabic. One possible translation is "armpit of the giant."

HOW TO SPOT

Where: Northern or Southern Hemisphere
When: Evening in January and February
How: Naked eyes
Location: Orion
Distance: 530 light-years from Earth
Magnitude: Up to 0.0
Color: Red

CANOPUS

Canopus is the second-brightest star in the night sky, but in many parts of the Northern Hemisphere it is never visible. In the Southern Hemisphere, this supergiant star rises high in the sky. It is part of the southern constellation Carina, which represents the keel of a ship. In many parts of southern Africa, Canopus is called Naka, meaning "the Horn Star." Traditionally, the first person to see the star rise would play a horn and might earn a cow as a reward.

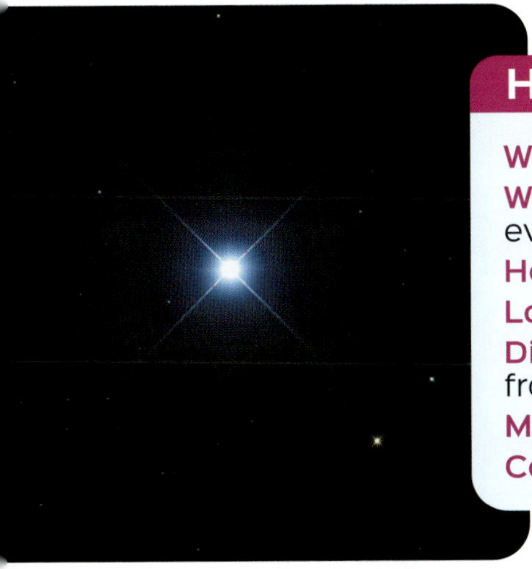

HOW TO SPOT

Where: Southern Hemisphere
When: Best viewed in the evening in February
How: Naked eyes
Location: Carina
Distance: 309 light-years from Earth
Magnitude: -0.7
Color: Yellow-white

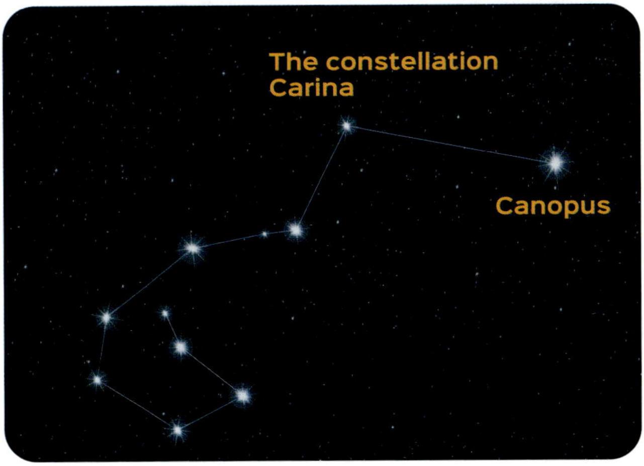

CAPELLA

Capella is also called the Goat Star. Today it is part of the constellation Auriga, which represents a person driving a chariot. But in some ancient stories, the constellation was a person herding goats. A faint group of three stars near Capella represented baby goats. Capella itself is actually a four-star system. The two brightest stars are almost the same size and color. It takes a powerful telescope at an observatory to see them separately. The other two stars are small red dwarfs.

HOW TO SPOT

Where: Best viewed in the Northern Hemisphere
When: Evening in December and January
How: Naked eyes
Location: Auriga
Distance: 43 light-years from Earth
Magnitude: +0.1
Color: Yellow

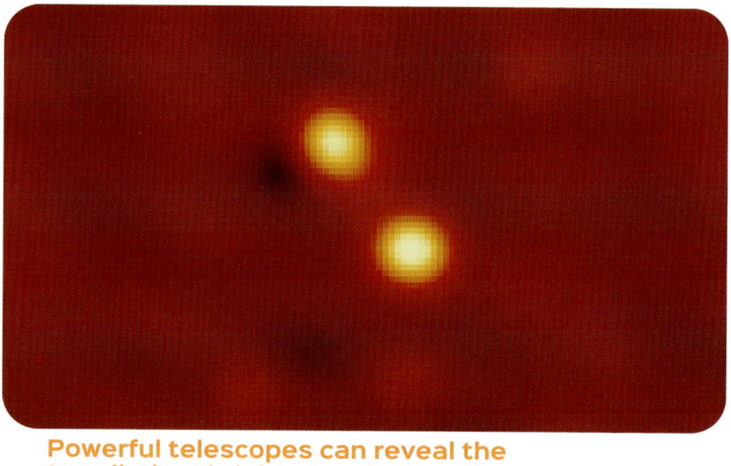

Powerful telescopes can reveal the two distinct bright stars in Capella.

CASTOR AND POLLUX

The twin stars of the constellation Gemini, Castor and Pollux, appear right next to each other in the sky. In fact, several light-years separate these stars. And they certainly aren't identical twins. Castor is actually a star system containing six separate stars. Pollux is a larger red giant that shines more brightly than Castor with a distinctive yellow-orange or golden color.

FUN FACT
An exoplanet named Thestias orbits Pollux. It is at least twice the size of Jupiter.

HOW TO SPOT

Where: Northern or Southern Hemisphere

When: Evening in February to March

How: Naked eyes

Location: Gemini

Distance: 51 light-years (Castor) and 33 light-years (Pollux) from Earth

Magnitude: +1.6 (Castor) and +1.2 (Pollux)

Color: Blue-white (Castor) and yellow-orange (Pollux)

DENEB

Deneb is one of the most distant stars that is visible to the naked eye. Astronomers estimate that it is more than 2,000 light-years away. The farther away a light source is, the dimmer it appears. Yet Deneb is one of the brighter stars in the sky. It shines up to 200,000 times brighter than the sun. Deneb and the stars Altair and Vega form a shape called the Summer Triangle because in northern skies they rise very high in the summer. In Chinese, Japanese, and Korean mythologies, Altair and Vega represent a pair of lovers who are allowed to meet only once a year. Deneb represents a bridge between them.

FUN FACT

If Deneb took the sun's place in our solar system, Earth would have to be located much farther away from it to get the same amount of light it does currently. Earth would need to be nine times farther away from the sun than Pluto is now.

HOW TO SPOT

Where: Best viewed in the Northern Hemisphere
When: Evening in August and September
How: Naked eyes
Location: Cygnus
Distance: More than 2,000 light-years from Earth
Magnitude: +1.3
Color: Blue-white

ETA CARINAE

Eta Carinae is a dying star system containing two huge stars that orbit each other closely. Back in 1838, these stars seemed to explode in an event called the Great Eruption. For more than a decade, Eta Carinae was the second-brightest star in the entire sky. It then faded and is now barely visible to the naked eye. Twin clouds of dust and gas from that eruption form a peanut shape around the star system.

HOW TO SPOT

Where: Southern Hemisphere
When: Best viewed in the evening in February
How: Naked eyes
Location: Carina
Distance: 7,500 light-years from Earth
Magnitude: Varies; currently +4.5
Color: Multicolored

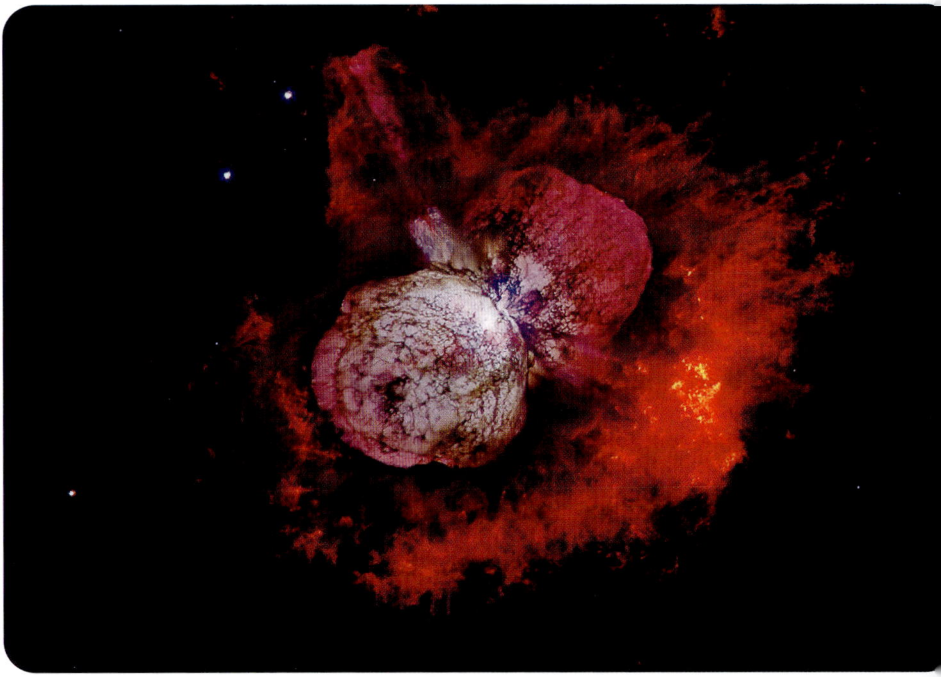

FOMALHAUT

Fomalhaut comes from a phrase meaning "mouth of the fish" in Arabic. This star is the brightest one in the constellation Piscis Austrinus, also known as the Southern Fish. Fomalhaut is one of the sun's nearest neighbors. It is just 100 to 300 million years old, which is young for a star. Most stars shine for billions of years. Fomalhaut is nicknamed "the lonely one" since it shines from a fairly dark and empty part of the sky. The western side of the Great Square of Pegasus points toward this star.

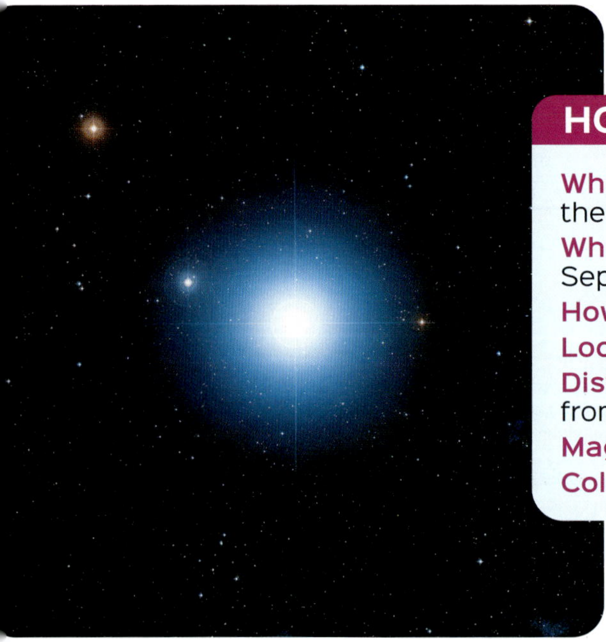

HOW TO SPOT

Where: Best viewed in the Southern Hemisphere
When: Evening in September and October
How: Naked eyes
Location: Piscis Austrinus
Distance: 25 light-years from Earth
Magnitude: +1.2
Color: Blue-white

THE ROYAL STARS

The ancient Persians recognized four "royal stars" as guardians of the sky and markers of the seasons. Regulus, the leader of the stars, indicated spring. Antares brought summer. Fomalhaut was the autumn star, and Aldebaran marked winter.

MIZAR AND ALCOR

Mizar is located in the middle of the Big Dipper's handle. In a very dark sky or through binoculars, a second, fainter star is visible just beside Mizar. This is Alcor. This pair was the first binary star system ever discovered. Astronomers later realized that these twins are actually sextuplets. Mizar is a set of four stars, and Alcor is a set of two.

HOW TO SPOT

Where: Northern Hemisphere
When: Best viewed in the evening in March and April
How: Naked eyes
Location: Ursa Major
Distance: 80 light-years from Earth
Magnitude: +2.0 (Mizar) and +4.0 (Alcor)
Color: White to blue-white

FUN FACT

In ancient Arabia, Mizar and Alcor were called the horse and rider.

POLARIS *(THE NORTH STAR)*

Polaris may be the most famous star in the northern sky, even though it is not very bright. Commonly known as the North Star, it seems to remain in place above Earth's North Pole while all the other stars spin around it. This means it is always visible from the Northern Hemisphere, but it can never be seen from any location south of the equator. For centuries, navigators have used it to locate north and to determine latitude, or how close someone is to the equator. In Mongolian mythology, Polaris holds the world together.

HOW TO SPOT

Where: Northern Hemisphere
When: All year
How: Naked eyes
Location: The end of the Little Dipper's handle
Distance: 433 light-years from Earth
Magnitude: +2.0
Color: Yellow-white

FUN FACT

The indigo bunting and some other bird species migrate at night, using the rotation of stars around Polaris to find their way.

THE HIGHEST PEAK

In a story from the Paiute of North America, Polaris is the mountain sheep Na-gah. He climbed the highest mountain peak and had no way back down. His sorrowful father transformed him into a star that lights the way for anyone who is lost.

PROCYON

Procyon is part of the constellation Canis Minor, or Smaller Dog. Along with Betelgeuse in Orion and Sirius in Canis Major, Procyon forms a shape called the Winter Triangle. Procyon is one of the sun's closest neighbors. It is a binary system of two stars, one of which is a white dwarf. In ancient Arabian mythology, Procyon and Sirius represented two sisters and Canopus was their brother. After a tragic event, Canopus and Sirius fled across the Milky Way. Procyon was left behind.

HOW TO SPOT

Where: Northern or Southern Hemisphere

When: Evening in January and February

How: Naked eyes

Location: Canis Minor

Distance: 12 light-years from Earth

Magnitude: +0.3

Color: Yellow

REGULUS

Regulus has long been associated with royalty. Its name is Latin for "little king." Regulus is also nicknamed "heart of the lion" because of its position in the zodiac constellation Leo. A lion is often called the king of the beasts. Regulus is located near the path that the sun and planets take through the sky. This means that occasionally a planet passes in front of Regulus, hiding the star from view. Venus will eclipse Regulus in 2044.

HOW TO SPOT

Where: Northern or Southern Hemisphere
When: Evening in March and April
How: Naked eyes
Location: Leo
Distance: 79 light-years from Earth
Magnitude: +1.4
Color: Blue-white

FUN FACT

Regulus spins so quickly that it has a distinct oval shape. If it spun a little faster, it would fly apart.

RIGEL

Rigel is an extremely hot star, more than twice as hot as the sun. It is a supergiant star that is 75 times the width of the sun. Rigel is part of a multistar system. Rigel A is orbited by a pair of smaller stars called Rigel B. This star system marks one foot of the constellation Orion. In one Inuit story, Orion's belt is a trio of hunters following a polar bear. Rigel is a fourth hunter who dropped his glove and had to stop to get it.

HOW TO SPOT

Where: Northern or Southern Hemisphere
When: Evening in January and February
How: Naked eyes
Location: Orion
Distance: 863 light-years from Earth
Magnitude: +0.1
Color: Blue-white

STAR COLORS

A star's color reveals the temperature of its outer layer. The hottest stars appear blue-white, average ones like the sun appear yellow, and the coolest stars seem orange or red. The constellation Orion contains the red star Betelgeuse and the blue-white star Rigel. Star colors are easiest to see using binoculars or telescopes.

SIRIUS

Sirius is the brightest star in the entire night sky. It is larger than the sun and puts out much more light. However, the main reason it outshines all other stars is that it is located fairly near Earth. Sirius is called the Dog Star because it is part of Canis Major, which represents a dog. Though it is the brightest star, Sirius is not the brightest object in the night sky. The moon and planets can all outshine it because they are so much closer to Earth. Sirius can be found by following the line formed by the three stars in Orion's belt toward the southeast.

Sirius B can be seen immediately below and to the right of Sirius A.

HOW TO SPOT

Where: Best viewed in the Southern Hemisphere

When: Evening in January and February

How: Naked eyes

Location: Canis Major

Distance: 8.6 light-years from Earth

Magnitude: -1.5

Color: Blue-white

COMPANION STARS

Sirius is officially known as Sirius A. It is part of a binary star system, meaning two stars that orbit each other. Astronomers discovered Sirius B in 1862. Nicknamed "the Pup," Sirius B is smaller than Earth. It is a white dwarf, a type of star that has burned through all its fuel.

VEGA

Vega is a bright star more than twice the size of the sun. It is part of the summer triangle with Altair and Deneb. Vega's constellation is Lyra, a very small but bright constellation. Vega is most likely a young star. Astronomers believe that a cloud of dust around the star could mean that planets are forming there. In Chinese, Japanese, and Korean mythologies, Vega represents a king's daughter who is separated from her lover, the star Altair. They are separated by a river represented by the Milky Way.

FUN FACT

Vega was the North Star in 12,000 BCE. It will be in this position in the sky again by 13,700 CE.

HOW TO SPOT

Where: Best viewed in the Northern Hemisphere
When: Evening in July and August
How: Naked eyes
Location: Lyra
Distance: 25 light-years from Earth
Magnitude: 0.0
Color: Blue-white

ALPHA PERSEI MOVING GROUP

The brightest star in the constellation Perseus is called Mirfak, Arabic for “elbow.” It shines brightly even in a night sky with light pollution. But it’s not alone. In a very dark sky, it’s possible to see dozens of other stars surrounding it. Binoculars help improve the view. These stars form the Alpha Persei Moving Group. As the name implies, the stars are not staying in place. They have been moving through space for the past 30 to 50 million years, since they formed. These stars are also called the Attendants of Mirfak.

FUN FACT

In native Hawaiian tradition, Mirfak marked the separation point between Earth and sky during the creation of the Milky Way.

HOW TO SPOT

Where: Northern Hemisphere
When: Best viewed in the evening in November and December
How: Naked eyes or binoculars
Location: Perseus
Distance: 506 light-years from Earth
Magnitude: +1.8 (Mirfak)

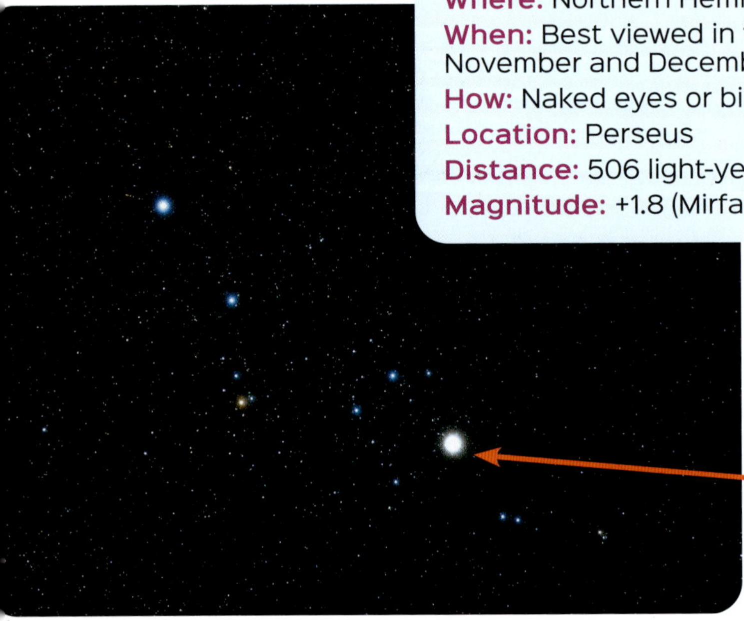

BEEHIVE CLUSTER

The Beehive Cluster is a group of about 1,000 stars sitting in the middle of the constellation Cancer. It fills a space in the sky the width of three full moons. In a very dark sky, it appears as a blurry patch or misty cloud to the naked eye. With binoculars or small telescopes, it's possible to see many stars shining out from a blurry background. The Romans called it Praesepe, which means "manger" or "crib." To astronomers, it is known as Messier 44, or M44 for short.

HOW TO SPOT

Where: Northern or Southern Hemisphere

When: Evening in March and April

How: Naked eyes, binoculars, or a small telescope

Location: Cancer

Distance: 577 light-years from Earth

Magnitude: +3.7

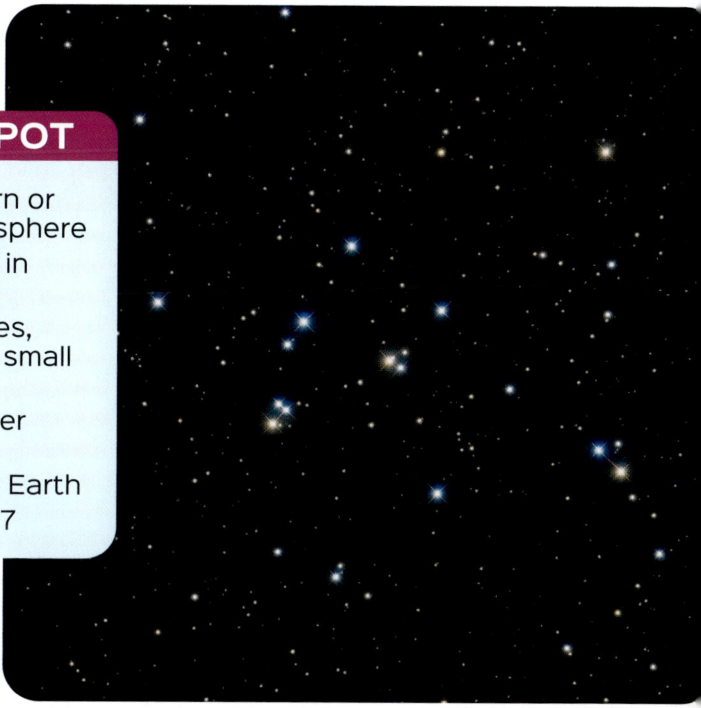

MESSIER OBJECTS

In the 1700s, astronomer Charles Messier mistook the Crab Nebula for a comet. He wanted to make it easier for others to avoid such mistakes in the future. He cataloged 110 star clusters, nebulae, and galaxies in the Northern Hemisphere skies. These are still called Messier objects today. Each one is named with M plus a number.

DOUBLE CLUSTER

Not many deep sky sights are visible to the naked eye, but the Double Cluster can be, especially when it rises high above the horizon in a very dark sky. Through binoculars, these clusters appear as twin masses of stars packed closely together. There are more than 300 supergiant stars in each cluster. These stars are all relatively young at around 12.8 million years old, and they are very hot. They shine with blue-white light. The clusters are separated from each other by just a few light-years. But they are about 7,500 light-years from Earth, located on a separate arm of the Milky Way galaxy.

HOW TO SPOT

Where: Northern Hemisphere
When: Best viewed in the evening in November and December
How: Naked eyes or binoculars
Location: Between Cassiopeia and Perseus
Distance: 7,500 light-years from Earth
Magnitude: +3.8

HERCULES GLOBULAR CLUSTER

The Hercules Globular Cluster is one of the most famous clusters in the northern sky. It contains as many as 300,000 stars and is 11.65 billion years old. It may be visible to the naked eye in a dark sky as a faint smudge. Through a telescope it looks like a pile of spilled salt. Every single "grain" is a star. The Hercules Globular Cluster's official name is Messier 13, or M13. It is located within the Keystone shape that marks the center of the constellation Hercules.

HOW TO SPOT

Where: Best viewed in the Northern Hemisphere

When: Evening in July and August

How: Binoculars

Location: Hercules

Distance: 22,200 light-years from Earth

Magnitude: +5.8

FUN FACT

The stars in this cluster are packed so closely together that they occasionally merge to form new stars.

The Hubble Space Telescope has spotted two colliding galaxies within the Hercules Globular Cluster.

HYADES

The Hyades is the nearest star cluster to Earth and is fairly easy to see with the naked eye. Its V shape marks out the face of the constellation Taurus, which represents a bull. The bright star Aldebaran marks the bull's eye and one end of the V. Aldebaran is not actually a member of the cluster, though. It just appears nearby from Earth's perspective. The stars in the Hyades are relatively young and likely formed alongside the stars of the Beehive Cluster.

HOW TO SPOT

Where: Northern or Southern Hemisphere
When: Evening in January and February
How: Naked eyes
Location: Taurus
Distance: 153 light-years from Earth
Magnitude: +0.5

FUN FACT

The Milky Way's gravity is tearing stars away from the Hyades, forming two tails that are hundreds of light-years long.

JEWEL BOX

The Jewel Box is a cluster that got its name when astronomer John Herschel compared it to fancy jewelry. Usually, the stars in one cluster are all the same type and color. But the stars of the Jewel Box cluster are different and shine in varying shades of red, yellow, and blue, resembling gems. The Jewel Box is visible only in the Southern Hemisphere. It can be found in the constellation Crux, the Southern Cross. To the naked eye, the Jewel Box appears as a fuzzy star. The colors become visible in large binoculars or telescopes. The Jewel Box is around 14 million years old, which is very young for a star cluster.

HOW TO SPOT

Where: Southern Hemisphere

When: Best viewed in the evening in May

How: Naked eyes

Location: Crux

Distance: 6,440 light-years from Earth

Magnitude: +4.2

The Jewel Box cluster through a telescope

OMEGA CENTAURI GLOBULAR CLUSTER

Omega Centauri, home to a whopping 10 million stars, is the largest star cluster in the Milky Way. It is ten times larger than a typical globular cluster. The stars are packed very closely together. Strangely, the stars in this cluster did not form all at once. Some scientists think this cluster is all that's left of a small galaxy that got absorbed into the Milky Way. In the Southern Hemisphere, Omega Centauri looks like a fuzzy glowing spot to the naked eye. A telescope brings a colorful swarm of stars into view.

HOW TO SPOT

Where: Southern Hemisphere
When: Best viewed in the evening in April and May
How: Naked eyes
Location: Centaurus
Distance: 15,600 light-years from Earth
Magnitude: +5.3

PLEIADES

The Pleiades, also known as the Seven Sisters, is one of the most famous sights in the entire night sky. Even in an area with some light pollution, five of the seven brightest stars should be easy to find. A line from Orion's belt through the star Aldebaran leads to the Pleiades. They form the same shape as the Big Dipper but much, much tinier. Binoculars or telescopes will reveal even more stars—the cluster contains around 3,000 of them. Many different cultures worldwide have told stories about the Pleiades. In Greek mythology, they were the seven daughters of Atlas, the giant who held the world on his shoulders.

HOW TO SPOT

Where: Northern or Southern Hemisphere

When: Evening in January and February

How: Naked eyes

Location: Taurus

Distance: 444 light-years from Earth

Magnitude: +2.9 to +4.2

FUN FACT

The Inuit of Greenland have seen the Pleiades as a pack of dogs hunting a polar bear.

CARINA NEBULA

The Carina Nebula is one of the largest and brightest nebulae in the sky, but it is visible only from the Southern Hemisphere. From a very dark location on a clear night, it appears to the naked eye as a faint, fuzzy cloud a bit larger than the full moon surrounding the star Eta Carinae. This star is dying, but in other parts of the nebula new stars are being born. Binoculars can reveal interesting shapes and structures inside the nebula. Professional space photographs reveal the nebula's stunning pink and red colors.

HOW TO SPOT

Where: Southern Hemisphere

When: Best viewed from February to July

How: Naked eyes or binoculars

Location: Carina

Distance: 7,500 light-years from Earth

Magnitude: +3.0

WHAT IS A NEBULA?

A nebula is a like a gigantic cloud in outer space. A nebula contains dust and gas spread out over an area many light-years across. Some are places where new stars are born. Others are the remnants left after a star has exploded. Some glow with light or brilliant colors. Others are dark and block light.

COALSACK NEBULA

The Coalsack Nebula got its name because it is as dark as coal. It is a vast cloud made of cold gas and dust that blocks out almost all the light from stars behind it. Any light that does make it through appears reddish. To the naked eye, the Coalsack Nebula looks like an oddly empty patch of sky in the midst of the Milky Way, right next to the constellation Crux. The Coalsack Nebula won't remain dark forever. In several million years, the dust and gas will come together to form stars.

HOW TO SPOT

Where: Southern Hemisphere
When: Best viewed in the evening in May
How: Naked eyes
Location: Crux
Type: Dark nebula
Distance: 600 light-years from Earth
Magnitude: Dark

A photo taken by an astronaut on the International Space Station shows the Coalsack Nebula in the bottom left.

FUN FACT
The Coalsack Nebula forms the head of the Emu in the Sky, a constellation from Australian Aboriginal cultures.

CRAB NEBULA

In the year 1054, astronomers in China, Arabia, and elsewhere noticed that a new, very bright star had appeared in the sky. Scientists today know it was a supernova, an exploding star. The explosion left behind a cloud of dust and gas that has been expanding ever since. This is the Crab Nebula, also called M1. The nebula got its name from an early drawing that made it look crab-like. Through a backyard telescope, it looks more like a blurry oval. Professional photographs of the nebula reveal brilliant red and blue colors.

HOW TO SPOT

Where: Northern or Southern Hemisphere

When: Evening in January and February

How: Telescope

Location: Taurus

Type: Supernova remnant

Distance: 6,500 light-years from Earth

Magnitude: +8.4

FUN FACT

The supernova that created the Crab Nebula was so bright it was visible in the daytime sky for almost a month in 1054.

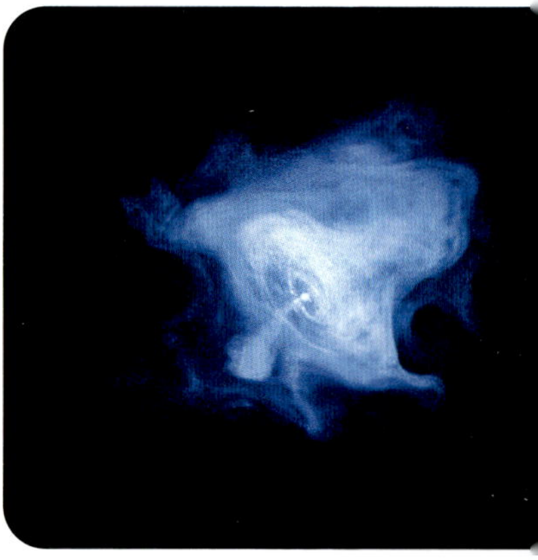

Images from X-ray telescopes reveal different shapes inside the Crab Nebula.

DUMBBELL NEBULA

The Dumbbell Nebula, or M27, got its name because it looks a bit like a weight people use for exercising. It also resembles an apple core or hourglass. It was the first planetary nebula ever discovered. This type of nebula actually has nothing to do with planets. It is the remnants of a star that ran out of fuel and collapsed. Our sun will eventually become this type of nebula. The Dumbbell Nebula is located inside the Southern Triangle between Vulpecula (the Fox) and Sagitta (an arrow).

HOW TO SPOT

Where: Best viewed in the Northern Hemisphere
When: Evening in September
How: Telescope
Location: Between Vulpecula and Sagitta
Type: Planetary nebula
Distance: 1,400 light-years from Earth
Magnitude: +7.4

EAGLE NEBULA

One of the most well-known images of outer space shows the Eagle Nebula, or M16. The Hubble Space Telescope took the picture in 1995. It shows only the very center of the nebula. Dark, towering, cloud-like forms made of dust rise like pillars. Inside, stars are being born. The photo is named *The Pillars of Creation*. Through a typical telescope, the Eagle Nebula looks like a misty cloud sprinkled with bright stars. These newly formed stars are 6 million years old or younger. This nebula is located between the teapot shape in Sagittarius and the tail end of the constellation Serpens.

HOW TO SPOT

Where: Northern or Southern Hemisphere

When: Evening in June and July

How: Telescope

Location: Between Sagittarius and Serpens

Distance: 7,000 light-years from Earth

Magnitude: +6.0

FUN FACT

The sun likely formed inside a nebula similar to the Eagle Nebula.

HORSEHEAD NEBULA

The Horsehead Nebula, a dark cloud that looks like a horse or seahorse's head, may be even more famous than the Eagle Nebula. However, it's much more difficult to spot through a backyard telescope. The good news is that it's just one small part of a vast area of amazing deep sky sights, the Orion Molecular Cloud Complex. This area takes up most of the sky around the constellation Orion. The Horsehead Nebula and its neighbor, the Flame Nebula, are located next to Alnitak, the lowest star in Orion's belt. Stars are being formed inside both of these nebulae.

HOW TO SPOT

Where: Northern or Southern Hemisphere
When: Evening in January and February
How: Large telescope
Location: Orion
Distance: 1,400 light-years from Earth
Magnitude: Dark

ORION NEBULA

Just below Orion's distinctive belt, there is a line of three faint stars, usually called Orion's sword. The middle star isn't actually a star at all. It's the Orion Nebula, or M42, one of the only nebulae bright enough to see with the naked eye. It looks like a slightly fuzzy star. It is actually 20,000 times larger than our solar system. New stars are being formed in the nebula. Through a telescope, billowing cloudy shapes and a sprinkle of baby stars become visible. Professional space photography equipment captures the brilliant green and red colors of this star nursery.

FUN FACT

The ancient Maya of South America saw the belt and feet of Orion as a hearth. The Orion Nebula was known as the Fire of Creation.

HOW TO SPOT

Where: Northern or Southern Hemisphere
When: Evening in January and February
How: Naked eyes or binoculars
Location: Orion
Distance: 1,300 light-years from Earth
Magnitude: +4.0

RING NEBULA

The Ring Nebula reveals what happens soon after a star the size of the sun dies. The nebula, also called M57, looks like a donut lit up from the center. The donut shape is a cloud of expanding gas. A white dwarf, all that is left of the star, sits at the center. A backyard telescope can pick up the distinctive ring shape of this nebula, which will appear silvery grey. However, professional space photographs reveal a rainbow of blue, yellow, green, and red extending outward from the middle of the ring.

HOW TO SPOT

Where: Best viewed in the Northern Hemisphere
When: Evening in July and August
How: Telescope
Location: Lyra
Distance: 2,300 light-years from Earth
Magnitude: +8.8

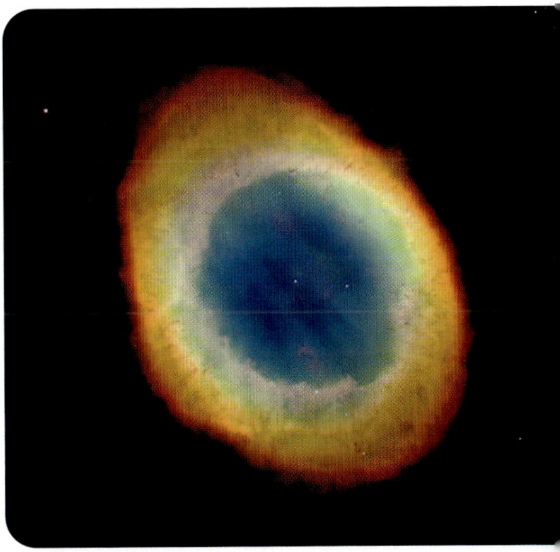

The Ring Nebula from the Hubble Space Telescope

The Ring Nebula through a backyard telescope

ANDROMEDA GALAXY

The Andromeda Galaxy, officially named M31, is the most distant object that can be seen with the naked eye. It can be seen only in a dark, clear sky. It looks like a fuzzy blur wider than the full moon and slightly oval in shape. Early astronomers thought it was a nebula inside the Milky Way. Then, in 1925, Edwin Hubble proved that it was so far away it had to be a separate galaxy. It is the closest large spiral galaxy to the Milky Way and moving closer. The two galaxies will eventually collide with each other, but not for another 4 billion years or so.

HOW TO SPOT

Where: Best viewed from the Northern Hemisphere
When: Evening in November
How: Naked eyes
Location: Between Cassiopeia and Pegasus
Distance: 2.5 million light-years from Earth
Magnitude: +3.4

LARGE AND SMALL MAGELLANIC CLOUDS

The Large and Small Magellanic Clouds are dwarf spiral galaxies that orbit the Milky Way. They are visible only from the Southern Hemisphere, appearing as cloudy patches in the sky near the point that all the southern constellations rotate around. In some parts of South America, people called them feathers of a rhea, an ostrich-like bird. In an Australian Aboriginal tale, the two clouds are an old man and woman.

The Large Magellanic Cloud

HOW TO SPOT

Where: Southern Hemisphere
When: All year
How: Naked eyes
Location: Opposite from Crux, near the south celestial pole
Distance: 163,000 light-years (large) and 200,000 light-years (small) from Earth
Magnitude: +0.9 (large) and +2.7 (small)

The Small Magellanic Cloud

FUN FACT

There is a North Star, but no South Star. The southern constellations rotate around a dark patch of sky.

THE MILKY WAY

The Milky Way is where Earth is located. The galaxy is shaped like a gigantic, flat disk with a black hole in the center and long, curving, spiral arms. The sun rotates around the center of the galaxy in a small arm called the Orion arm. From Earth, the galaxy appears as a band of cloudy light stretching across the entire sky. Unfortunately, even a small amount of light pollution hides the Milky Way from view. A very dark sky is required to see it. The Milky Way got its name from a Greek myth in which the goddess Hera spills milk across the sky.

FUN FACT

Some cultures named dark patches within the Milky Way. The Incas saw a llama and a serpent, while the Māori of New Zealand saw a shark.

HOW TO SPOT

Where: Anywhere with a very dark sky

When: All year, but best viewed in July and August

How: Naked eyes

Location: Stretching across the entire sky

Magnitude: Varies

WHIRLPOOL GALAXY

The Whirlpool Galaxy, also known as M51, is one of the most incredible sights to see with a telescope. It faces toward Earth, showing off its entire spiraling shape. This galaxy can be found near the last star in the handle of the Big Dipper, part of Ursa Major. A large enough telescope will reveal a smaller galaxy right next to this one. The Whirlpool Galaxy is slowly absorbing the smaller galaxy.

The Whirlpool Galaxy from the NuSTAR space telescope

HOW TO SPOT

Where: Northern Hemisphere
When: Evening in May
How: Telescope
Location: Near the Big Dipper
Distance: 23 million light-years from Earth
Magnitude: +8.4

The Whirlpool Galaxy through a backyard telescope

HALLEY'S COMET

Comets are often described as dirty snowballs because they are made mainly of ice, rock, and dust. As they approach the hot sun, comets grow long tails of glowing dust and gas. Halley's Comet is the most famous one because it returns about every 75 years and can be seen with the naked eye when it arrives. Throughout history, many people have noted its arrival. Astronomer Edmond Halley was the first to realize these sightings were connected.

HOW TO SPOT

Where: Northern or Southern Hemisphere

When: Most recently came near Earth in 1986; will return in 2061

How: Naked eyes

A European spacecraft studied Halley's Comet up close in 1986.

FUN FACT

A comet may have smashed into Earth about 66 million years ago, leading to the extinction of the dinosaurs.

FUTURE BRIGHT COMETS

Comets are tricky to predict. Most comets that zip past Earth are too small and dim to see without a telescope. For a comet to appear very brightly and clearly, a lot of things have to line up just right, including the comet's orbit, Earth's orbit, the comet's composition, and more. The news and social media will get the word out when a bright comet is approaching. A few to watch out for include Hartley 2, PanSTARRS, and Pons-Brooks. Some comets stick around in the sky for a while. The comet Hale-Bopp was visible for 18 months in 1996 and 1997. It won't return for more than 2,000 years, though.

HOW TO SPOT

Where: Check online for news
When: Check online for news
How: Naked eyes

The comet NEOWISE appeared in the night sky in 2020. It will return in about 6,800 years.

HOW DOES A COMET FORM?

Some comets come from the Oort Cloud, a gigantic shell made of trillions of icy objects. This shell surrounds the solar system. Sometimes an object gets knocked out of the shell and moves toward the sun. The sun's heat causes gas and dust to stream away in a glowing tail. Other comets come from the Kuiper Belt, a collection of icy objects that orbit the sun past the planet Neptune.

QUADRANTIDS

During a meteor shower, streaks of light regularly appear in the sky. People call them shooting stars, but they are not stars. They are bits of ice and dust vaporizing in the atmosphere, shining with heat and light. Single meteors may fall at any time of the year. But when Earth passes through a field of debris, usually left behind by a comet, many fall at once. This is a meteor shower. The Quadrantid meteor shower has fireball meteors that shine more brightly and last longer in the sky than typical meteors. However, this shower usually lasts for just a few hours on one night of the year.

HOW TO SPOT

Where: Northern Hemisphere

When: December or January; check NASA's website for the specific date and time

Meteors per hour: 60 to 200

How: Naked eyes

Location: In the area around Boötes

FUN FACT

The Quadrantids come from the pieces of an asteroid that circles the sun every five and a half years.

PERSEIDS

The Perseids is one of the most popular meteor showers to watch in the Northern Hemisphere. It has a high rate of meteors and happens in midsummer when the temperatures outside at night are pleasant. The debris for this shower comes from a comet named Swift-Tuttle, which swings nearby every 130 years. In China and Japan, there is a famous story about lovers represented by the stars Altair and Vega. They are separated by the Milky Way, and they reunite once a year. If they are unable to meet that day, the woman cries. Some say the Perseids represent her tears.

HOW TO SPOT

Where: Northern Hemisphere
When: July or August; check NASA's website for the specific date and time
Meteors per hour: Up to 100
How: Naked eyes
Location: Across the entire sky

Time-lapse images show multiple meteors at once.

HOW TO WATCH A METEOR SHOWER

The peak of a meteor shower doesn't last very long. A clear and moonless night and an area well away from any light pollution are best for viewing. At the correct time, hopeful viewers should lie down outside on a blanket, look up, and wait for meteors to fall. Patience is key.

LEONIDS

On November 13, 1833, people around the United States witnessed a night sky filled with shining meteors. It was the Leonids, but it wasn't a typical meteor shower. It was a meteor storm! Throughout the night, 50,000 to 150,000 meteors fell every hour. A similar storm happened in 1966. The Leonids may storm like this whenever their parent comet, Tempel-Tuttle, passes close to the sun. This happens every 33 years. The next chance to witness a sky filled with Leonid meteors will come in 2031.

HOW TO SPOT

Where: Northern or Southern Hemisphere

When: November; check NASA's website for the specific date and time

Meteors per hour: Usually around 15

How: Naked eyes

Location: Across the entire sky

An illustration from the 1800s shows Earth crossing the path of meteoroids that make up the Leonids.

GEMINIDS

Many consider the Geminids to be the best meteor shower of the year. The meteors move at about half the speed of those in a Leonid or Perseid shower. Instead of flashing by in the blink of an eye, each one shines for a few seconds and may follow a jagged path. These meteors may appear tinted yellow, red, orange, blue, or even green. An asteroid named 3200 Phaethon is the source of the debris for this shower. It's a very unusual asteroid because it is colored blue and has a tail like a comet.

HOW TO SPOT

Where: Best viewed in the Northern Hemisphere

When: December; check NASA's website for the specific date and time

Meteors per hour: Around 50

How: Naked eyes

Location: Gemini

FUN FACT

The Eta Aquarids in May is considered to be the best meteor shower of the year in the Southern Hemisphere.

THE NORTHERN AND SOUTHERN LIGHTS

In the most northern and southern parts of planet Earth, colorful sheets of light occasionally dance across the night sky. The technical names for them are aurora borealis in the north and aurora australis in the south. Most people know them as the northern and southern lights. They happen when the sun sends out streams of charged particles called solar wind. Earth's magnetic field deflects solar wind toward the poles. When enough particles hit gases in the atmosphere, the sky lights up.

HOW TO SPOT

Where: Near the Arctic or Antarctica

When: Best viewed during March or September

How: Naked eyes

Location: Near the horizon in the direction of the closest pole

FUN FACT

Many cultures have associated the northern lights with ghosts or the spirits of people who have died.

Astronauts can see auroras from space.

SPRITES

Sprites are bursts of electricity similar to lightning strikes. But sprites never come near the ground. They look sort of like red jellyfish that appear high in the sky for a brief moment. For years, scientists thought sprites were a myth. But in 1989, a pilot took a video of them. They don't come from the same storm clouds as rain and regular lightning. They happen in the very top layer of the atmosphere, a region called the mesosphere. Though they look small from the ground, they can be 30 miles (48 km) wide.

HOW TO SPOT

Where: Best viewed in the Midwestern United States

When: During a thunderstorm at night

How: Naked eyes

Location: High in the sky

INTERNATIONAL SPACE STATION

The International Space Station (ISS) looks like a rapidly moving bright star. In fact, it can shine as brightly as the planet Venus in the sky. It is easy to see, but viewing it requires some planning. The ISS moves so quickly that it takes just two to four minutes for it to zip across the sky from the eastern horizon to the western horizon. It will make several passes in one night, though, and it will be visible during the night in any given area for several weeks. Several people are inside the ISS at all times.

HOW TO SPOT

Where: Northern or Southern Hemisphere

When: Check online at the NASA website Spot the Station

How: Naked eyes

Altitude: 280 miles (451 km) above Earth

Magnitude: As bright as -3.9

From the ground, the ISS can be seen zooming across the night sky.

SATELLITES

Satellites are machines that orbit Earth. Some track weather, some take pictures, and some assist with communications. As of 2021, more than 4,000 active satellites orbited the planet. That number is only going to grow in the future. Companies are planning to launch thousands of satellites that will beam internet connections to people on the ground. Seeing satellites is easy. On a clear night, most people can see one approximately every 15 minutes. It looks like a speck of white light moving steadily in a line across the sky. However, if the light has flashing or colored lights, it's an airplane.

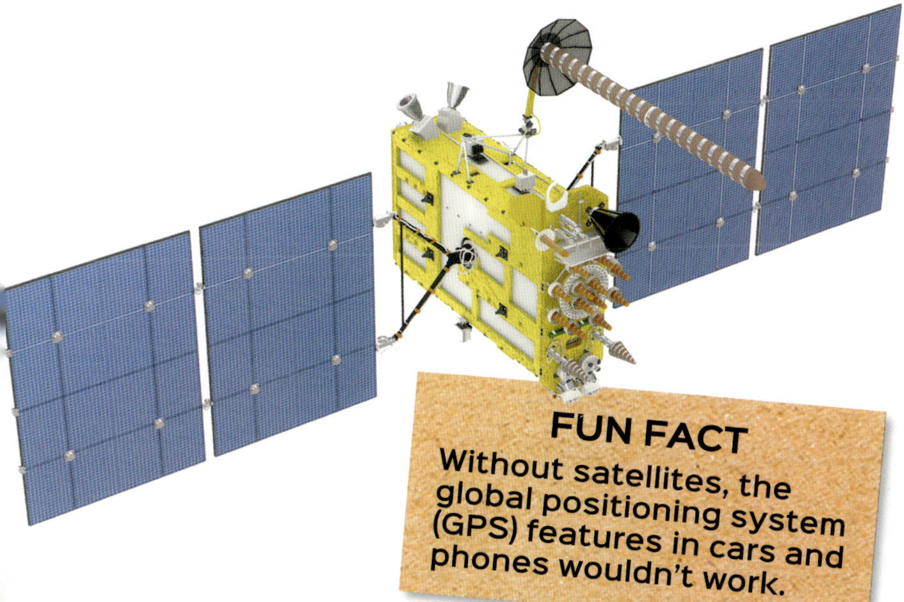

FUN FACT

Without satellites, the global positioning system (GPS) features in cars and phones wouldn't work.

HOW TO SPOT

Where: Northern or Southern Hemisphere

When: Anytime

How: Naked eyes

Altitude: Most are between 100 and 1,200 miles (161 and 1,930 km) above Earth

Magnitude: Varies

GLOSSARY

asteroid
A rocky object that orbits the sun but isn't large enough to be a planet.

astronomer
A person who studies outer space.

atmosphere
The gases surrounding a planet.

axis
The line that a planet, moon, or other object rotates around.

crater
A bowl-like hole left on the surface of a planet or moon after an object strikes it.

distinctive
A quality that sets something apart or helps identify it.

equator
The line that separates the northern and southern halves of Earth.

hemisphere
One half of a planet or sphere.

immortal
Lasting forever or unable to die.

meteor
An object from space that vaporizes in Earth's sky. Also called a shooting star.

mythology
A group of stories that all belong to one culture.

nebula
A massive, cloud-like collection of dust and gas in outer space.

orbit
The path an object such as a planet or moon follows around a separate object.

TO LEARN MORE

FURTHER READINGS

Oseid, Kelsey. *What We See in the Stars: An Illustrated Tour of the Night Sky*. Ten Speed Press, 2017.

Read, John A. *50 Things to See with a Telescope*. Stellar Publishing, 2018.

Thacher, Meg. *Sky Gazing*. Storey Publishing, 2020.

ONLINE RESOURCES

Booklinks
NONFICTION NETWORK
FREE! ONLINE NONFICTION RESOURCES

To learn more about the night sky, please visit **abdobooklinks.com** or scan this QR code. These links are routinely monitored and updated to provide the most current information available.

PHOTO CREDITS

Cover Photos: iStockphoto, front (Saturn), front (moon), front (aurora); Shutterstock Images, front (asteroid), front (meteor shower), front (nebula), back (Mars), back (Jupiter); JSC/NASA, front (space station); Red Line Editorial, front (big dipper), back (Orion); JPL-Caltech/NASA, front (galaxy); Denis Belitsky/Shutterstock Images, front (milky way); Yurij Omelchenko/Shutterstock Images, back (satellite)
Interior Photos: Shutterstock Images, 4 (Neptune), 4 (Leo), 5 (Libra), 5 (satellite), 5 (Scorpio), 5 (Venus), 8 (bottom), 13, 15 (top), 15 (bottom), 16 (left), 17, 18 (top), 20 (bottom), 21, 23, 24 (top), 26 (top), 26 (bottom), 27, 28, 30, 31 (top), 31 (bottom), 32, 33 (top), 34, 35 (top), 36, 37 (top), 38 (bottom), 39 (top), 39 (bottom), 40, 41 (top), 41 (bottom), 42, 43 (bottom), 44, 45 (top), 46, 47 (bottom), 48 (top), 49, 50 (right), 51, 52, 53 (bottom), 55, 56 (top), 57, 58 (top), 58 (bottom), 65 (bottom), 66 (top), 67, 68, 69, 71 (bottom), 74 (bottom), 78, 79, 80, 81 (top), 82, 83 (bottom), 96, 107, 112 (Venus), 112 (satellite), 112 (Callisto), 112 (stargazer); iStockphoto, 4 (meteorite), 29 (bottom), 59; Aleksandr Morrisovich/Shutterstock Images, 4 (moon), 22 (top); Pavel Chagochkin/Shutterstock Images, 5 (asteroids), 112 (asteroids); Johns Hopkins University Applied Physics Laboratory/Carnegie Institution of Washington/NASA, 8 (top); JPL/NASA, 9, 20 (top); JPL/USGS/NASA, 10; JPL-Caltech/UCLA/MPS/DLR/IDA/NASA, 11 (right), 12 (top), 12 (bottom); JPL-Caltech/NASA, 11 (left), 85, 86, 94; Vadim Sadovski/Shutterstock Images, 14; MSFC/NASA, 16 (right); JSC/NASA, 18 (bottom), 87 (bottom), 104 (bottom), 106 (top); Harm Kruyshaar/Shutterstock Images, 19; David Hajnal/Shutterstock Images, 22 (bottom), 97 (bottom); KSC/NASA, 24 (bottom); JPL/JHUAPL/NASA, 25; Digital Storm/Shutterstock Images, 29 (top); Natalia Hubbert/Shutterstock Images, 33 (bottom), 54 (bottom); Massimo Todaro/Shutterstock Images, 35 (bottom); Nastya Moon/Shutterstock Images, 37 (bottom); Alexandr Yurtchenko/iStockphoto, 43 (top); Hoika Mikhail/Shutterstock Images, 45 (bottom); Roman Voloshyn/Shutterstock Images, 47 (top);

Juan Aunion/Shutterstock Images, 48 (bottom); Morphart Creation/Shutterstock Images, 50 (left); Vera Shestak/iStockphoto, 53 (top); Dorota Janus/Shutterstock Images, 54 (top); Alberto Clemares Exposito/Shutterstock Images, 56 (bottom); Tragoolchitr Jittasaiyapan/Shutterstock Images, 60, 61 (top), 62 (bottom), 63, 65 (top), 77; M. Kornmesser/ESO, 61 (bottom); K. Ohnaka/ESO, 62 (top); Cristian Cestaro/Shutterstock Images, 64, 72 (top); Mullard Radio Astronomy Laboratory/Science Source, 66 (bottom); Davide De Martin/ESA/Hubble/NASA, 70; Nitish Waila/Shutterstock Images, 72; Neven Krcmarek/Shutterstock Images, 73; John Chumack/Science Source, 74 (top); Genevieve de Messieres/Shutterstock Images, 75, 103; QA International/Science Source, 76; K. Noll/Hubble Collaboration/AURA-ESA/NASA, 81 (bottom); Brian Donovan/Shutterstock Images, 83 (top), 98 (top); JPL-Caltech/NOAO/AURA/NSF/NASA, 84; Rev. Ronald Royer/Science Source, 87 (top); ESA/JPL/Arizona State University/NASA, 88 (top); NASA Goddard/NASA, 88 (bottom); JPL-Caltech/Harvard-Smithsonian CfA/NASA, 89; STScI/AURA/NASA, 90 (top); JPL-Caltech/Institut d'Astrophysique Spatiale/NASA, 90 (bottom); STScI/ESA/NASA, 91; JPL-Caltech/UCLA/NASA, 92; JPL-Caltech/ESA/Hubble Heritage Team/STScI/AURA/NASA, 93 (top); Albert Barr/Shutterstock Images, 93 (bottom); JPL-Caltech/STScI/NASA, 95 (top), 95 (bottom); JPL-Caltech/IPAC/NASA, 97 (top); Giotto Project/ESA/NASA, 98 (bottom); Mark A. Lee/Shutterstock Images, 99; Ben Pong/Shutterstock Images, 100; NASA/Science Source, 101; Science Source, 102 (right); SPL/Science Source, 102 (left); John A Davis/Shutterstock Images, 104 (top); ESO/Petr Horalek/Science Source, 105; Sergey Kamshylin/Shutterstock Images, 106 (bottom)

ABDOBOOKS.COM
Published by Abdo Publishing, a division of ABDO, PO Box 398166, Minneapolis, Minnesota 55439.

102021
012022

THIS BOOK CONTAINS
RECYCLED MATERIALS

Editor: Arnold Ringstad
Series Designer: Colleen McLaren
Content Consultant: Dr. Douglas Duncan; Department of Astrophysical & Planetary Sciences; University of Colorado

Library of Congress Control Number: 2021941707
Publisher's Cataloging-in-Publication Data
Names: Hulick, Kathryn, author.
Title: The night sky / by Kathryn Hulick
Description: Minneapolis, Minnesota : Abdo Publishing, 2022 | Series: Field guides | Includes online resources and index.
Identifiers: ISBN 9781532196980 (lib. bdg.) | ISBN 9781098218799 (ebook)
Subjects: LCSH: Sky--Juvenile literature. | Astronomy--Juvenile literature. | Moon--Juvenile literature. | Stars--Juvenile literature. | Field guides--Juvenile literature.
Classification: DDC 520--dc23

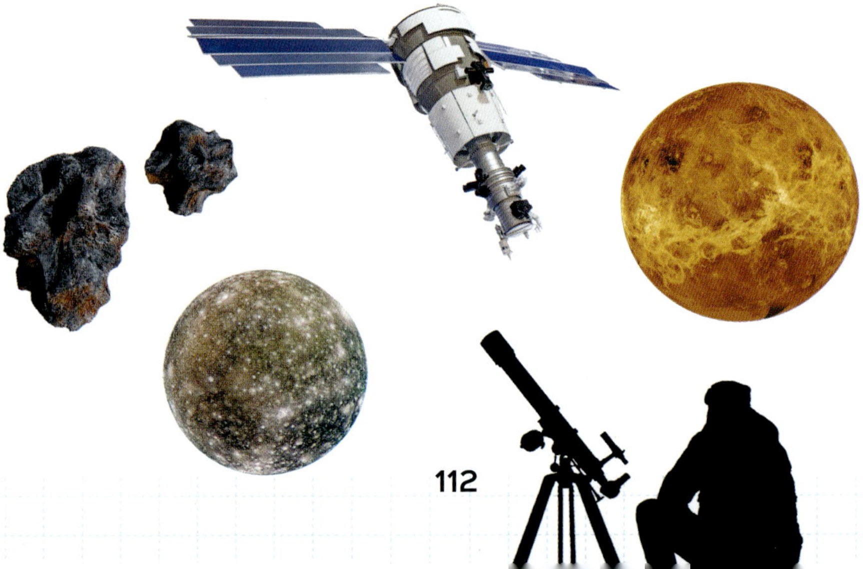

FIELD GUIDES

INSECTS AND ARACHNIDS

Carla Mooney

Abdo Reference

An Imprint of Abdo Publishing | abdobooks.com

CONTENTS

True Bugs

Other Insects

Spiders

Daddy Longlegs

Ticks and Mites

Scorpions

WHAT ARE INSECTS AND ARACHNIDS?

Insects and arachnids are some of the most abundant creatures on Earth. They live almost everywhere, from rain forests to deserts, and they come in a vast array of shapes and colors. Among them are some of the oldest creatures on the planet. Scientists estimate that some species date back as far as 400 million years.

WHAT ARE INSECTS LIKE?

Insects are the largest group in the animal kingdom, with about 1.5 million known species. And there may be many more insect species that people have not yet identified. In fact, some scientists estimate that there may be more than ten million insect species on Earth. Insects include flies, beetles, butterflies, moths, ants, wasps, bees, and more. While many insects are tiny, some can grow to be more than 7 inches (18 cm) long.

Insects are highly diverse, but they all have these things in common:

- All insects have hard external coverings called exoskeletons.
- Insect bodies are divided into three regions: the head, thorax, and abdomen.
- On their heads, insects have a pair of antennae that they use to sense smell and taste.
- Insects have three pairs of legs attached to the thorax. Some insects also have wings attached to the thorax.

WHAT ARE ARACHNIDS LIKE?

There are more than 60,000 species of arachnids. This group includes spiders, ticks, mites, scorpions, pseudoscorpions, and harvestmen, which are also known as daddy longlegs.

Arachnids have some key features in common:

- Arachnids have eight jointed legs and hard exoskeletons.
- An arachnid's body is made up of two sections: the cephalothorax and the abdomen.
- The cephalothorax is the front part of the body. It contains the head and thorax. An arachnid has four pairs of legs attached to the cephalothorax.
- The rear section of the body is called the abdomen.
- Arachnids have a pair of jointed jaws called chelicerae. Unlike insects, arachnids do not have antennae or wings. To feed, arachnids typically suck blood and fluids from the bodies of other organisms.

WHAT ROLES DO INSECTS AND ARACHNIDS PLAY?

Insects and arachnids crawl, walk, jump, swim, and fly in a variety of habitats around the globe. They are an essential part of the food chain. Some serve as food for larger animals. Others hunt for prey. These creatures also serve as pollinators for many flowering plants. Insects and arachnids are an important part of the world's ecosystems.

HOW TO USE THIS BOOK

Tab shows the insect or arachnid category.

The insect's or arachnid's common name appears here.

MOTHS AND BUTTERFLIES

MONARCH *(DANAUS PLEXIPPUS)*

The monarch is one of the most recognizable butterflies in the United States. The butterfly's body is black with white … It has reddish-orange wings … nd veins. The wings … ts along a black … with pale-orange … onarch migrates … south. The caterpillar has black, white, and yellow bands that look a bit like a tiger's stripes.

HOW TO SPOT

Size: Wingspan of 3.4 to 4.9 inches (9 to 12 cm)
Range: North America up to southern Canada, Central and South America
Habitat: Fields, meadows, weedy areas, marshes, and roadsides
Diet: Adults eat nectar; larvae eat milkweed

FUN FACT
The monarch butterfly is said to be named after King William III of England, often known as William of Orange.

How to Spot boxes give information about the insect's or arachnid's size, range, habitat, and diet.

Fun Facts give interesting information about insects and arachnids.

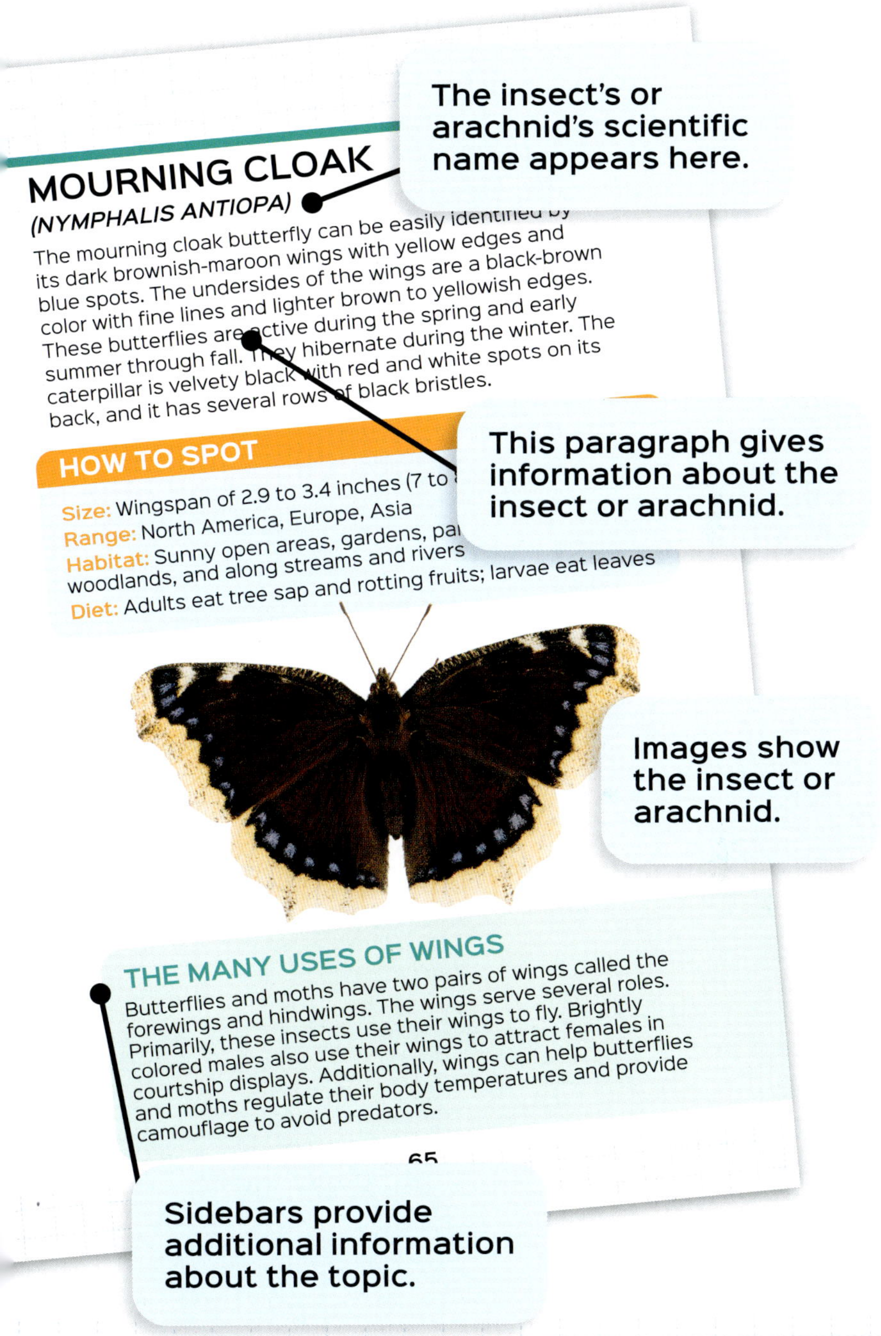
MOURNING CLOAK
(NYMPHALIS ANTIOPA)
The mourning cloak butterfly can be easily identified by its dark brownish-maroon wings with yellow edges and blue spots. The undersides of the wings are a black-brown color with fine lines and lighter brown to yellowish edges. These butterflies are active during the spring and early summer through fall. They hibernate during the winter. The caterpillar is velvety black with red and white spots on its back, and it has several rows of black bristles.
HOW TO SPOT
Size: Wingspan of 2.9 to 3.4 inches (7 to
Range: North America, Europe, Asia
Habitat: Sunny open areas, gardens, pa
woodlands, and along streams and rivers
Diet: Adults eat tree sap and rotting fruits; larvae eat leaves
THE MANY USES OF WINGS
Butterflies and moths have two pairs of wings called the forewings and hindwings. The wings serve several roles. Primarily, these insects use their wings to fly. Brightly colored males also use their wings to attract females in courtship displays. Additionally, wings can help butterflies and moths regulate their body temperatures and provide camouflage to avoid predators.
65
The insect's or arachnid's scientific name appears here.
This paragraph gives information about the insect or arachnid.
Images show the insect or arachnid.
Sidebars provide additional information about the topic.

BLUE BOTTLE FLY

(CALLIPHORA VOMITORIA)

Blue bottle flies live near humans or domestic animals. These flies are large and hairy with metallic-blue abdomens. A blue bottle fly has a gray head, black sides, and large red eyes. Adult blue bottle flies are most active during the spring and fall. Females lay their eggs on meat, decaying plant matter, or infected wounds. Females are attracted to meat and often enter open houses. When they can't find an exit, they buzz loudly.

HOW TO SPOT

Size: 0.4 to 0.6 inches (10 to 14 mm) long

Range: Europe, Africa, and the Americas

Habitat: Pastures, barnyards; near decaying meat, rotting vegetation, open wounds, and dung

Diet: Rotting meat, wounds, and liquid from decaying flesh

FUN FACT

The blue bottle fly has an area of reddish coloring on its head that is known as a beard.

BULB FLY *(MERODON EQUESTRIS)*

The bulb fly has a black body with bands of yellow, orange, or tan hairs. With its colored bands, this fly often looks like a small bumblebee. Its legs are black, and its wings are clear. This fly has a wide head that is broader than its thorax. During the spring and summer, bulb flies travel from flower to flower to drink nectar.

HOW TO SPOT

Size: 0.4 to 0.5 inches (10 to 13 mm) long

Range: Most of North America, Europe, and Asia

Habitat: Parks, gardens, meadows, and other places where flowers grow

Diet: Nectar and pollen

CRANE FLY *(TIPULA PALUDOSA)*

The crane fly looks like a giant mosquito. It has six long, thin legs that are very fragile. Often, the fly's legs drop off and regrow. Its abdomen can be gray, brown, or yellow. Sometimes it has a dark mark along its body. The male crane fly has a blunt tip on the end of its abdomen. The female has a pointed tip that she uses to push her eggs into the dirt. The fly has large, translucent wings and large, black antennae with up to 19 segments.

HOW TO SPOT

Size: About 1 inch (25 mm) long
Range: Across the Northern Hemisphere
Habitat: Grasslands, parks, and gardens
Diet: Adults rarely feed but sometimes drink nectar

HALTERES

The crane fly uses its halteres to help it balance during flight. These are small, dumbbell-shaped organs located behind the wings. During flight, the halteres tell the fly how its body is rotating. They send signals to the fly's wing muscles to correct its position in the air.

DRONE FLY *(ERISTALIS TENAX)*

The drone fly looks similar to a honeybee in size and color. It has a dark-brown to black body with yellow-orange markings on its abdomen. Short brownish-yellow hairs cover its thorax and part of its abdomen. The drone fly has two wings. Males have large, close-set eyes, while females have smaller eyes that are more widely spaced.

HOW TO SPOT

Size: About 0.5 to 0.6 inches (13 to 15 mm) long

Range: Every continent except Antarctica

Habitat: Meadows, fields, and near flowers

Diet: Nectar and pollen

FUN FACT

The female drone fly can lay eggs in carcasses.

DUNG FLY *(SCATOPHAGA STERCORARIA)*

The dung fly is often found on the fresh feces of large mammals, including horses, cattle, sheep, and deer. The fly is bright yellow to yellow-brown in color. It is covered with short, upright hairs. Its legs are long and hairy, and it has red eyes. Its wings are yellow-brown near the base and clear near the tips. The dung fly lays its eggs on manure. When the larvae hatch, they tunnel into the dung and feed. The dung fly is predatory. It attacks and eats other flies.

HOW TO SPOT

Size: 0.3 to 0.4 inches (8 to 10 mm) long

Range: Across the Northern Hemisphere

Habitat: Barnyards and pastures near the fresh feces of large mammals

Diet: House flies and other adult insects

FRUIT FLY *(DROSOPHILA MELANOGASTER)*

The fruit fly is attracted to the smell of ripe or rotting fruit, which is how it got its name. It has a short body that is yellow-brown in color. Its oval wings extend past its abdomen. The fruit fly has a round head with short antennae and large, bright-red, compound eyes. The fruit fly does not have biting mouthparts. Instead, its mouth sucks up liquids such as nectar and plant juice. The female is slightly bigger than the male. The female's abdomen has a pointed tip while the male's abdomen is rounded.

HOW TO SPOT

Size: 0.1 inches (3 mm) long
Range: Every continent except Antarctica
Habitat: Orchards, fields, forests, and other places near fruit
Diet: Plant juices

FUN FACT
The fruit fly has a very short life cycle. It may be as brief as ten days in warm weather.

GIANT ROBBER FLY

(PROCTACANTHUS RODECKI)

The giant robber fly is a large, hairy fly. It has a long, slender body with a tapering abdomen. Its body and legs are covered with stiff bristles that are blackish brown or beige in color. The legs have white hair too. The giant robber fly is a fast and powerful flier and an aggressive hunter. In the air it uses its long legs to capture prey. It attacks wasps, bees, dragonflies, grasshoppers, and other flies. It makes a loud buzzing sound when in flight.

HOW TO SPOT

Size: 1 to 1.1 inches (25 to 28 mm) long
Range: Worldwide
Habitat: Pastures, meadows, and open fields
Diet: Bees and other insects

FUN FACT

The male giant robber fly is territorial. It chases or captures any male that enters its territory.

GREATER BEE FLY

(BOMBYLIUS MAJOR)

The greater bee fly has long hairs on its thorax and abdomen. The hairs are black, brown, and yellow and give the fly the appearance of a fuzzy bee. Its wings are clear with a brown or black pattern along the bottom half. This fly is often active on bright, sunny days. It is commonly spotted sipping nectar from wildflowers using the long, stiff proboscis jutting from its head. It is also seen in sunny woodland areas. As it hovers over flowers, the fly's wings beat rapidly and create a high-pitched whine.

HOW TO SPOT

Size: 0.5 to 0.6 inches (13 to 15 mm) long

Range: North America, Europe, and Asia

Habitat: Woodlands, meadows, open fields, and gardens

Diet: Nectar

GREEN BOTTLE FLY

(LUCILIA SERICATA)

The common green bottle fly is metallic green with black markings. Some have a coppery green color. This fly has black, bristle-like hairs on its back. It also has black antennae and legs. Its wings are mostly clear with light-brown veins. The green bottle fly can often be spotted near garbage, feces, and dead animals. These flies are usually active on bright, sunny days in places where humans and animals live.

HOW TO SPOT

Size: 0.4 inches (10 mm) long

Range: Worldwide, especially in the Northern Hemisphere

Habitat: Dead animals and fish, garbage, feces, and open wounds

Diet: Decomposing animals and plant matter

HOUSE MOSQUITO *(CULEX PIPIENS)*

The house mosquito is a common night-flying mosquito. This mosquito has a light-brown or grayish-brown body and matching brown wings. It has lighter-colored bands on its abdomen. The mosquito's brown-colored mouthpart is long and thin to help it suck up fluids.

HOW TO SPOT

Size: 0.2 to 0.4 inches (5 to 10 mm) long

Range: Found in many regions worldwide and throughout North America

Habitat: Swamps, ponds, and bodies of stagnant water

Diet: Blood from humans and birds, plant juices, and nectar

FUN FACT

Only the female house mosquito bites to feed on the blood of humans and other animals. Males do not bite.

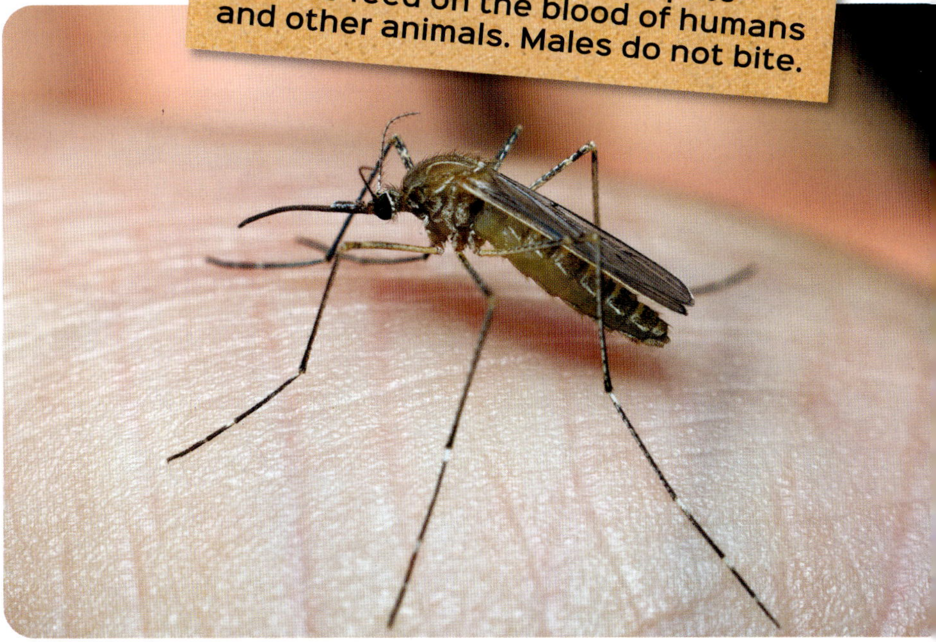

HOUSEFLY *(MUSCA DOMESTICA)*

The housefly is a well-known pest often found in homes, on farms, and around garbage dumps. It has a gray thorax with four narrow black stripes running from front to back. Its abdomen is gray or yellowish with dark markings at the midline and on the sides. The fly's clear wings are set at an angle, giving the insect a triangular shape. The housefly produces chemicals from its mouthparts to liquefy its food. Then it sucks up the partially digested food. The housefly is active during the day and rests on ceilings, trees, grasses, and other spots at night.

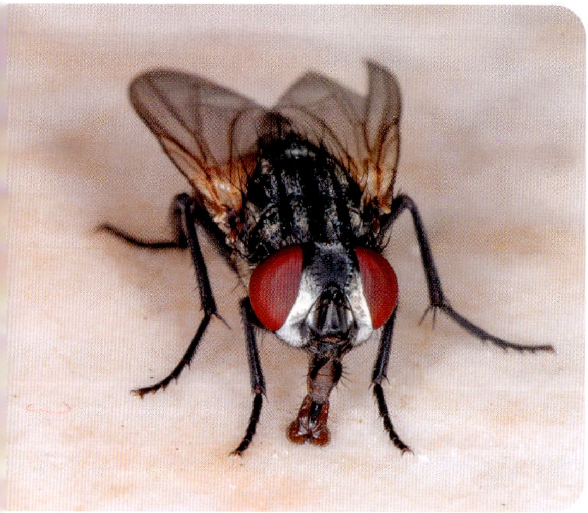

HOW TO SPOT

Size: 0.2 to 0.3 inches (5 to 8 mm) long

Range: Every continent except Antarctica

Habitat: Near horse manure, garbage, or exposed human food

Diet: Liquids from sweet or decaying matter

FUN FACT

A female housefly can lay up to 500 eggs in only three to four days.

THICK-HEADED FLY

(PHYSOCEPHALA TEXANA)

The thick-headed fly has a long, thin body. As its name suggests, the fly's head is thicker than its thorax. Thick-headed flies are reddish brown in color and often have yellow markings. The back of the thick-headed fly's thorax has three black stripes. The abdomen is red with bands of yellow dusting and large, black spots. The two wings are usually clear and sometimes have dark markings. These flies are often found near flowers and use their long mouthparts to sip nectar.

HOW TO SPOT

Size: Flies in the *Physocephala* genus are 0.2 to 0.6 inches (5 to 15 mm) long

Range: North America

Habitat: Open areas such as meadows, parks, and brushlands near flowers

Diet: Nectar

ASIAN LONG-HORNED BEETLE

(ANOPLOPHORA GLABRIPENNIS)

The Asian long-horned beetle has a glossy black body. It has approximately 20 white spots on each wing cover. The beetle also has long antennae, about 1.3 to 1.5 times the length of its body. Its antennae are striped with white and black. The beetle's legs are a white-blue color. Female beetles lay eggs in hardwood trees. Larvae bore into the trees and feed on the bark and wood. Adult beetles depart the infested trees. They leave behind round exit holes and piles of sawdust.

HOW TO SPOT

Size: 0.8 to 1.4 inches (20 to 36 mm) long

Range: Temperate zones of East Asia and the United States

Habitat: Hardwood forests and other areas with hardwood such as warehouses

Diet: Leaves, twigs, and plant matter

BIG SAND TIGER BEETLE

(CICINDELA FORMOSA)

The big sand tiger beetle has a distinctive patch of dark-red or purple coloring on its back over a white-ivory background. The shape of this coloring varies by beetle, but it is typically wider at the top and thinner at the bottom. This beetle has six legs and two very long antennae. The big sand tiger beetle is one of the insect world's fiercest predators. It uses the two mandibles located below its antennae to hunt insects and spiders. Because of its large size, this beetle warms up more slowly and becomes active later in the morning than other beetles.

HOW TO SPOT

Size: 0.6 to 0.7 inches (15 to 18 mm) long

Range: North America

Habitat: Dry, sandy areas of blowouts, sand dunes, and sand hills

Diet: Small insects and spiders

FUN FACT

The big sand tiger beetle is better at flying than landing. It often tumbles to the ground when it tries to land.

BOLL WEEVIL *(ANTHONOMUS GRANDIS)*

The adult boll weevil is a small, round-bodied beetle. It has a long snout that extends about half of its body length. Its color is typically grayish black to brown with yellowish hair-like scales. On the inside of its front legs, the boll weevil has a distinct double-toothed spur. In the spring, the boll weevil mates and lays eggs inside a cotton plant. This beetle is active during the summer.

HOW TO SPOT

Size: 0.2 to 0.3 inches (4 to 8 mm) long
Range: Central America, Mexico, Cuba, and the southern United States
Habitat: Areas where cotton is grown
Diet: Cotton seedpods (bolls), cotton flower buds, and related plants

FUN FACT

To protect cotton crops, scientists have inserted a gene into the cotton plant's DNA that causes the plant to produce a compound that is toxic to the boll weevil.

DESTROYING COTTON CROPS

Historically, the boll weevil was a pest for cotton farmers in the southern United States. When weevils infested the cotton bolls, the bolls turned yellow and fell off the plant. This ruined the cotton fibers. Sometimes an infestation caused the entire cotton plant to produce few bolls.

BOMBARDIER BEETLE

(PHEROPSOPHUS AEQUINOCTIALIS)

The bombardier beetle is a species of ground beetle common in Central and South America. The beetle's head and body can be yellow to red in color. Its hardened wing cases usually have two large, black spots that join where the cases meet. The bombardier beetle is nocturnal and spends the day hiding under logs, stones, or grasses. At night it emerges from its hiding spot to run along river beaches and sandy trails.

HOW TO SPOT

Size: 0.6 to 0.8 inches (15 to 20 mm) long
Range: Central and South America
Habitat: Riverbanks, sandbars, and soils near fresh water
Diet: Crickets, insects, plants, and fruits

A DEFENSIVE SPRAY

When in danger, the bombardier beetle can produce a hot, powerful defensive chemical spray. The spray shoots as a fine mist from the tip of the beetle's abdomen, creating a popping sound. The beetle can aim its spray in any direction to deter a potential predator.

DELTA FLOWER SCARAB

(TRIGONOPELTASTES DELTA)

The delta flower scarab is a medium-size beetle. The plate-like structure on its back has a yellow border with a yellow triangle in the middle. The beetle's wing cases are orange-brown with dark spots or markings. Yellowish scales line the beetle's underside. It has antennae with ten segments. It uses its mouthparts to sip pollen or nectar. This beetle is most active during the late spring and summer. It is commonly found near flowers in meadows and grassy areas.

FUN FACT

The word ***delta*** in the beetle's name comes from the Greek letter delta, which looks like a triangle.

HOW TO SPOT

Size: 0.3 to 0.4 inches (8 to 10 mm) long

Range: Southeastern United States from Florida to eastern Texas

Habitat: Woodlands, meadows, and tall grasses near flowers

Diet: Pollen and nectar

DOGBANE LEAF BEETLE

(CHRYSOCHUS AURATUS)

Dogbane leaf beetles have long, oval shapes. These beetles have a distinct iridescent blue-green color. A dogbane leaf beetle's wing cases are shiny with a coppery color. Its legs and antennae are blue-black in color. Its antennae are long and have 12 joints. The beetle's mandibles are blunt and made for eating plants. It moves from plant to plant within an area of host plants.

HOW TO SPOT

Size: 0.3 to 0.4 inches (8 to 10 mm) long

Range: Southern Canada and most of the United States

Habitat: Near dogbane plants, especially Indian hemp and spreading dogbane

Diet: Dogbane plant leaves and milkweed

DRUGSTORE BEETLE

(STEGOBIUM PANICEUM)

The drugstore beetle is a tiny, reddish-brown beetle. It has rows of fine hairs on its wing cases. The wing cases also have parallel rows of deep pits. The beetle's antennae are smooth and end in three segments. The drugstore beetle eats a wide variety of food and materials, including flour, dry mixes, breads, cookies, chocolates, and spices. It also feeds on materials such as wood, hair, leather, horn, and museum specimens. It is a common pest in processed and packaged foods.

HOW TO SPOT

Size: 0.1 inch (3 mm) long

Range: Worldwide; more common in warmer regions

Habitat: Inside stored foods

Diet: A variety of dried herbs and plant material

FUN FACT

The drugstore beetle got its name because it sometimes feeds on prescription drugs.

KITCHEN INVADERS

Drugstore beetles are commonly found in kitchens and pantries. They often live in foods that are kept in open or unsecured containers. They lay their eggs in grain, flour, bread, pasta, cereals, and rice. When they can't find these things, they can survive for weeks without food.

EASTERN EYED CLICK BEETLE

(ALAUS OCULATUS)

Eastern eyed click beetles are thin, long beetles. They are known for the clicking noises they make when moving fast to escape danger. The beetle has a stiff spine on its belly that snaps with force to propel the beetle away from a predator. The snap makes the click sound. When a beetle is stuck on its back, the snap's force can be so powerful that it flips the beetle onto its feet.

HOW TO SPOT

Size: 1 to 1.8 inches (25 to 46 mm) long

Range: United States east of the Rocky Mountains

Habitat: Woodlands, especially near rotting timber

Diet: Adults eat little; larvae eat plant roots

FUN FACT

There are more than 900 species of click beetles living in North America.

GIANT STAG BEETLE

(LUCANUS ELAPHUS)

The giant stag beetle is the largest stag beetle in North America. It has a long, thin body with a flattened back. This beetle is reddish brown and shiny in color. It has black antennae and legs. A male giant stag beetle has a wide head with a crest above the eyes. It also has giant jaws that look like antlers. A female has a narrower head and a smaller jaw. Males use their giant jaws to fight other males for females. At night, the beetles are attracted to light, and they can often be spotted flying at dusk.

HOW TO SPOT

Size: 1.2 to 2.4 inches (30 to 60 mm) long
Range: North America, from North Carolina to the northeastern United States
Habitat: Woodlands and forests
Diet: Sap, plant fluids, and ripe fruit juices

FUN FACT

Female stag beetles release chemicals that attract male beetles.

JAPANESE BEETLE

(POPILLIA JAPONICA)

The Japanese beetle has a bright metallic-green or copper body. Its hardened wing covers are grooved and reddish brown in color. The beetle's underside has grayish hair. On the sides of its abdomen, the beetle has five distinct white tufts of hair. The tip of the beetle's abdomen has two white patches. The beetle feeds during the day, eating nearly 300 species of plants, vegetables, shrubs, and trees.

HOW TO SPOT

Size: 0.4 to 0.5 inches (10 to 12 mm) long

Range: East Asia, southeastern Canada, and the eastern and midwestern United States

Habitat: Open woods, meadows, farms, and gardens

Diet: Foliage and flowers

FUN FACT

A swarm of Japanese beetles can strip a peach tree in only 15 minutes, leaving nothing but bare branches and fruit pits.

PYRALIS FIREFLY *(PHOTINUS PYRALIS)*

The pyralis firefly, also known as the big dipper firefly, is actually a type of beetle. The firefly is dark brown. Its head has a rounded cover with a yellow border and two orange spots. The firefly has two pairs of wings. The first pair of wings is dark brown with a yellow border. This pair forms covers, known as elytra, over the second pair of wings. The firefly has a light-producing organ on its abdomen. When it lights up, it flashes a bright yellow-green color.

FUN FACT

The firefly uses its flashing signals to attract a mate and deter predators.

HOW TO SPOT

Size: 0.4 to 0.6 inches (10 to 15 mm) long
Range: East of the Rocky Mountains
Habitat: Meadows, gardens, parks, and woodland edges
Diet: Insects, earthworms, and snails

RED MILKWEED LEAF BEETLE

(TETRAOPES TETROPHTHALMUS)

The red milkweed leaf beetle has a narrow, elongated body. It is reddish in color and has four black dots on its pronotum. The beetle's wing cases have patterns of black dots and streaks. Its legs are grayish black with traces of red. Its antennae are smooth. Adult red milkweed leaf beetles are generally solitary. Because they can fly, they easily move from place to place. Adults are active in the early summer to autumn.

HOW TO SPOT

Size: 0.3 to 0.6 inches (8 to 15 mm) long

Range: Eastern United States and Canada

Habitat: Near milkweed plants

Diet: Leaves, stems, and flowers of the milkweed plant

SEVEN-SPOTTED LADYBUG

(COCCINELLA SEPTEMPUNCTATA)

The seven-spotted ladybug is a medium-size beetle. Its head and thorax are black with yellow or white markings. Its legs and underside are also black. It has orange-red–colored wing cases with up to nine black spots. The ladybug can fly and is mostly active during the day. Adults are active during the spring and dormant in the summer. During the winter months, adult ladybugs gather in groups of about ten to 15, hibernating together in low-lying grasses or between boulders.

HOW TO SPOT

Size: 0.3 inches (8 mm) long

Range: North America, the Middle East, and India

Habitat: Open fields, grasslands, marshes, gardens, and parks

Diet: Small, sap-sucking insects called aphids

FUN FACT

A female ladybug can eat up to 75 aphids in a single day.

SOUTHERN DUNG BEETLE

(ONTHOPHAGUS AUSTRALIS)

The southern dung beetle is black and shiny. It has a short, broad head with prominent, oval eyes. The beetle has large wings and distinctive segmented antennae. Southern dung beetles are typically active during the late summer and fall. They are known for rolling the feces, or dung, of larger animals into balls. The balls of dung serve as food or as places to lay eggs.

HOW TO SPOT

Size: Dung beetles in the genus *Onthophagus* are 0.1 to 0.4 inches (2 to 11 mm) long

Range: Southeastern Australia

Habitat: Manure in open pastures

Diet: Dung

BALD-FACED HORNET

(DOLICHOVESPULA MACULATA)

The bald-faced hornet is actually a wasp. It got the name "bald-faced" from its white face and black body. This wasp has three white stripes at the end of its body. Bald-faced hornets are a social species. They live in colonies of hundreds to thousands of wasps. The wasps build a ball-shaped paper nest in trees or shrubs. They create the nest by collecting and chewing wood fibers, then forming those fibers into a nest.

HOW TO SPOT

Size: Workers are 0.5 to 0.6 inches (13 to 15 mm) long; queens are 0.7 to 0.8 inches (18 to 20 mm) long

Range: Southern Canada and the United States

Habitat: Forest edges, meadows, parks, and gardens

Diet: Yellow jackets, flies, nectar, and sap

BLACK-AND-GOLD BUMBLEBEE

(BOMBUS AURICOMUS)

The black-and-gold bumblebee is one of the largest bumblebee species. Its body is covered with short hairs of even length. The female workers and the queen have black faces with a few scattered yellow hairs. The male bumblebee has a mostly yellow face and large eyes. The bee's thorax is largely black with some yellow hairs. Its abdomen has yellow and black hairs, and the tip is black. The black-and-gold bumblebee is social and lives in a colony with other bumblebees.

HOW TO SPOT

Size: Workers are 0.3 to 0.5 inches (8 to 13 mm) long; queens are 0.8 to 1 inch (20 to 25 mm) long

Range: Eastern United States and Canada

Habitat: Grasslands, farmlands, and fields

Diet: Nectar and pollen

FUN FACT

The bumblebee carries pollen and nectar totaling about 25 percent of its body weight back to the nest.

THE QUEEN'S ROLE

Each spring, the black-and-gold bumblebee queen emerges from hibernation. She finds a new nest site for the colony and lays eggs. She forages for food and takes care of the colony until the first worker bees emerge. Then the queen stays in the nest to lay more eggs.

BLACK-AND-YELLOW MUD DAUBER *(SCELIPHRON CAEMENTARIUM)*

The black-and-yellow mud dauber is a common black wasp with yellow markings, black antennae, and black eyes. A long, thin, black waist connects its thorax and abdomen. Yellow markings vary by individual wasp. The wasp's abdomen is mostly black, and it has mainly yellow-marked legs. This wasp is not aggressive, and it seldom stings. Adults are active from spring through the fall.

HOW TO SPOT

Size: 1 inch (25 mm) long

Range: The Americas, Asia, Europe, Australia, and some Pacific islands

Habitat: A variety of structures, including rock ledges, bridges, barns, garages, attics, porches, and more

Diet: Nectar

FUN FACT

Black-and-yellow mud daubers collect mud balls at the edges of bodies of water and use them to build rectangular nests.

BROWN-WINGED STRIPED SWEAT BEE *(AGAPOSTEMON SPLENDENS)*

The brown-winged striped sweat bee has a distinctive metallic blue-green color and brown wings. It has black antennae and legs. The male bee has black and yellow bands on its abdomen. Like all species of sweat bees, the brown-winged striped sweat bee is attracted to perspiration because of the moisture and salts. This bee builds its nest in the ground or in wood. The bee is an important pollinator of many wildflowers. Females collect pollen to put in the nest for larvae to eat after hatching.

Male

HOW TO SPOT

Size: 0.4 inches (10 mm) long

Range: North Dakota to Maine, south to Texas and Florida

Habitat: Fields, gardens, grasslands, and other open spaces with flowers

Diet: Nectar and pollen

Female

CALIFORNIA CARPENTER BEE

(XYLOCOPA CALIFORNICA)

The California carpenter bee is a large, black bee with some blue-green tint. This bee appears similar to a bumblebee, but its head is larger and it has only short hairs or no hairs on its abdomen. The male bee's face has a yellow-white center. The male has some lighter markings on its pronotum and first abdominal segment. Female bees chew tunnels into dry wood or lumber, where they store food and lay eggs. The California carpenter bee is an important pollinator of many flowers and plants. This bee is active during the spring and summer.

HOW TO SPOT

Size: 0.8 to 1 inch (20 to 25 mm) long
Range: Western United States and Mexico
Habitat: Forests and meadows
Diet: Nectar and pollen

CICADA KILLER WASP

(SPHECIUS SPECIOSUS)

Cicada killer wasps are among the largest wasps in North America. This wasp has a rust-colored head and thorax. Its abdomen has bright-yellow and black bands. The wasp has six legs that can be yellow to red in color. It also has large, dark-amber wings. Female cicada killer wasps have stingers on the ends of their abdomens. They hunt insects called cicadas to feed their larvae.

FUN FACT
Cicada killer wasps build their nests underground.

HOW TO SPOT

Size: 1.2 to 2 inches (30 to 50 mm) long

Range: United States and Europe

Habitat: Forests, grasslands, parks, and gardens

Diet: Nectar and cicadas

THE CICADA KILLER LIFE CYCLE

Female cicada killer wasps use cicadas as hosts for their eggs. The wasp paralyzes and poisons a cicada. Then she brings it back to the nest and deposits her eggs inside it. When the larvae hatch, they feed off the host cicada.

COMMON EASTERN BUMBLEBEE *(BOMBUS IMPATIENS)*

The common eastern bumblebee is one of North America's most common bumblebees. This bumblebee has short pale-yellow hairs on its thorax. Black hairs cover its head, abdomen, and legs. The male bee has a yellow face, and the female's face is black. The common eastern bumblebee is a social bee. It can form large colonies. The older bees gather pollen during the day while younger bees care for the young. While the bees gather pollen and nectar, they pollinate many plants and flowers. Adult bees chew pollen with their saliva to feed growing bee larvae. When the common eastern bumblebee feels threatened, it may sting.

HOW TO SPOT

Size: 0.3 to 0.8 inches (8 to 20 mm) long

Range: Ontario to Florida, west to North Dakota and East Texas

Habitat: Grasslands, forests, marshes, farms, parks, and gardens

Diet: Nectar and pollen

BEE COMMUNICATION

As social insects, common eastern bumblebees communicate with other bees through touch, vision, wing vibrations, and chemicals called pheromones. The bees send messages about where to find food, the safety of the nest, and their daily activities.

EASTERN CARPENTER BEE

(XYLOCOPA VIRGINICA)

The eastern carpenter bee is large and black or metallic blue-black in color. It lives in the eastern regions of North America and in Central America. It has a large, rounded body with yellow hairs. Its abdomen is black, hairless, and shiny. A female bee has a black face, and a male has a white spot on its face. Female bees can sting. Adults are active in the late spring and again in the late summer before hibernating over the winter months. Females bore tunnels into wood, where they store food and lay eggs.

HOW TO SPOT

Size: 0.8 to 0.9 inches (19 to 23 mm) long

Range: Central America and eastern North America

Habitat: Forests, woodlands, gardens, parks, and houses

Diet: Nectar

FUN FACT

Eastern carpenter bees vibrate their strong muscles to shake pollen from flowers, a method called buzz pollination.

EASTERN YELLOWJACKET

(VESPULA MACULIFRONS)

The eastern yellowjacket is a small wasp with distinct black and yellow lines on its head, thorax, and abdomen. Its body is slightly wider than its head. Males, workers, and queens have differing patterns on their abdomens. The female has a stinger at the end of her abdomen that she can use to repeatedly sting animals in defense of her hive. The yellowjacket has strong jaws that let it capture and chew prey. It also has a tongue for sipping nectar and juices from plants. The eastern yellowjacket is usually peaceful. However, it will attack when it feels threatened. The yellowjacket builds its nest underground.

HOW TO SPOT

Size: 0.5 to 0.7 inches (13 to 18 mm) long

Range: Eastern North America

Habitat: Forests, woodlands, gardens, and parks

Diet: Adults eat nectar and juices; larvae eat insects and arthropods

EXECUTIONER WASP

(POLISTES CARNIFEX)

The executioner wasp is known for its extremely painful sting. The wasp is mostly yellow with brown bands on its abdomen. It has large, narrow wings that are reddish brown in color. Its antennae are yellow with a dark base. The wasp's head is yellow, and its crown is black. The executioner wasp is a paper wasp. Paper wasps build their nests by chewing wood fibers until they become paste-like. The wasps use the paste to build nests under the eaves of buildings or hanging from tree branches. When dry, the nests have the consistency of paper.

FUN FACT

Wasps can repeatedly sting their victims because their stingers are smooth. Bees, whose stingers are barbed, can sting only once because the stinger gets stuck in the victim.

HOW TO SPOT

Size: 0.9 to 1.1 inches (23 to 28 mm) long

Range: Parts of the southern United States; Mexico; Central and South America

Habitat: Humid coastal areas such as tropical forests and woodlands

Diet: Adults eat nectar and juices; larvae eat nectar and insects

GOLDEN NORTHERN BUMBLEBEE *(BOMBUS FERVIDUS)*

The golden northern bumblebee is a large, hairy bee. Most of its body is covered in yellow hair, and it has a black stripe of hairs on the thorax between the wings. Its face and head are mostly black, while its wings are dark and smoky colored. Like other bees, golden northern bumblebee workers fly from flower to flower to collect pollen and nectar. They pollinate the flowers along the way. The nectar and pollen are brought back to the nest to feed the queen and bee larvae. These bees have long tongues that allow them to reach into long flowers.

HOW TO SPOT

Size: 0.6 to 0.8 inches (15 to 20 mm) long

Range: North America

Habitat: Open grassy areas, meadows, forest clearings, and open roadsides

Diet: Nectar and honey

FUN FACT

The golden northern bumblebee's hind legs have pollen baskets. These body structures are used to store pollen so the bee can carry it back to the nest.

GREAT GOLDEN DIGGER WASP

(SPHEX ICHNEUMONEUS)

The great golden digger wasp is one of the larger members of the wasp family. It has a bright-orange body, a black-tipped abdomen, and golden hairs. The great golden digger is a solitary wasp and does not live as part of an organized colony. This wasp is most active during the summer. Female wasps tunnel in the open ground, where they lay eggs and store food. Females hunt for insects such as crickets, katydids, and grasshoppers to feed their larvae.

HOW TO SPOT

Size: 0.6 to 0.9 inches (15 to 23 mm) long

Range: The Americas and the Caribbean

Habitat: Meadows with open, sandy areas

Diet: Adults eat nectar and juices; larvae eat crickets, katydids, and grasshoppers

MURDER HORNET *(VESPA MANDARINIA)*

The murder hornet, also known as the Asian giant hornet, is the world's largest hornet. It has a large, yellow head with powerful jaws that it uses to overpower prey. The hornet's thorax is black, while its abdomen has alternating bands of yellow and black. Its body is covered in hair. The hornet also has two pairs of wings. A female murder hornet has a smooth stinger that is nearly 0.4 inches (10 mm) long. Murder hornets are social hornets and live in colonies.

HOW TO SPOT

Size: 1.5 to 2 inches (38 to 51 mm) long
Range: Asia; some colonies spotted in North America in 2019
Habitat: Dense woodlands
Diet: Bees, honeybees, insects, and wasps

FUN FACT
One murder hornet can kill up to 40 honeybees in a single minute.

ATTACKING HONEYBEES

A murder hornet kills a honeybee by detaching the bee's head from its body. Then the hornet chews the bee into a gummy paste that it takes back to the nest for its larvae. Sometimes a group of ten to 20 murder hornets will stage a coordinated attack on an entire honeybee colony.

WESTERN HONEYBEE

(APIS MELLIFERA)

The western honeybee is mostly reddish brown and black in color, with orange and yellow rings on its abdomen. Its head, antennae, and legs are black. Short, pale hairs cover its thorax and lightly cover its abdomen. The honeybee's wings are translucent. The bee has a pollen basket on its hind legs. The western honeybee is a social bee that lives in colonies of up to 80,000 workers and a single queen bee. Colonies build hives in hollow trees and similar spaces.

HOW TO SPOT

Size: 0.4 to 0.8 inches (10 to 20 mm) long

Range: Worldwide

Habitat: Meadows, open wooded areas, and gardens near flowering plants

Diet: Nectar and honey

FUN FACT

Honeybees build their hives out of wax secretions from their bodies. The honeybee queens lay eggs in cells in the wax.

ONE CHANCE TO STING

A honeybee worker has a barbed stinger. The bee can sting only once. When the bee stings its victim, the bee's stinger sticks in the target. The stinger rips out of the bee's abdomen, causing the bee to die.

AFRICAN WEAVER ANT

(OECOPHYLLA LONGINODA)

The African weaver ant is a large ant that varies from orange to dark brown in color. The thorax is covered with fine hairs, while short hairs cover the abdomen. The ant's feet have suction pads that allow it to firmly cling to surfaces. Its antennae have 12 segments. The African weaver has large mandibles with long, triangular teeth. It uses silk produced by its larvae to stitch leaves together and build nests in trees. African weaver ants are aggressive and will attack other ants and insects.

FUN FACT

If their nest is disturbed, thousands of African weaver ants will drop down to attack, bite, and secrete a mild acid on the intruder.

HOW TO SPOT

Size: 0.2 inches (5 mm) long
Range: Sub-Saharan Africa
Habitat: Tropical rain forests
Diet: Insects and ants

ARGENTINE ANT *(LINEPITHEMA HUMILE)*

The Argentine ant is small and brown in color with a flattened head. It has a thin petiole, a structure that connects its thorax and abdomen. The ant's mandibles, antennae, and legs can be yellow, red, or brown. This ant is active year-round and often found near human homes. It lives in large colonies that sometimes join together to form super colonies. Argentine ants are aggressive predators. They will attack other ants and insects to defend their colonies.

HOW TO SPOT

Size: 0.08 to 0.1 inch (2 to 3 mm) long

Range: All continents except Antarctica

Habitat: Forests; fields; and near rivers, homes, buildings, and other areas where humans live

Diet: Insects; nectar; honeydew, liquid secreted by aphids and other insects; and human food

BLACK CARPENTER ANT

(CAMPONOTUS PENNSYLVANICUS)

One part of the black carpenter ant's name comes from its black color. The other part comes from the fact that it creates its nests in damaged wood. It has one petiole connecting its thorax and abdomen. The ant's abdomen has long, pale-yellow or grayish hairs. Carpenter ants are active during the spring and summer. In hot weather, they search for food at night. This ant species does not sting, but individuals will bite and spray a type of acid at predators.

HOW TO SPOT

Size: Workers are 0.2 to 0.6 inches (5 to 16 mm) long; queens average 0.75 inches (19 mm) long

Range: Eastern United States and Canada

Habitat: Logs, tree trunks, timber, and buildings

Diet: Insects, honeydew, fruit juices, sugar grains, and other sweets

FIRE ANT *(SOLENOPSIS GEMINATA)*

The fire ant ranges in color from dull yellow to red or black. It has a large head and jaws. It has two segments between its thorax and abdomen. Fine hair covers its head and abdomen. Its antennae have ten segments, with two at the end forming a structure called a club. Fire ants live in large colonies that may contain hundreds of thousands of worker ants. This species builds nests in the soil that often take the form of large soil mounds. Workers have powerful stings and bites that produce a burning sensation like fire.

FUN FACT

Worker fire ants dig underground tunnels that can stretch up to 25 feet (8 m) away from the nest's large soil mound.

HOW TO SPOT

Size: 0.06 to 0.3 inches (2 to 8 mm) long

Range: Most of the United States and southern Canada

Habitat: Fields, woodlands, and open areas in dry to moist soil

Diet: Insects, seeds, poultry, fruits, honeydew, vegetables, and flowers

ODOROUS HOUSE ANT

(TAPINOMA SESSILE)

Odorous house ants are one of the most widespread ant species across North America. This small ant ranges in color from brown to black, with lighter jaws and legs. Worker ants have oval-shaped heads, short thoraxes, and slightly arched bodies. They may have a few light-yellow hairs on their bodies. These ants do not sting, but they can bite. When crushed, odorous house ants emit an unpleasant smell similar to that of rotten coconuts. These ants often build nests in mulch, debris piles, and buildings. Once the ants establish a colony, they are difficult to move.

FUN FACT

Once an odorous house ant finds food, it leaves an invisible scent trail back to its nest so the other worker ants can find the food too.

HOW TO SPOT

Size: 0.09 to 0.17 inches (2 to 4 mm) long

Range: Southern Canada to northern Mexico

Habitat: Forests, meadows, grasslands, parks, gardens, mulch, and dirt piles

Diet: Honeydew, nectar, small insects and spiders, and human food

PHARAOH ANT

(MONOMORIUM PHARAONIC)

The pharaoh ant is a very small ant that is a common indoor pest. The ant's body is yellow to light brown to red and almost transparent. It is smooth and shiny with a tiny waist featuring two knobs that connect its thorax and abdomen. The ant's antennae have 12 segments with a three-segment club at the tip. Pharaoh ants use their antennae to sense vibrations and help them navigate dark areas. These ants often establish colonies in hard-to-reach places in buildings. They do not sting, but they are among the most difficult ants to remove from a home.

HOW TO SPOT

Size: 0.04 to 0.08 inches (1 to 2 mm) long

Range: Worldwide

Habitat: Heated structures and soil in subtropical regions

Diet: Insects and household foods

ROUGH HARVESTER ANT

(POGONOMYRMEX RUGOSUS)

The rough harvester ant is reddish brown in color. It has a two-segment waist between its thorax and abdomen. The ant's head has strong mouthparts for chewing seeds and grains. The ant also has hairs on the underside of its head that it uses to carry objects. A female rough harvester ant has a stinger at the tip of the abdomen. During the day, these ants spread out from the colony to gather plants and seeds for the nest. When threatened, harvester ants can sting or bite. When the colony is attacked, these ants will swarm to defend it.

HOW TO SPOT

Size: 0.3 to 0.5 inches (8 to 13 mm) long

Range: Southwestern United States into Mexico

Habitat: Lowlands, bare areas, and sandy areas near roads

Diet: Seeds, grains, and plant materials

WINTER ANT *(PRENOLEPIS IMPARIS)*

The winter ant is common across the United States. Worker winter ants are light to dark brown in color. Queen ants are reddish brown, and males are black. The ant's head is sometimes darker than its midsection and legs. Overall, the ant's body is smooth, shiny, and shaped like an hourglass. It has a one-segment waist between its thorax and abdomen. The winter ant is most active during cool weather, when other ant species are less likely to gather food. During warmer months, these ants close off their nest entrance and become dormant.

HOW TO SPOT

Size: 0.1 to 0.3 inches (3 to 8 mm) long
Range: North America
Habitat: Wooded areas and damp soil with clay
Diet: Dead insects, earthworms, small arthropods, seeds, nectar, honeydew, and decaying fruits

STORING FOOD

Some winter ants act as food storage units for the colony. These ants fill their bellies with nectar. Too big and bloated to move, they hang from the roof of the nest. When food is scarce, the ants will regurgitate the food in their bellies to feed the members of their colony.

BANDED WOOLLYBEAR MOTH

(PYRRHARCTIA ISABELLA)

The banded woollybear moth is a type of tiger moth. It has yellowish-brown forewings with rows of small, black spots. The moth's hindwings are paler than its forewings, are tinted pinkish orange, and have black or gray spots. Adult moths are active from the late winter through the late fall. They are nocturnal and are attracted to lights. The woollybear's caterpillar form is covered in a band of red-orange hair in the middle and a band of black hair on each end.

HOW TO SPOT

Size: Wingspan of 1.6 to 2.1 inches (4 to 5 cm)

Range: Southern Canada, the United States, and northern Mexico

Habitat: Fields, meadows, pastures, and roadsides

Diet: Adults eat nectar; larvae eat plants and trees

FUN FACT

Wet weather lengthens the black bands on the woollybear caterpillar. The red band lengthens as the caterpillar matures.

CABBAGE WHITE *(PIERIS RAPAE)*

The cabbage white is a small- to medium-size butterfly. This butterfly is known for its white wings. The forewings have black tips and black spots, with one spot on males and two spots on females. The butterfly's hindwings can be white, pale yellow, or gray-white. Adult butterflies are active from early spring through late fall. They fly mostly during the day and rest at night. The caterpillar form is a bright-green color and is covered with short hairs. It has yellow stripes on its sides and back.

HOW TO SPOT

Size: Wingspan of 1.8 to 2.3 inches (5 to 6 cm)

Range: Worldwide

Habitat: Open spaces including gardens, grasses, roadsides, and parks in urban and suburban areas

Diet: Adults eat nectar; larvae eat cabbages and other plants in the mustard family

CASEMAKING CLOTHES MOTH

(TINEA PELLIONELLA)

The casemaking clothes moth is a small moth. It has long, narrow forewings that are brownish gray in color and fringed with small hairs. The forewings also have one or more dark spots. The moth's hindwings are a pale brown-gray. These moths are active year-round in homes. They prefer dark areas such as closets, basements, and attics. Adult casemaking clothes moths do not feed. However, their larvae eat fabric and can destroy clothing. The casemaking clothes moth encloses itself in an open-ended, silken, tube-shaped case. It makes the case from fibers of materials the larva has eaten. The larva drags the case wherever it goes.

HOW TO SPOT

Size: Wingspan of 0.4 to 0.6 inches (1 to 1.5 cm)

Range: Worldwide

Habitat: Birds' nests and indoors in buildings and structures

Diet: Adults do not feed; larvae eat wool, fur, feathers, and hair

CECROPIA MOTH

(HYALOPHORA CECROPIA)

The cecropia moth is the largest moth in North America. Its wingspan can reach up to 6 inches (15 cm). The wings are brownish with white, red, and tan bands. Each wing has a large crescent shape outlined in black. The forewings also have a crescent in an eyespot near the tip. The moth's body is hairy with red and white bands on its abdomen. Adult cecropia moths are active at night during the spring and summer and are attracted to lights. The cecropia caterpillar is pale green with orange, yellow, and blue knobs.

HOW TO SPOT

Size: Wingspan of 4.3 to 6 inches (11 to 15 cm)

Range: Southern Canada and much of the United States

Habitat: Open areas with trees

Diet: Adults do not feed; larvae eat leaves

FUN FACT

Moths have hairy bodies to help them maintain their internal body temperatures.

EYESPOTS

Some butterflies and moths have eyespots. An eyespot is a marking on the wing or tail of a butterfly or moth that looks like an eye. Eyespots may deter predators or trick them into attacking parts of the insect's body that aren't needed for survival.

COMMON WOOD-NYMPH

(CERCYONIS PEGALA)

The common wood-nymph is a familiar butterfly in North America. Common wood-nymphs are brown and have two ringed eyespots on each forewing. Some may have additional smaller eyespots on the hindwings. Butterflies that live in southern and coastal regions are larger and have yellowish patches on the outer forewings. Butterflies that live more inland are smaller and may not have yellow patches. The caterpillar is bright green with two yellow stripes on each side. It has fine, fuzzy hair and two short red tails.

HOW TO SPOT

Size: Wingspan of 1.8 to 3 inches (5 to 8 cm)

Range: Southern Canada and most of the continental United States, except the Southwest and Florida

Habitat: Large, sunny, grassy areas including prairies, open meadows, bogs, and fields

Diet: Adults eat rotting fruits and nectar; larvae eat grasses

GIANT SWALLOWTAIL

(PAPILIO CRESPHONTES)

The giant swallowtail is the largest butterfly in North America. It is a dark-brown to black butterfly with a striking diagonal band of yellow spots across its forewings. The undersides of the wings are mostly yellow. This butterfly is active year-round, though only rarely during midwinter. The caterpillar is brown or olive with buff spots and can sometimes look like a bird dropping.

HOW TO SPOT

Size: Wingspan of 4 to 6.3 inches (10 to 16 cm)
Range: The Americas
Habitat: Woodlands, gardens, and citrus groves
Diet: Adults eat nectar; larvae eat leaves and young plant shoots

FUN FACT

When threatened, the giant swallowtail caterpillar sticks out an orange gland and gives off a bad smell to deter predators.

GRAY HAIRSTREAK

(STRYMON MELINUS)

The gray hairstreak is a small butterfly with gray-purple wings. The undersides of its wings are gray with a white line along the edges. On its hindwings, the butterfly has a black dot within an orange spot. An orange spot can also be found on its head, between the eyes. The gray hairstreak also has a tail on each of its hindwings.

FUN FACT

When a predator approaches, the grey hairstreak can wriggle the tails on its hindwings. The moving tails look like antennae and may trick the predator into attacking the wrong end of the insect.

HOW TO SPOT

Size: Wingspan of 0.9 to 1.4 inches (2 to 4 cm)

Range: Southern Canada to northwestern South America

Habitat: Tropical forests, open woodland areas, meadows, fields, open roadsides, parks, and yards

Diet: Adults eat nectar; larvae eat flowers, fruits, and leaves

LUNA MOTH *(ACTIAS LUNA)*

Luna moths are large, pale-green moths. Each wing has a transparent eyespot. The hindwings have long, curving tails. In the summer, the moth's forewings have a pink, yellow, or reddish-brown color along the leading edge. These beautiful moths are active at night and are drawn to lights. The caterpillar form is bright green and covered with small spots that are black and pink. Yellow lines fall between the caterpillar's segments.

HOW TO SPOT

Size: Wingspan of 3 to 4 inches (8 to 10 cm)

Range: Southern Canada, the United States, and Mexico

Habitat: Hardwood forests

Diet: Adults do not feed; larvae eat leaves of hardwood trees

MONARCH *(DANAUS PLEXIPPUS)*

The monarch is one of the most recognizable butterflies in the United States. The butterfly's body is black with white spots on its head and thorax. It has reddish-orange wings with a pattern of wide black borders and veins. The wings have small white and pale-orange spots along a black border. The tips of the wings are black with pale-orange spots. From August to October, the monarch migrates south. The caterpillar has black, white, and yellow bands that look a bit like a tiger's stripes.

HOW TO SPOT

Size: Wingspan of 3.4 to 4.9 inches (9 to 12 cm)

Range: North America up to southern Canada, Central and South America

Habitat: Fields, meadows, weedy areas, marshes, and roadsides

Diet: Adults eat nectar; larvae eat milkweed

FUN FACT

The monarch butterfly is said to be named after King William III of England, often known as William of Orange.

MOURNING CLOAK

(NYMPHALIS ANTIOPA)

The mourning cloak butterfly can be easily identified by its dark brownish-maroon wings with yellow edges and blue spots. The undersides of the wings are a black-brown color with fine lines and lighter brown to yellowish edges. These butterflies are active during the spring and early summer through fall. They hibernate during the winter. The caterpillar is velvety black with red and white spots on its back, and it has several rows of black bristles.

HOW TO SPOT

Size: Wingspan of 2.9 to 3.4 inches (7 to 8 cm)

Range: North America, Europe, and Asia

Habitat: Sunny open areas, gardens, parks, open woodlands, and along streams and rivers

Diet: Adults eat tree sap and rotting fruits; larvae eat leaves

THE MANY USES OF WINGS

Butterflies and moths have two pairs of wings called the forewings and hindwings. The wings serve several roles. Primarily, these insects use their wings to fly. Brightly colored males also use their wings to attract females in courtship displays. Additionally, wings can help butterflies and moths regulate their body temperatures and provide camouflage to avoid predators.

PAINTED LADY *(VANESSA CARDUI)*

The painted lady butterfly has orange-brown wings. Its forewings have black, rounded tips with white spots. Its hindwings have a row of black spots along the edges. The wing's underside has a black, brown, and gray pattern with small eyespots. Painted lady butterflies are active from spring through fall. While they prefer open areas such as fields and meadows, they are very adaptable and can live in a variety of habitats. The caterpillar is grayish brown with black marbling, a yellow stripe on its back, and gray spines.

FUN FACT

The painted lady butterfly makes an annual mass migration that can be up to 9,300 miles (15,000 km) long.

HOW TO SPOT

Size: Wingspan of 2 to 2.9 inches (5 to 7 cm)

Range: Worldwide, except Australia and Antarctica

Habitat: Areas with wide-open areas of vegetation such as fields and meadows

Diet: Adults eat nectar; larvae eat leaves

SPRING AZURE *(CELASTRINA LADON)*

The spring azure butterfly is widespread across most of North America. The butterfly's wings are pale to bright blue in color. The wing's edges have a checkered border on males and a wider black-gray border on females. The undersides of the wings are gray with several darker spots. Adults are active during spring and summer in northern and western regions. In southern regions, these butterflies are active year-round.

HOW TO SPOT

Size: Wingspan of 0.8 to 1.2 inches (2 to 3 cm)

Range: Most of North America

Habitat: Gardens, woodlands, desert foothills, tundra, and other habitats

Diet: Adults eat nectar; larvae eat flowers and fruits

BEDBUG *(CIMEX LECTULARIUS)*

The bedbug is a parasite that feeds on the blood of humans and other animals. The insect is flat, round, and covered in short, stiff hairs. It has small leathery wings that are wider than they are long. Its pronotum is notched and fringed with hairs. The bedbug is active at night. It crawls to find a human host for a blood meal. Before feeding, the bedbug is usually brown in color. After feeding, its body swells and becomes redder.

FUN FACT

The lump or swelling experienced after a bedbug bite is caused by an allergic reaction to the bedbug's saliva.

HOW TO SPOT

Size: 0.2 to 0.3 inches (4 to 7 mm) long

Range: Worldwide

Habitat: Human dwellings in beds, bedding, clothing, carpets, and furniture

Diet: Human blood

GIANT WATER BUG

(LETHOCERUS AMERICANUS)

The giant water bug is brown and flat with an oval shape. It sometimes looks like a dead leaf. It has flattened hind legs that it uses as oars when swimming. It is a fierce predator. When hunting, the bug uses a hook-shaped claw on its forelegs to grab and hold prey. Then the water bug pierces its prey with its sharp beak. It injects a powerful toxin that paralyzes the prey. Then it liquefies the internal parts of the prey's body. The bug sucks up the resulting liquid.

FUN FACT

Water bugs are also called toe biters because they have painful bites.

HOW TO SPOT

Size: 1.6 to 2.5 inches (41 to 64 mm) long

Range: Worldwide

Habitat: Freshwater ponds, marshes, and slow-moving streams

Diet: Insects, tadpoles, and small fish

BREATHING UNDERWATER

The giant water bug has a unique adaptation for living in water. It has breathing tubes at the end of its abdomen. These tubes reach the water's surface like snorkels. The water bug can draw in air through the tubes. The air enters the body through holes in the abdomen.

GREEN PEACH APHID

(MYZUS PERSICAE)

The green peach aphid is a small bug that may be winged or wingless. Winged green peach aphids have black heads and thoraxes and yellow-green abdomens with a large dark patch. Wingless aphids are yellow to green in color. Some have green stripes down the middle or sides of their bodies. The aphid also has cornicles, or tubes, that project from the abdomen. The tubes secrete a defensive fluid. The green peach aphid is considered a pest because of its ability to spread plant viruses.

HOW TO SPOT

Size: 0.08 inches (2 mm) long
Range: Worldwide
Habitat: A variety of host plants
Diet: Host plants including lettuce, peach, potato, spinach, tomato, and other vegetables and ornamental crops

LARGE MILKWEED BUG
(ONCOPELTUS FASCIATUS)

The large milkweed bug is bright orangish red and black in color. On the thorax, a black diamond shape is surrounded by an orange border. A thick, black band crosses the middle of the bug's body. The lower ends of its wings are also black. Adult milkweed bugs are active from spring to fall and are typically found in large groups. They can fly from plant to plant to gather food. The bug uses its long mouthpart to pierce and suck food.

FUN FACT

The bright colors of the giant milkweed bug warn predators of its bitter taste, which is caused by the bug's diet.

HOW TO SPOT

Size: 0.4 to 0.7 inches (10 to 18 mm) long

Range: North and Central America

Habitat: Fields and meadows containing milkweed

Diet: Seeds, leaves, and stems of milkweed

PALE GREEN ASSASSIN BUG

(ZELUS LURIDUS)

The pale green assassin bug has a slender, green body with a narrow head and wings that range from tan to brown. The male is smaller and darker than the female of this species. The bug's head is dark brown or black with red eyes. It has a shield-like shoulder plate with a pair of spines. As its name suggests, the assassin bug preys on other insects. It captures small, soft-bodied prey using a sticky secretion on its forelegs.

FUN FACT

Sometimes the assassin bug waits on a leaf to attack an unsuspecting insect. Other times, it actively hunts its prey.

HOW TO SPOT

Size: 0.5 to 0.8 inches (13 to 20 mm) long

Range: Southeastern Canada, the United States, and Mexico

Habitat: Wooded habitats and along roadsides

Diet: Other insects

RED-BANDED LEAFHOPPER

(GRAPHOCEPHALA COCCINEA)

The red-banded leafhopper is a brightly colored, slender bug native to North and Central America. It has yellow legs and a yellow head with a black stripe through the eyes. Its thorax and wings are striped with bright blue-green and red-orange. As its name suggests, the leafhopper moves by hopping or leaping. It is often found near blackberry and raspberry bushes and ornamental plants such as roses and rhododendrons. When threatened, the leafhopper springs away from potential predators. These bugs are active from the spring through fall.

HOW TO SPOT

Size: 0.3 to 0.4 inches (8 to 10 mm) long
Range: Northern and eastern North America and Central America
Habitat: Meadows and woodlands
Diet: Sap of vines, plants, and shrubs

SQUASH BUG *(ANASA TRISTIS)*

The squash bug is a common pest found on pumpkins and squash. The adult squash bug has an oval body that ranges from gray to black in color. It has orange and brown stripes along the edges of its abdomen. Its wings fold flat over the body. The squash bug uses its mouthparts to suck sap from plants. When it feeds, the squash bug damages the plant and injects a toxic substance that causes the plant to wilt and blacken.

HOW TO SPOT

Size: 0.5 to 1 inch (13 to 25 mm) long

Range: North and Central America

Habitat: Agricultural fields and gardens

Diet: Sap from the stems, leaves, and fruits of melon and squash plants

STINK BUG *(BANASA DIMIATA)*

The stink bug is widespread in North America. This bug gets its name from the unpleasant odor it emits when threatened. It produces a smelly chemical in a gland on its abdomen as a way to deter predators. Although its color can vary, the stink bug typically has a two-color pronotum that is green near the head and dark green or reddish brown toward the abdomen. The stink bug has two pairs of wings. The forewings are longer and cover the hindwings. Stink bugs are active from spring to fall in many types of trees and shrubs.

FUN FACT

The stink bug's smelly chemical attracts other stink bugs. In the fall, the bugs release the chemical when they find a warm place to gather.

HOW TO SPOT

Size: 0.3 to 0.4 inches (8 to 10 mm) long

Range: Southern Canada to northern Mexico

Habitat: Orchards, gardens, and farms

Diet: A variety of trees and shrubs

FAMILIAR BLUET DAMSELFLY

(ENALLAGMA CIVILE)

The familiar bluet damselfly's bright-blue color makes it easy to see as it flies from plant to plant in search of insects to eat. The male has blue around the eyes and black stripes down the thorax. It has a long, thin abdomen that is mostly blue with black spots. The female familiar bluet has a similar shape and markings but has pale-blue or light-brown coloring. The familiar bluet is active in the late spring through fall in most areas. It lives near water and lays its eggs just under the water's surface.

HOW TO SPOT

Size: 1.3 to 1.7 inches (34 to 44 mm) long

Range: North America

Habitat: Lakes, ponds, bogs, streams, and slow rivers

Diet: Small insects

FIELD CRICKET

(GRYLLUS PENNSYLVANICUS)

Adult field crickets are black and brown with long antennae. They use their large hind legs to jump powerfully and rapidly. All field crickets make the recognized chirping sound. A cricket's chirping sound occurs when it rubs scrapers on its left forewing across a row of teeth-like structures on its right forewing. The male field cricket creates a three-note song. The female answers with a two-note song. Field crickets are active during the summer and fall. They typically live in small burrows in grassy areas and on the ground underneath plant matter.

HOW TO SPOT

Size: 0.6 to 1 inch (15 to 25 mm) long
Range: North America
Habitat: Grassy areas
Diet: Plants, small fruits, seeds, and insects

FUN FACT

The field cricket chirps more rapidly in warmer weather. Taking the number of chirps in 13 seconds and adding 40 gives an approximate temperature in degrees Fahrenheit.

GREEN DARNER DRAGONFLY

(ANAX JUNIUS)

The green darner dragonfly got its name because it looks like a darning needle. It has large eyes and a short, thick, green thorax with four wings. Its abdomen is long and thin with a black stripe on the back. Males are mostly green with some blue segments on their abdomens. Females can be green, brown, and grayish green in color. Adults are active during the day, dawn, and dusk. They often rest in foliage around ponds and other water sources. As strong fliers, they are successful at hunting prey in the air.

FUN FACT

The green darner dragonfly's four wings move independently. This allows the dragonfly to fly forward and backward and rapidly change directions.

HOW TO SPOT

Size: 2.7 to 3.1 inches (68 to 79 mm) long

Range: North and Central America, the Caribbean, and parts of Asia

Habitat: Areas near rivers, streams, ponds, and other water sources

Diet: Insects

ORIENTAL COCKROACH
(BLATTA ORIENTALIS)

The oriental cockroach, also called a water bug, lives in every country in the world. It is shiny black or dark brown in color. The male has wings that cover approximately 75 percent of its body, while the female has short wing pads. Neither the male nor the female can fly. The oriental cockroach is active year-round. It lives in a variety of places, including basements, cellars, crawl spaces, hollow trees, and stumps. Sometimes a large infestation of oriental cockroaches can be detected by a strong, musty odor.

HOW TO SPOT

Size: 0.7 to 1.2 inches (18 to 30 mm) long

Range: Worldwide

Habitat: Areas containing natural debris and warm, damp, shady areas near the ground

Diet: Garbage, sewage, and decaying organic matter

MAKING PEOPLE SICK

As the oriental cockroach crawls through unsanitary areas, it spreads dirt, bacteria, and other germs wherever it walks. By shedding skin and excreting waste products, these cockroaches can contaminate food and spread allergens that trigger allergic reactions and other illnesses in nearby humans.

PRAYING MANTIS *(MANTIS RELIGIOSA)*

The praying mantis gets its name from the way its long front legs sometimes appear to be folded in prayer. The praying mantis has a large, elongated, green or tan body. It has two pairs of wings that stretch past its abdomen. The mantis also has a mobile, triangle-shaped head with large eyes. Adults are active during the late summer and fall. They hunt a variety of insects by day. The praying mantis is a solitary insect. It interacts with another mantis only to mate in late summer.

FUN FACT

The praying mantis can swivel its head 180 degrees to look at its surroundings.

HOW TO SPOT

Size: 2 to 2.6 inches (51 to 66 mm) long

Range: Southern Europe, Asia, Africa, Australia, and North America

Habitat: Meadows

Diet: Caterpillars, butterflies, flies, and some species of moth

SPUR-THROATED GRASSHOPPER

(MELANOPLUS PONDEROSUS)

The spur-throated grasshopper is one of the most common grasshoppers in North America. The grasshopper is typically yellow, green, or pale brown in color. Its body may have bands, spots, or blotches of color on it. It has a blunt projection between the bases of its forelegs that looks like a spur. Its hind legs are often orange or reddish with yellow and brown markings. The spur-throated grasshopper's chewing mouthparts tear away plant tissue. It is known for causing damage to corn, small grains, and other crops.

HOW TO SPOT

Size: 1 to 1.8 inches (25 to 45 mm) long

Range: North America

Habitat: Open fields, meadows, and grasslands

Diet: Grasses and leaves

BANDED GARDEN SPIDER

(ARGIOPE TRIFASCIATA)

The banded garden spider is a large spider with an egg-shaped body and bright markings. The spider's color varies. Some are reddish brown with white bands. Others are black with white and yellow bands. The spider's legs also have bands in colors similar to its body. Silver hairs cover the spider's neck area. The banded garden spider builds an orb-shaped web in gardens between plants. It sits and waits in the center of its web with its body upside down until prey become stuck in the web.

HOW TO SPOT

Size: Females are 0.6 to 1 inch (15 to 25 mm) long; males are 0.2 inches (5 mm) long

Range: The Americas

Habitat: Open areas with tall grasses, plants, and shrubs

Diet: Insects

SPINNERETS

A spinneret is a spider's silk-producing organ. Spinnerets are shaped like tubes or cones. Liquid silk emerges from the spinneret's tip. When the liquid silk hits the air, it forms a filament. The spider draws the silk filament into a thread. Then the spider uses the silk thread to create a web or cocoon covering.

BARN SPIDER *(ARANEUS CAVATICUS)*

The barn spider creates intricate wheel-shaped webs to catch prey. This spider ranges from light brown to dark brown in color. Its abdomen is often reddish brown and covered with tiny hairs that are red and brown. The spider's long legs are thicker at the base and become thin and pointy at the ends. The legs have striped bands of red, brown, and white. Barn spiders capture their prey in sticky webs. Every day at dusk, the spider builds a new web. In the morning it consumes the web and is ready to build again that night.

HOW TO SPOT

Size: Males are 0.2 to 0.4 inches (6 to 10 mm) long; females are 0.5 to 0.6 inches (12 to 16 mm) long

Range: North America

Habitat: Barns, caves, mine openings, and cliff overhangs

Diet: Insects such as mosquitoes, flies, beetles, and moths

BOLD JUMPING SPIDER

(PHIDIPPUS AUDAX)

The bold jumping spider is black with spots and stripes on its abdomen and legs. In young spiders the spots are orange, but they turn white in older spiders. The spider's mouthparts are bright metallic-blue or green. This spider has eight eyes and very good eyesight. It uses its good eyesight to hunt its prey. Like other jumping spiders, the bold jumping spider does not build webs to catch prey. Instead, it actively hunts and stalks its prey during the day. First it watches the prey. Then it sneaks up on the prey and jumps on it.

FUN FACT

When a bold jumping spider leaps, it releases a line of webbing. If the jump fails, the line catches the spider as it falls.

HOW TO SPOT

Size: Males are 0.3 to 0.5 inches (8 to 13 mm) long; females are 0.4 to 0.6 inches (10 to 15 mm) long

Range: Southern Canada and the United States east of the Rocky Mountains

Habitat: Grasslands, prairies, and open woodlands

Diet: Insects

BROWN RECLUSE SPIDER

(LOXOSCELES RECLUSA)

The brown recluse spider has a yellow-brown neck with a brown patch shaped like a violin. Its abdomen is covered with short hairs that look like soft fur. The rest of the spider's body is a darker, reddish brown. This spider has six eyes arranged in three pairs. It also has long, thin legs covered in small hairs. The bite of a brown recluse spider releases a small amount of highly toxic venom. Wounds can be slow to heal. Some bites lead to infections or cause the affected tissue to die.

HOW TO SPOT

Size: Males are 0.3 inches (8 mm) long; females are 0.4 inches (9 mm) long

Range: Midwestern and southern United States

Habitat: Outdoors under rocks and debris; may be found in homes and outbuildings

Diet: Small insects

CAROLINA WOLF SPIDER

(HOGNA CAROLINENSIS)

The Carolina wolf spider is the largest wolf spider species in North America. It is dark brown in color with gray hairs on its neck area. Its underside is black, while its brown abdomen has a dark stripe down the middle. This wolf spider is active during the summer. It is a skilled hunter that seeks out its prey. Though sometimes seen during the day, the giant wolf spider is mainly nocturnal. Its dark coloring helps camouflage it on the ground. The female spins a large egg sac and attaches it to her spinneret. Then she drags the egg sac until her spiderlings hatch.

FUN FACT

After the spiderlings hatch, they climb onto the back of the female Carolina wolf spider. She carries them until they are ready to live on their own.

HOW TO SPOT

Size: Males are 0.8 inches (20 mm) long; females are 0.9 to 1.4 inches (23 to 36 mm) long

Range: United States

Habitat: Various habitats

Diet: Insects

COBWEB SPIDER

(ENOPLOGNATHA OVATA)

The small cobweb spider varies in color and pattern. Its abdomen can be white, cream, or green in color. The spider may also have dark spots on the side of the abdomen, a broad red stripe, or two red stripes in a V pattern. Its legs are translucent. The cobweb spider is a predator. It preys on insects that are much bigger than itself. The female lays eggs in a white sac that gradually becomes blue-gray. The spider hides the egg sac in a rolled-up leaf tied with silk. The female guards the egg sac until the eggs hatch.

HOW TO SPOT

Size: 0.2 inches (5 mm) long

Range: Europe and North America

Habitat: Shrubs, grasslands, and gardens

Diet: Small insects

COMMON HOUSE SPIDER

(ACHAEARANEA TEPIDARIORUM)

Common house spiders are among the most widespread spiders in North America. This spider is often found in houses, barns, storage sheds, fences, and other structures. It ranges in color from yellowish tan to black and has patches of faded color on its back. Its yellow legs have lightly ringed segments, while its abdomen ranges from dull white to brown. The common house spider spins uneven webs that can be spotted in wall and window corners.

HOW TO SPOT

Size: Males are 0.2 inches (4 mm) long; females are 0.2 to 0.3 inches (5 to 8 mm) long
Range: Southern Canada and the United States
Habitat: Dwellings and other structures
Diet: Insects

FUN FACT

A house spider's web is made of many crisscrossing strands of sticky silk.

DESERT TARANTULA

(APHONOPELMA CHALCODES)

The desert tarantula can be found in the deserts and woodlands of the southwestern United States. The spider is mostly black with a brownish-gray neck and a patch of rust-colored stinging hairs on its abdomen. The stinging hairs ward off potential predators. Females are larger and heavier than males and are also lighter in color. The spider is nocturnal and solitary. It often hides in its burrow or under rocks during the day. At night it emerges to search for food. The tarantula bites prey with its fangs and injects it with venom.

HOW TO SPOT

Size: Up to 2.8 inches (71 mm) long

Range: Southwestern United States

Habitat: Desert soil

Diet: Lizards, crickets, beetles, grasshoppers, cicadas, and caterpillars

LONG-BODIED CELLAR SPIDER *(PHOLCUS PHALANGIOIDES)*

The long-bodied cellar spider has a pale, yellow-brown body with a large, gray patch in the center of its cephalothorax. This small spider has a narrow abdomen and very long, thin legs. It spins an irregular web in dark cellars, garages, and other structures. Then it hangs upside down in the web where it waits to capture prey such as insects and other spiders.

FUN FACT

The long-bodied cellar spider is commonly known as the daddy longlegs spider, but it should not be confused with another order of arachnids called harvestmen, which are also nicknamed daddy longlegs.

HOW TO SPOT

Size: 0.2 to 0.4 inches (5 to 10 mm) long

Range: Worldwide

Habitat: Under stones and ledges and in low-light locations such as cellars and caves

Diet: Insects and other spiders

RABID WOLF SPIDER

(LYCOSA RABIDA)

The rabid wolf spider is brownish yellow in color with dark stripes. As a nocturnal spider, it actively hunts insect prey at night. The female spins a silk cocoon around her eggs. She attaches the cocoon to her spinnerets and carries it with her. After they hatch, the spiderlings ride on the female's back until they are ready to move on their own.

HOW TO SPOT

Size: Males are 0.5 inches (13 mm) long; females are 0.6 to 0.8 inches (15 to 20 mm) long

Range: Eastern and midwestern United States

Habitat: Woods, meadows, in litter, and on low foliage

Diet: Small insects

FUN FACT

Although they are called rabid wolf spiders, these arachnids do not carry the rabies virus. They get their name from their erratic movements.

SOUTHERN BLACK WIDOW SPIDER *(LATRODECTUS MACTANS)*

The southern black widow spider is a species of venomous spider found in North America. The southern black widow is shiny and black. The female has a red hourglass marking on the underside of her abdomen and red spots on her back. The male has red and white stripes on the sides of his elongated abdomen. The spider has curved bristles on its hind legs that form a comb foot that is used to throw silk over prey. The female black widow's venom is extremely toxic to people. Male black widows do not bite.

HOW TO SPOT

Size: Males are 0.1 inches (3 mm) long; females are 0.4 inches (10 mm) long

Range: Southeastern United States

Habitat: Among fallen branches and under objects such as furniture, trash, and more

Diet: Insects

FUN FACT

After mating, the female black widow sometimes eats the male spider. This is the reason for the word *widow* in the spider's name.

SPITTING SPIDER

(SCYTODES THORACICA)

The spitting spider has a pale, yellow body with black markings that resemble a musical instrument known as a lyre. The spider's long legs have black bands and taper away from the body. Adults are active during the summer inside dwellings. At night they hunt. When it finds prey, the spider spits a sticky substance at it. It covers the prey in numerous overlapping bands of the goo. The material paralyzes the prey. Once the sticky substance dries, the spider bites the prey and injects venom to liquefy its insides. The spider eats its prey by sucking its liquefied tissues.

HOW TO SPOT

Size: Males are 0.1 to 0.2 inches (3 to 4 mm) long; females are 0.2 inches (5 mm) long

Range: Southeastern Canada, the eastern United States, and parts of Europe

Habitat: Temperate forests, dark corners, cellars, cupboards, and closets

Diet: Insects

SYDNEY FUNNEL-WEB SPIDER

(ATRAX ROBUSTUS)

The Sydney funnel-web spider is a venomous spider found in Australia. It has venom sacs and large fangs. The spider is a glossy, blue-black color with fine hairs that cover its abdomen. This spider's legs are shiny. It remains solitary except when mating. The spider builds white silk webs at ground level. It weaves the entrance into a funnel. When an insect lands on the web, the spider quickly approaches the prey and bites it. Then the spider takes the prey into the funnel to feed.

HOW TO SPOT

Size: Males are 1 inch (25 mm) long; females are 1.4 inches (36 mm) long

Range: Australia

Habitat: Gullies, moist soil, and compost heaps

Diet: Beetles, cockroaches, insect larvae, native land snails, millipedes, frogs, and other small vertebrates

FUN FACT

Sydney funnel-web spiders are very fast runners and will bite humans if disturbed. Without immediate treatment, the spider's bite can be fatal.

ZEBRA SPIDER *(SALTICUS SCENICUS)*

Zebra spiders are named for the black and white stripes on their abdomens. Males have large, black fangs that point forward. The zebra spider is a jumping spider. It catches its prey by leaping on it. The spider can leap up to 4 inches (10 cm). When the spider spots large prey, it approaches from behind. The zebra spider jumps on the prey, bites to immobilize it, and then eats it.

HOW TO SPOT

Size: 0.2 to 0.3 inches (4 to 7 mm) long

Range: Europe and the United States

Habitat: Dry, sunny locations; often seen on walls, on fences, and in gardens

Diet: Insects such as flies and mosquitoes

BROWN HARVESTMAN

(PHALANGIUM OPILIO)

The brown harvestman is one of the most widespread species of harvestmen in the world. It has a short, sphere-shaped body and long, thin legs. The upper part of the body is covered with a light-gray or brown pattern, while the lower part is generally light cream in color. Its chelicerae, or jaws, are large and pincer-like. Adults are active in the late spring through early fall. In agricultural fields, they prey on several crop pests.

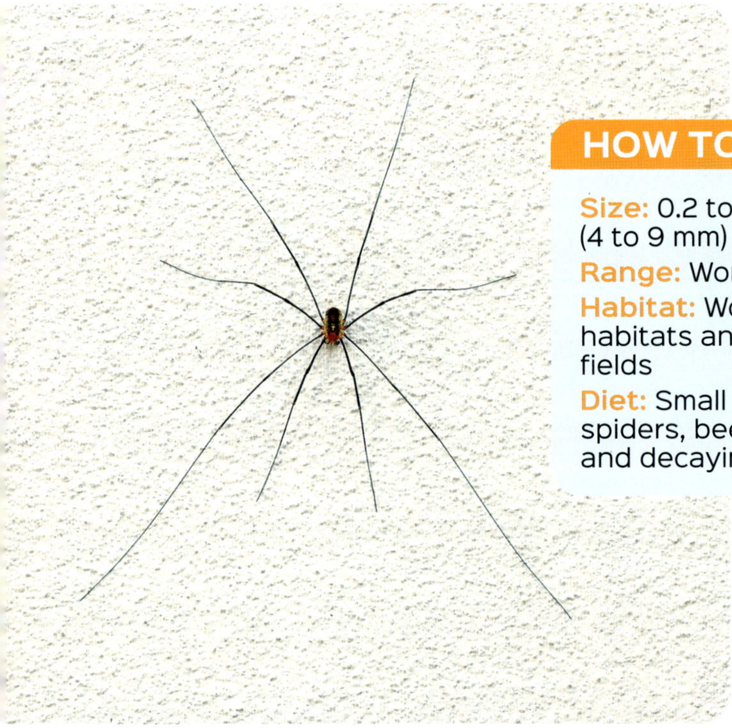

HOW TO SPOT

Size: 0.2 to 0.4 inches (4 to 9 mm) long

Range: Worldwide

Habitat: Wooded, open habitats and agricultural fields

Diet: Small insects, spiders, beetles, slugs, and decaying vegetation

HARVESTMEN

Although they may look similar, a harvestman is not a spider. Harvestmen have two eyes, while spiders can have up to eight eyes. Unlike spiders, harvestmen do not have silk glands and do not spin webs. Harvestmen also do not have fangs or venom as spiders do.

EASTERN HARVESTMAN

(LEIOBUNUM VITTATUM)

The eastern harvestman is also known as the striped harvestman because of the large, blackish stripe down the middle of its back and sides. It is yellow to greenish brown in color with long legs that are either pale or dark. The eastern harvestman is active during the late spring through early fall. It is often found resting on leaves, tree trunks, or the walls of buildings in cool, shady areas. To keep warm on cool fall nights, eastern harvestmen will huddle together in tree holes and other sheltered areas.

HOW TO SPOT

Size: 0.2 to 0.3 inches (6 to 8 mm) long

Range: North America

Habitat: Forests, woodlands, parks, and backyards

Diet: Small insects, fungi, and plant fluids

FUN FACT
Harvestmen use the sensitive tips of their legs as sense organs.

AMERICAN DOG TICK

(DERMACENTOR VARIABILIS)

The American dog tick is a species that is known for carrying diseases such as Rocky Mountain spotted fever and rabbit fever. As its name suggests, the tick is typically found on dogs. It will sometimes feed on larger animals such as cattle, horses, and humans. The tick moves from host to host to feed on blood. The adult tick is typically brown to reddish brown in color with a round, oval body and eight legs. It also has distinctive gray and silver markings that form diamonds and other geometric designs on its upper back.

HOW TO SPOT

Size: 0.2 to 0.6 inches (5 to 15 mm) long
Range: United States and parts of Canada
Habitat: Forests, wooded areas, and grasslands
Diet: Blood of animals including dogs, rabbits, humans, and raccoons

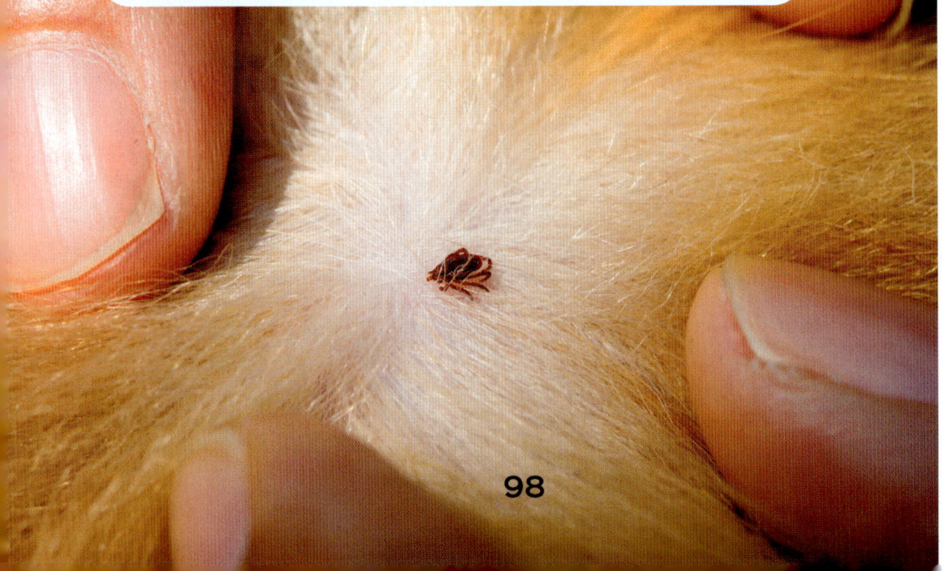

CLOVER MITE *(BRYOBIA PRAETIOSA)*

The clover mite is a widespread plant-feeding mite. Adults are reddish brown to dark, greenish brown in color. They have eight legs, but their front two legs are twice the size of the other legs. Because the large front legs extend forward near the mite's head, they are sometimes mistaken for antennae. The mite's body is oval-shaped with feather-like plates on its abdomen. Large populations of clover mites can cause damage to lawns, flowers, and other plants. Although they are primarily plant feeders, they can sometimes enter buildings. They do not attack humans.

HOW TO SPOT

Size: 0.03 inches (0.8 mm) long
Range: Worldwide
Habitat: Lawns and other areas with host plants
Diet: A wide range of plants including lawn grasses, ornamental flowers, clovers, dandelions, and more

FUN FACT

When crushed, the clover mite leaves a red stain from its body fluids, which is sometimes mistaken for blood.

DEER TICK *(IXODES SCAPULARIS)*

The deer tick, also known as the black-legged tick, is the main carrier of the human illness called Lyme disease. The tick is generally dark brown to black in color. Females are orange or red behind the scutum, the hard shield behind the tick's head. The adult deer tick has no significant markings and does not have eyes. The tick feeds on the blood of mammals, particularly the white-tailed deer. When it feeds on human hosts, it can spread Lyme disease.

FUN FACT

Deer ticks generally need to feed for about 24 to 48 hours to transmit diseases such as Lyme disease.

HOW TO SPOT

Size: 0.1 inch (3 mm) long

Range: Eastern United States

Habitat: Forests and fields where host animals are common

Diet: Blood of animals such as mice, birds, and deer

AN INFREQUENT FEEDER

Most ticks can survive for 200 days without feeding. In fact, the deer tick only needs to feed three times during its entire life cycle. It needs to feed once during the larval stage, once in the nymph stage, and once as an adult tick.

HARVEST MITE

(NEOTROMBICULA AUTUMNALIS)

The harvest mite is a parasite. Its larvae infest domestic mammals, humans, and some birds. The female lays her eggs in damp soil. After they hatch, the larvae climb grass blades and wait for a host. When one comes near, the larvae attach to the host and feed on its tissue. After several days of feeding, they fall off and develop into nymphs and then, later, adult mites. The larvae are red or orange in color. They have three pairs of long legs covered by claws and bristly hairs. Adult mites are reddish in color and have pentagon-shaped back plates.

HOW TO SPOT

Size: 0.01 inches (0.3 mm) long

Range: Western Europe to southwestern Asia

Habitat: Varied

Diet: Larvae eat the liquefied tissue of hosts; adults eat plant fluids, other insects, and insect eggs

LONE STAR TICK

(AMBLYOMMA AMERICANUM)

The lone star tick is primarily brown in color. It has eight legs and long mouthparts. The name *lone star* refers to a pale white spot near the center of the female's back shield. The male has white streaks or spots around the edges of its body. At all three life stages of the tick (larvae, nymph, and adult), it will feed on humans and other animals. Although the lone star tick does not transmit Lyme disease, it does transmit other diseases. These include Rocky Mountain spotted fever, tularemia (rabbit fever), and ehrlichiosis.

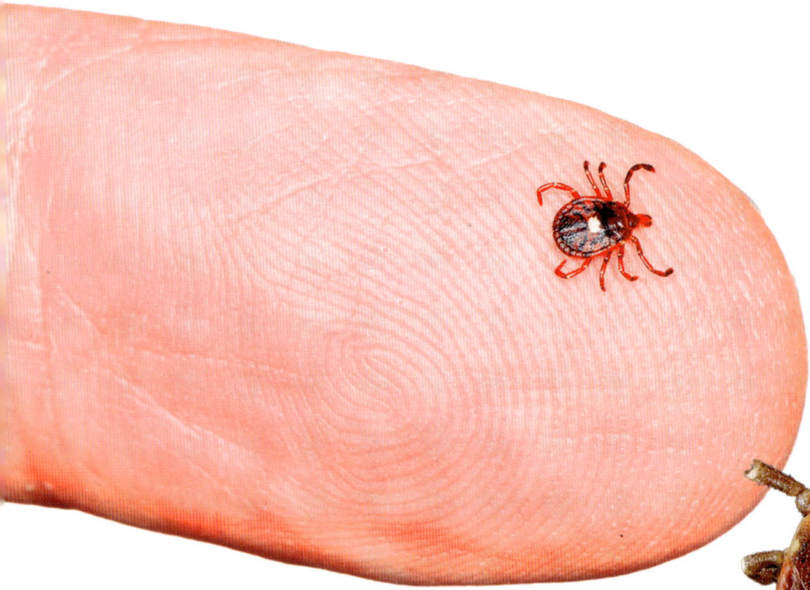

HOW TO SPOT

Size: 0.2 inches (4 mm) long

Range: Eastern, southeastern, and midwestern United States

Habitat: Woodlands where white-tailed deer live

Diet: Blood of mammals and birds

TWO-SPOTTED SPIDER MITE

(TETRANYCHUS URTICAE)

The tiny two-spotted spider mite is a plant-feeding mite that is generally considered a pest. The oval-shaped mite is typically yellowish and almost translucent in color. It has eight legs and a distinct dark spot on each side of its body. As winter approaches, some mites turn reddish orange. Active in the spring through fall, the spider mite can invade areas where plants are abundant, such as greenhouses, gardens, and nurseries. The mite feeds on the plant and removes sap from leaf tissues, which causes the leaves to appear speckled. If severely infested with spider mites, the plant may die.

HOW TO SPOT

Size: Less than 0.01 to 0.03 inches (0.3 to 0.8 mm) long

Range: North America and Europe

Habitat: Gardens, orchards, and greenhouses

Diet: Foliage and fruit

FUN FACT

The dark spots on the two-spotted spider mite's body are food particles that can be seen through the body wall.

ARIZONA BARK SCORPION

(CENTRUROIDES EXILICAUDA)

Arizona bark scorpions are yellowish, medium-size scorpions. They have long, thin pincers and tails. A bark scorpion has a dark stripe down its back. It is one of the most venomous scorpions in the United States and can give a very painful sting. The bark scorpion typically rests during the day under stones, litter, or loose bark. At night it emerges to hunt for food on the ground, tree trunks, and walls. It grabs prey with its claws and quickly kills the prey with a venomous sting.

HOW TO SPOT

Size: Up to 3 inches (7.6 cm) long

Range: Southwestern United States

Habitat: Temperate and dry areas, often under rocks, logs, tree bark, and other objects

Diet: Soft-bodied insects, worms, and other invertebrates

SCORPION VENOM

All scorpions are venomous. A pair of glands produce the scorpion's venom. When the scorpion stings its victim, muscles around the venom glands squeeze. The squeezing forces venom through the stinger and into the wound. The venom causes stinging and burning in the prey. It also contains neurotoxins that affect different parts of the prey's body.

EMPEROR SCORPION

(PANDINUS IMPERATOR)

The emperor scorpion is one of the largest scorpions in the world. Its body is shiny black with two large pincers in front. It has four walking legs and a long tail that ends in a stinger. Its venom is generally mild. To kill prey, the emperor scorpion typically uses its enormous claws to tear its prey apart. Despite its fearsome appearance, the emperor scorpion is often timid. When threatened, it will flee before fighting. However, if cornered, this scorpion will become aggressive. Emperor scorpions are social and live in colonies of up to 15 scorpions. The scorpion rests during the day and emerges at night.

HOW TO SPOT

Size: 7.9 inches (20 cm) long
Range: West Africa
Habitat: Hot and humid forests
Diet: Insects and sometimes small vertebrates

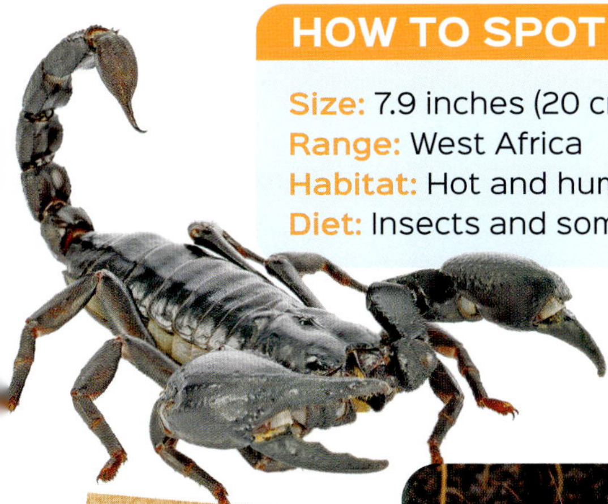

FUN FACT

Because their eyesight is poor, emperor scorpions have sensory structures called pectines behind their legs that help them sense their surroundings.

GIANT DESERT HAIRY SCORPION *(HADRURUS ARIZONENSIS)*

The giant desert hairy scorpion is the largest scorpion in North America. It has a tan to olive-green color with a darker back and yellowish claws, legs, and tail. The scorpion's tail is covered with stiff, brown hairs, explaining the word *hairy* in its name. The scorpion is a solitary predator that is active on warm nights. When hunting, it hides and grabs prey with its front claws and stings the victim with its tail. During the day, the scorpion hides under rocks, in caves, or in burrows. Although not aggressive, the giant desert hairy scorpion will attack when provoked. Its sting is painful but not life-threatening to humans.

HOW TO SPOT

Size: 5.5 inches (14 cm) long
Range: Southwestern United States
Habitat: Deserts
Diet: Insects, lizards, small mammals, and other scorpions

STRIPED BARK SCORPION

(CENTRUROIDES VITTATUS)

The striped bark scorpion is yellowish to tan in color and has two broad, black stripes on its abdomen. It has a dark triangle on top of its head. Like most scorpions, the striped bark scorpion has a flattened, elongated body. It has four pairs of walking legs and a pair of pincers in the front of its body. Its long, curling tail ends in a stinger. The scorpion uses its pincers to capture and hold its prey. Then it stings and kills the prey with its venom-filled tail.

HOW TO SPOT

Size: 1 to 1.5 inches (2.5 to 3.8 cm) long

Range: Southern central United States and northern Mexico

Habitat: Varied, from woodlands to deserts

Diet: Soft-bodied prey such as spiders, cockroaches, ants, crickets, beetles, and butterflies

FUN FACT

Striped bark scorpions are born live rather than in eggs, usually in litters that average about 31 scorpions.

GLOSSARY

abdomen
One of three main body parts of an insect. It is the third segment of the insect's body, after the thorax.

aphid
A small, soft-bodied insect that sucks the juices of plants.

blowout
A valley created by wind in an area with sand or light soil.

cephalothorax
The front part of an arachnid's body.

colony
A group of one species whose members live and interact together.

hibernate
To spend the winter in a dormant state.

larva
The active, juvenile form of an insect.

mandibles
Jaws or jawbones.

mouthpart
A structure near the mouth of an insect that is used to gather or eat food.

nocturnal
Active at night.

pollinator
An insect or animal that moves pollen from one flower to another flower.

predator
An animal that preys on another animal.

prey
An animal that is hunted or killed by another animal for food.

proboscis
In insects, a tube-shaped mouthpart used for feeding.

pronotum
A plate-like structure found on the thorax of some insect species.

secrete
To give off a substance.

thorax
One of three main body parts of an insect. It is the second segment of the insect's body, behind the head and in front of the abdomen.

translucent
Allowing light to pass through.

TO LEARN MORE

FURTHER READINGS

Daniels, Jaret C. *Insects & Bugs for Kids: An Introduction to Entomology*. Adventure Publications, 2021.

Honovich, Nancy. *1,000 Facts about Insects*. National Geographic, 2018.

Romero, Libby. *Insects*. National Geographic, 2017.

ONLINE RESOURCES

Booklinks
NONFICTION NETWORK
FREE! ONLINE NONFICTION RESOURCES

To learn more about insects and arachnids, please visit **abdobooklinks.com** or scan this QR code. These links are routinely monitored and updated to provide the most current information available.

PHOTO CREDITS

Cover Photos: Cathy Keifer/iStockphoto, front (moth); iStockphoto, front (green moth), front (Hercules beetle), front (scorpion); Anneliese Gruenwald-Maerkl/iStockphoto, front (ladybug); Tracy Wesolek/iStockphoto, front (tarantula); Shutterstock Images, front (butterfly), front (tick), back (water bug); Andrew Banham/Shutterstock Images, front (long-horned beetle); Cristina Romero Palma/Shutterstock Images, front (fly); Meister Photos/Shutterstock Images, front (harvestman); Alexsander Ovsyannikov/Shutterstock Images, front (spider); Ayhan Turan Menekay/Shutterstock Images, front (hornet); Danut Vieru/Shutterstock Images, back (mosquito); Eric Isselee/Shutterstock Images, back (praying mantis); Tom Biegalski/Shutterstock Images, back (dragonfly)
Interior Photos: Kasira Suda/Shutterstock Images, 1 (beetle), 23; Tig Tillinghast/Shutterstock Images, 1 (hornet), 34 (top); Michael Siluk/Shutterstock Images, 1 (cricket), 77; Shutterstock Images, 1 (tarantula), 5 (fruit fly), 5 (bombardier beetle), 5 (wasp), 11 (top), 13, 15 (top), 16 (top), 20 (bottom), 24, 28, 29 (top), 29 (bottom), 31 (top), 32 (top), 48, 56, 57 (bottom), 58 (top), 58 (bottom), 61, 63 (bottom), 67 (top), 67 (bottom), 69, 71, 72 (top), 76 (bottom), 82, 84, 87 (bottom), 89 (top), 90 (right), 92, 95 (top), 96, 97 (top), 98 (bottom), 100, 101 (top), 102 (right), 105 (top), 107, 112 (top left), 112 (center), 112 (top right); Tobias Hauke/Shutterstock Images, 1 (scorpion), 93 (top), 104; Clint H./Shutterstock Images, 4 (scorpion); Steve Collender/Shutterstock Images, 4 (spider); Sean McVey/Shutterstock Images, 4 (beetle); Gerald A. DeBoer/Shutterstock Images, 5 (milkweed bug); Petlin Dmitry/Shutterstock Images, 5 (cricket); Keith V./Shutterstock Images, 5 (bee); Super Prin/Shutterstock Images, 5 (butterfly); Sari Oneal/Shutterstock Images, 6 (top), 64 (top), 81 (top), 85 (bottom), 91; Jay Ondreicka/Shutterstock Images, 6 (bottom), 64 (bottom); Cosmin Manci/Shutterstock Images, 7, 65; Arno van Dulmen/Shutterstock Images, 8 (top), 8 (bottom left); Ant Cooper/Shutterstock Images, 8 (bottom right); Keith Hider/Shutterstock Images, 9; Ksenia Lada/Shutterstock Images, 10; iStockphoto, 11 (bottom), 38 (bottom), 44 (top), 50 (top), 85 (top), 103 (bottom); A. S. Floro/Shutterstock Images, 12 (top); Laurie K./iStockphoto, 12 (bottom); Steve Bower/Shutterstock Images, 14, 27 (top); David Birkenfeld/iStockphoto, 15 (bottom); Bildagentur Zoonar GmbH/Shutterstock Images, 16 (bottom); Mario Saccomano/Shutterstock Images, 17; Vinicius R. Souza/Shutterstock Images, 18 (top); Rudmer Zwerver/Shutterstock Images, 18 (bottom); Snelson Stock/Shutterstock Images, 19; Paul Kulinich/Shutterstock Images, 20 (top); Paul Sparks/Shutterstock Images, 21, 78 (bottom); Alf Ribeiro/Shutterstock Images, 22; D. L. Kugler/Shutterstock Images, 25 (top); Daniel Knop/Shutterstock Images, 25 (bottom); Tomasz Klejdysz/Shutterstock Images, 26, 70 (top), 70 (bottom);

William J. Weber/iStockphoto, 27 (bottom), 112 (bottom left); Elliotte Rusty Harold/Shutterstock Images, 30, 41 (left), 44 (bottom), 97 (bottom); Jason Ondreicka/iStockphoto, 31 (bottom); Ihor Hvozdetskyi/ Shutterstock Images, 32 (bottom); David McClenaghan/Science Image, 33; Manu M. Nair/Shutterstock Images, 34 (bottom); Paul Reeves Photography/Shutterstock Images, 35, 41 (right), 72 (bottom); Brett Hondow/Shutterstock Images, 36; Wirakorn Hanjo Hellmann/ Shutterstock Images, 37 (top); Deelert/Shutterstock Images, 37 (bottom); Irfan M. Nur/Shutterstock Images, 38 (top); Mark Lehigh/ Shutterstock Images, 39; J. J. Gouin/ Shutterstock Images, 40; Jeremy A. Casado/Shutterstock Images, 42 (top); Melinda Fawver/Shutterstock Images, 42 (bottom), 90 (left), 98 (top left), 98 (top right); Parashar Mangela/Shutterstock Images, 43; Marv Vandehey/Shutterstock Images, 45 (top); Jeff W. Jarrett/Shutterstock Images, 45 (bottom); Scott Camazine/ Science Source, 46; Daniel Prudek/ Shutterstock Images, 47; Heather Broccard-Bell/iStockphoto, 49 (top), 55; Javier Chiavone/Shutterstock Images, 49 (bottom); Shawn Coates/iStockphoto, 50 (bottom), 112 (bottom right); Nadim Mahmud Himu/iStockphoto, 51; MYP Studio/ Shutterstock Images, 52; Bani Suman Ghosh/Shutterstock Images, 53 (top); Hasyim/Shutterstock Images, 53 (bottom); Edward Snow/iStockphoto, 54 (top); Nature's Images, Inc./ Science Source, 54 (bottom); Manfred Ruckszio/Shutterstock Images, 57 (top); David Havel/Shutterstock Images, 59; Brian Lasenby/Shutterstock Images, 60 (top); Kerrie W./Shutterstock Images, 60 (bottom); Frode Jacobsen/ Shutterstock Images, 62; Lisa A. Ernst/Shutterstock Images, 63 (top); Vitalii Hulai/Shutterstock Images, 66; D. Kucharski K. Kucharska/ Shutterstock Images, 68 (left); Simon Berenyi/Shutterstock Images, 68 (right); Bill Kennedy/Shutterstock Images, 73; Gonzalo Jara/ Shutterstock Images, 74 (top); Young Swee Ming/Shutterstock Images, 74 (bottom); David Lehner/Shutterstock Images, 75; Danita Delimont/ Shutterstock Images, 76 (top); Craig Chaddock/Shutterstock Images, 78 (top); Oleksandr Kostiuchenko/ Shutterstock Images, 79; Eric Isselee/Shutterstock Images, 80, 88; David Byron Keener/Shutterstock Images, 81 (bottom); Alexsander Ovsyannikov/Shutterstock Images, 83 (top); Davide Bonora/Shutterstock Images, 83 (bottom); John Serrao/ Science Source, 86; Marius Dobilas/ Shutterstock Images, 87 (top); Melani Wright/Shutterstock Images, 89 (bottom); Stephen Dalton/Science Source, 93 (bottom); Ken Griffiths/ Shutterstock Images, 94; Stephan Morris/Shutterstock Images, 95 (bottom); Nik Bruining/Shutterstock Images, 99; Eye of Science/Science Source, 101 (bottom); Steve Heap/ Shutterstock Images, 102 (left); Nigel Cattlin/Science Source, 103 (top); Milan Vachal/Shutterstock Images, 105 (bottom); K. Hanley CHDPhoto/ Shutterstock Images, 106 (top); Viktor Loki/Shutterstock Images, 106 (bottom)

ABDOBOOKS.COM
Published by Abdo Publishing, a division of ABDO, PO Box 398166, Minneapolis, Minnesota 55439.

102021
012022

THIS BOOK CONTAINS
RECYCLED MATERIALS

Editor: Arnold Ringstad
Series Designer: Colleen McLaren
Content Consultant: Dr. Douglas Golick, Associate Professor, Department of Entomology, University of Nebraska-Lincoln

Library of Congress Control Number: 2021941708
Publisher's Cataloging-in-Publication Data
Names: Mooney, Carla, author.
Title: Insects and arachnids / by Carla Mooney
Description: Minneapolis, Minnesota : Abdo Publishing, 2022 | Series: Field guides | Includes online resources and index.
Identifiers: ISBN 9781532196973 (lib. bdg.) | ISBN 9781098218782 (ebook)
Subjects: LCSH: Insects--Juvenile literature. | Arachnids--Juvenile literature. | Insects--Behavior--Juvenile literature. | Bug watching--Juvenile literature. | Spiders--Juvenile literature | Field guides--Juvenile literature
Classification: DDC 595.7--dc23

FIELD GUIDES

FOSSILS, ROCKS, AND MINERALS

Marcia Amidon Lusted

Abdo Reference

An Imprint of Abdo Publishing | abdobooks.com

CONTENTS

Metamorphic Rocks

Minerals

WHAT ARE FOSSILS, ROCKS, AND MINERALS?

Choose any location in the world, and chances are good that there will be fossils, rocks, or minerals there. These objects form in different ways and have distinct characteristics. Fossils, rocks, and minerals can tell people how Earth formed, how it has changed, and the plants and animals that once inhabited it.

WHAT ARE MINERALS?

A mineral is an inorganic substance, meaning that it is not alive. There are more than 5,000 types of minerals on Earth. All minerals have certain features:

- All minerals occur naturally. They are not created by people.
- All minerals are solid.
- A mineral has a crystal structure. This is an orderly, symmetrical, and repeating arrangement of atoms.
- Every mineral has a set chemical composition. That means a mineral is always made up of the same elements. Sometimes it will just have one element.

WHAT ARE ROCKS?

Rocks are made up of minerals. They can appear in many different shapes and sizes. Some rocks may contain pieces of organic matter. Rocks can be classified in three ways, depending on how they formed. Rocks are either igneous, sedimentary, or metamorphic.

- Igneous rocks are created when molten magma or lava solidifies.
- Sedimentary rocks are formed by deposits of dead plants and sediments, which can include sand and silt.

- Metamorphic rocks are created when rocks underground are changed by heat or pressure.

Rocks have two things in common with minerals. First, both rocks and minerals are found in Earth's outer crust. Second, people view some rocks and minerals as valuable because they can be used in manufacturing or construction. Sometimes people extract useful minerals from rocks.

WHAT ARE FOSSILS?

Fossils are often found in sedimentary rocks. They are the remains of animals and plants. Over time, the remains are sometimes replaced with minerals.

Fossils preserve pieces of organisms, such as shells, feathers, leaves, or bones. Most living things decompose quickly after they die, and only a small number are preserved as fossils. Some experts think that only one bone in a billion ends up becoming a fossil. In addition, fossils must be at least 10,000 years old to be classified as such. Fossils often take on the color of the rock they are preserved in.

Geologic Time Scale

	Name	Date
Period	Cambrian	541 to 485.4 million years ago
Period	Ordovician	485.4 to 443.8 million years ago
Period	Silurian	443.8 to 419.2 million years ago
Period	Devonian	419.2 to 358.9 million years ago
Period	Carboniferous	358.9 to 298.9 million years ago
Period	Permian	298.9 to 251.9 million years ago
Period	Triassic	251.9 to 201.3 million years ago
Period	Jurassic	201.3 to 145 million years ago
Period	Cretaceous	145 to 66 million years ago
Epoch	Paleocene	66 to 56 million years ago
Epoch	Eocene	56 to 33.9 million years ago
Epoch	Oligocene	33.9 to 23 million years ago
Epoch	Miocene	23 to 5.3 million years ago
Epoch	Pliocene	5.3 to 2.6 million years ago
Epoch	Pleistocene	2.6 million years ago to 11,700 years ago
Epoch	Holocene	11,700 years ago to the present day

HOW TO USE THIS BOOK

SCALLOP (PECTEN)

scallop has two shells connected by a ligament. The shells ave broad ribs that start at the base and spread upward. callops have been around since the Late Eocene epoch. hey are found all over the world. These animals prefer to ve in clean sands and fairly shallow waters. They often dig depressions in seabed sands and rest in them. Scallop fossils are usually just the shells. The ligament connecting the shells is rarely preserved.

HOW TO SPOT

Size: 3.1 inches (7.9 cm) long
Identifying Features: Ribbed shell
Range: Worldwide
Habitat: Clean sands and shallow waters

FUN FACT

Scallops can swim by opening and closing their hinged shells.

GETTING PRESERVED

For something to be preserved as a fossil, it needs to meet certain conditions that stop the decaying process. For instance, the organism needs to be protected from water and air. Many fossils are found in marine or freshwater sediments. In these environments, the animals were buried in oxygen-deprived clay or silt. They were able to form into fossils.

15

DRAGONFLY *(PETALURA)*

Petalura is a genus of dragonfly. This creature has lived on Earth since the Jurassic period. A dragonfly has two forewings and two hindwings. It also has a long, slender tail. These features may be seen in fossils. The *Petalura* fossil forms when the dragonfly dies in a watery environment and is then buried in silt or clay. The sediment hardens into rock. Then, the decaying dragonfly leaves behind its imprint in the rock.

HOW TO SPOT

Size: 1.25 inches (3 cm) long

Identifying Features: A distinct dragonfly shape with four broad, veined wings

Range: Europe, Australia, New Zealand, and islands in the South Pacific Ocean

Habitat: Near fresh water

FUN FACT

Insect fossils from the Early Devonian period don't have wings. It's not until the Late Carboniferous period that many of them were able to fly.

WHERE ARE FOSSILS FOUND?

Fossils are usually found in sedimentary rocks. People can find fossils in cliffs and other exposed areas near coasts. They can also find fossils in quarries, in arid areas such as deserts, and in rugged terrain with layered rocks.

GIANT CERITH *(CAMPANILE)*

The giant cerith is a gastropod. It dates from the Late Cretaceous period to the present. Giant ceriths are found along the bottoms of shallow, warm seas. They feed on algae. The shell of the giant cerith is often what's fossilized. It is spiraled and grows to a point. The shell can have as many as 30 spiral whorls with rows of knobs. The giant cerith drags its shell as it crawls, so one side of its shell is often flattened.

HOW TO SPOT

Size: 12 to 24 inches (30 to 61 cm) long

Identifying Features: Spiral shell

Range: Worldwide

Habitat: Warm, shallow seas

FOSSIL SIZE

Fossils come in many different shapes and sizes. Microfossils, such as bacteria and pollen, can be seen only with microscopes. Macrofossils, such as dinosaur bones and petrified trees, can be many feet long and weigh several tons.

GLASS SPONGE *(RHIZOPOTERION)*

Glass sponges in the genus *Rhizopoterion* existed in Europe during the Cretaceous period. The glass sponge was an aquatic animal. It lived on the ocean floor. It had surface pores that let water flow in and out of it. The sponge had a tall, funnel-shaped body. Glass sponge fossils are found in sedimentary rocks that were once covered by ancient seas.

HOW TO SPOT

Size: 4 inches (10 cm) tall
Identifying Features: Funnel shaped
Range: Europe
Habitat: Muddy ocean floors at depths of more than 20,000 feet (6,096 m)

GOOSE BARNACLE *(STRAMENTUM)*

Goose barnacles lived during the Cretaceous period. They were aquatic animals. Their bodies and legs were enclosed in shells. These shells had hard, overlapping plates. Goose barnacles could be fossilized if their bodies were buried in silt. The silt would then have to become a sedimentary rock.

FUN FACT

People once believed that goose barnacle fossils grew into geese, which is how they got their common name.

HOW TO SPOT

Size: 0.75 inches (1.9 cm) long
Identifying Features: Oval shaped
Range: Europe, North Africa, and North America
Habitat: Often attached to gastropods, ammonites, or bivalves on seafloors

HORN CORAL *(SEPTASTRAEA)*

Horn corals lived in the Miocene to Pleistocene epochs. They resided in warm, shallow waters near reefs. They sometimes attached to the shells of other marine animals. Horn corals had hard, star-shaped cavities. These gave the corals honeycombed appearances.

HOW TO SPOT

Size: One cavity is 0.063 inches (0.16 cm) long

Identifying Features: Large, branching colonies

Range: Atlantic coastal plains of North America and Europe

Habitat: Warm, shallow waters near reefs

PHYLLOCERATID *(PHYLLOCERAS)*

Phylloceratids were common all over the world during the Early Jurassic to Late Cretaceous periods. However, they became extinct at the same time as the dinosaurs, about 65 million years ago. A phylloceratid is a type of ammonite. Its fossil has a smooth, curved shell with dark, wavy lines. The fossils are preserved in mud that hardens into sedimentary rocks.

HOW TO SPOT

Size: 4 inches (10 cm) long
Identifying Features: Curled, smooth shell
Range: Worldwide
Habitat: Seas

FUN FACT

Phylloceratid fossils can be found in quarries, seacoasts, river shores, deserts, and canyons.

MARY ANNING

Mary Anning was born in Lyme Regis, England, in 1799. At the time, women were not encouraged to get an education. However, Anning taught herself about fossils and paleontology. She found ammonite specimens and other fossils. Anning also discovered the first complete skeleton of an ichthyosaur, an extinct aquatic reptile.

SAND DOLLAR *(ENCOPE)*

Sand dollars have been around since the Miocene epoch. They bury themselves in the sand in warm, shallow waters. These animals have rigid skeletons. They are very flat and thin with slightly domed tops. Sand dollars have flower-like patterns on their tops. The edges of these animals have slits. Living sand dollars are deep brown or purplish red. When fossilized, sand dollars can be brown or white.

HOW TO SPOT

Size: 3.5 inches (8.9 cm) long

Identifying Features: Round with flower-like patterns

Range: North and South America

Habitat: Warm, shallow waters

FUN FACT

Sand dollars got their name because sometimes their remains are silvery white and look like silver dollars.

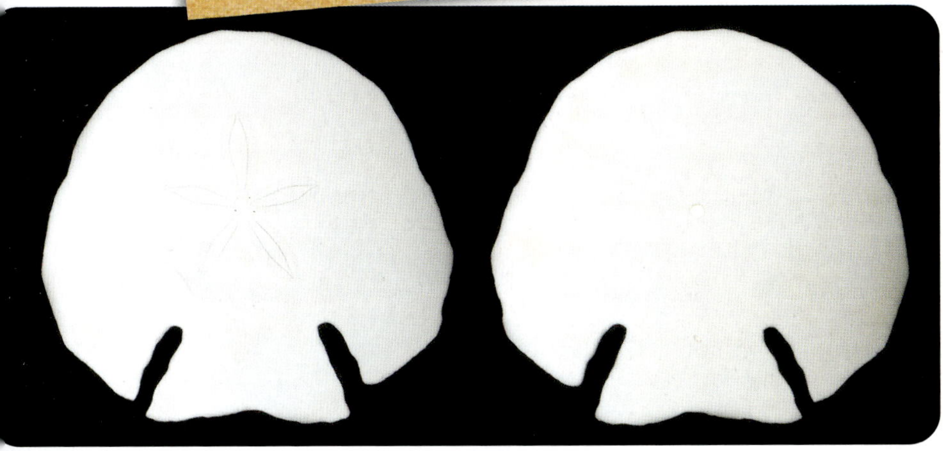

SCALLOP *(PECTEN)*

A scallop has two shells connected by a ligament. The shells have broad ribs that start at the base and spread upward. Scallops have been around since the Late Eocene epoch. They are found all over the world. These animals prefer to live in clean sands and fairly shallow waters. They often dig depressions in seabed sands and rest in them. Scallop fossils are usually just the shells. The ligament connecting the shells is rarely preserved.

HOW TO SPOT

Size: 3.1 inches (7.9 cm) long
Identifying Features: Ribbed shell
Range: Worldwide
Habitat: Clean sands and shallow waters

FUN FACT
Scallops can swim by opening and closing their hinged shells.

GETTING PRESERVED

For something to be preserved as a fossil, it needs to meet certain conditions that stop the decaying process. For instance, the organism needs to be protected from water and air. Many fossils are found in marine or freshwater sediments. In these environments, the animals were buried in oxygen-deprived clay or silt. They were able to form into fossils.

SEA LILY *(PARISANGULOCRINUS)*

Sea lilies belonging to the genus *Parisangulocrinus* lived during the Silurian to Carboniferous periods. Most were attached to seabeds by flexible stems. At the tops of the stems were cups. A series of feathery arms formed crowns on top of the cups. They filtered food from the water. Sea lilies sank to the ocean floor when they died. They were so numerous that the skeletons of their stems formed thick layers that became limestone, preserving them.

HOW TO SPOT

Size: Cup is 0.6 inches (1.5 cm) long
Identifying Features: Feathery arms
Range: Europe and North America
Habitat: Warm, shallow waters

SERPULID WORM *(GLOMERULA)*

The serpulid worm dates from the Early Jurassic period to the Paleocene epoch. The worm lived in a hard, narrow tube made of calcite. Many worms usually twisted together in tangled groups. Over many years, some of the tubes these worms made were fossilized.

FUN FACT
Serpulid worms filtered and ate plankton and organic debris that floated in the seas.

HOW TO SPOT

Size: 4 inches (10 cm) long
Identifying Features: Narrow tube or a tangled mass
Range: Worldwide
Habitat: Seabeds

TRILOBITE *(OLENELLUS)*

A trilobite gets its name from the three long lobes that make up its body. It also has a head shield, a thorax with dozens of segments, and a tail shield. This creature had large eyes and a small tail. Trilobites were alive during the Early Cambrian period. They are extinct today. These animals lived in ocean environments close to seabeds.

HOW TO SPOT

Size: 2.5 inches (6.4 cm) long

Identifying Features: Small tail, large head, and many segments making up the thorax

Range: North America and Scotland

Habitat: Near seabeds

FUN FACT

Many trilobites could roll themselves into balls. Some could even lock their tails onto their head shields.

TUSK SHELL *(DENTALIUM)*

Tusk shells come from invertebrates in the scaphopod and chiton families. They've been around since the Middle Triassic period. The animals live on seafloors. They survive at different temperatures and depths. A tusk shell has between four and 20 sharp, regularly spaced ribs running along its entire length. Its smaller end is curved. The larger end has the invertebrate's head and tentacled feet, though the soft tissue is rarely fossilized.

HOW TO SPOT

Size: 2 inches (5 cm) long; 0.25 inches (0.64 cm) wide

Identifying Features: Narrow, tubular shell shaped like a tusk

Range: Worldwide

Habitat: Seafloors

FUN FACT

A scaphopod will bury itself in the sand, but it makes sure that the narrow end of its shell sticks out. From this end, the scaphopod waves its delicate tentacles in the water. This helps the animal pick up small bits of food.

ARCHAEOPTERYX (ARCHAEOPTERYX)

Archaeopteryx is a genus of feathered dinosaurs. They lived during the Late Jurassic period. Scientists believe these vertebrates were a transitional species between non-avian dinosaurs and birds. Fossils show that *Archaeopteryx* had wings, feathers, teeth, functioning fingers, and bony tails.

HOW TO SPOT

Size: 20 inches (51 cm) long
Identifying Features: Chicken-sized dinosaur with a long, bony tail
Range: Europe
Habitat: Near inland seashores

An artist's depiction of what *Archaeopteryx* may have looked like

ARTHRODIRE *(COCCOSTEUS)*

The arthrodire belonged to a family of primitive fish. It lived in the Middle Devonian period. An arthrodire had slicing plates instead of teeth, which wore down with use. Its head was guarded by a bony shield. A circle of bony plates protected its eyes. Its fossils have been found in sandstone.

HOW TO SPOT

Size: 14 inches (36 cm) long

Identifying Features: Broad and flattened skull, plates, and protective head shield

Range: Europe and North America

Habitat: Shallow, freshwater lakes

Head of an arthrodire

FUN FACT

An arthrodire could open its jaw very wide. This made it possible for the animal to eat a large variety of prey.

BAROSAURUS

Barosaurus was a large dinosaur that lived during the Late Jurassic period. It was a plant eater, and its long neck helped it reach treetops. *Barosaurus* likely lived near water where trees and vegetation were found. Only parts of *Barosaurus* fossils have been discovered. In fact, *Barosaurus* fossils are so rare that the skull of this dinosaur has never been found.

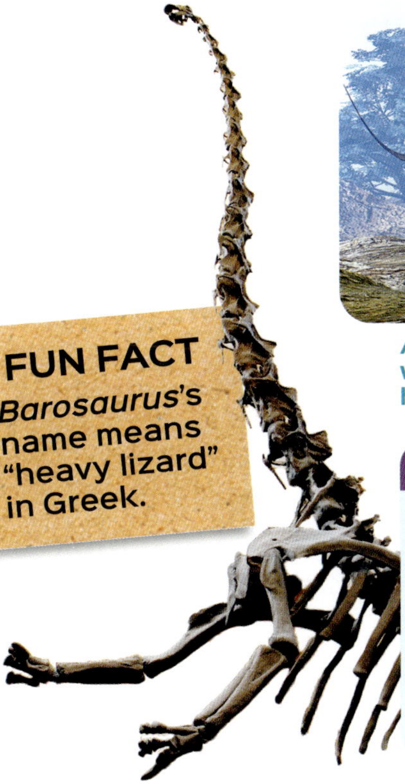

An artist's imagining of what *Barosaurus* may have looked like

FUN FACT
Barosaurus's name means "heavy lizard" in Greek.

HOW TO SPOT

Size: 75 feet (23 m) long; 20 feet (6.1 m) tall
Identifying Features: Long neck and tail
Range: North America
Habitat: Close to water with vegetation and trees

DISCOVERING *BAROSAURUS*

In the 1800s, a woman named E. R. Ellerman found the first *Barosaurus* specimen in South Dakota. She contacted a paleontologist at Yale University about the discovery, but it took years for professionals to come and excavate the skeleton. During that time, some people went to the site and took pieces of the skeleton for themselves.

DIMETRODON (DIMETRODON)

Dimetrodon lived during the Early Permian period. It is an extinct relative of early mammals. The most distinguishing feature of this animal is the large, sail-like structure that stood upright on its back. It also had a narrow skull and teeth of different sizes. At the front of its jaw were sharp canine teeth. These were used to rip into prey. At the back of its mouth were shearing teeth that helped *Dimetrodon* grind up bones and tough muscles.

HOW TO SPOT

Size: More than 11.5 feet (3.5 m) long
Identifying Features: Large dorsal sail and narrow skull
Range: North America
Habitat: Arid regions and wet, swampy areas

DIPLOMYSTUS (DIPLOMYSTUS)

Diplomystus lived from the Cretaceous period to the Eocene epoch. The fish had a bony internal skeleton. Its upturned mouth was typical in fish that fed from the water's surface. *Diplomystus* was common in many North American lakes. Its fossils have been found in the Green River Formation in Utah, Colorado, and Wyoming. This was a large lake with a muddy bottom.

HOW TO SPOT

Size: 8 inches (20 cm) long

Identifying Features: Notched tail; upturned mouth; and thin, oval scales

Range: North and South America

Habitat: Freshwater lakes

FUN FACT

Some *Diplomystus* fossils have smaller fish preserved in their mouths or intestines.

EOHIPPUS (*HYRACOTHERIUM*)

Eohippus lived during the Late Paleocene and Early Eocene epochs. This mammal is related to horses, and its feet were adapted for running. However, *Eohippus*'s body was more bent over than that of a modern horse. Its teeth were specially adapted for eating fruit and soft leaves.

HOW TO SPOT

Size: Shoulder height of 16 inches (41 cm) on average

Identifying Features: Four toes on its front feet and three toes on its back feet. Each toe had a tiny hoof.

Range: Europe and North America

Habitat: Tropical forests

FUN FACT

Many *Eohippus* fossils have been found in the Green River Formation in Utah, Colorado, and Wyoming.

ICHTHYOSAUR *(ICHTHYOSAURUS)*

The ichthyosaur was a marine reptile. It thrived during the Triassic and Jurassic periods. The animal may have swum like an eel, swinging from side to side. Its fins were like paddles. The ichthyosaur's strong eye bones indicate it could probably dive very deep in the ocean. However, the animal did not have gills, so it would have needed to surface often to breathe. Some of the best-preserved ichthyosaur fossils in the world were found in Nevada's limestone deposits.

FUN FACT
Ichthyosaur's name means "fish lizard."

HOW TO SPOT

Size: 6.5 feet (2 m) long on average

Identifying Features: Many teeth, a long jaw, and bony plates around its eye sockets

Range: Europe, Greenland, and North America

Habitat: Deep waters

IGUANODON (IGUANODON)

Iguanodon was a large, heavy, plant-eating dinosaur. It lived during the Late Jurassic and Early Cretaceous periods. *Iguanodon* primarily spent its time moving around on four legs, but it could also walk on its two hind ones. *Iguanodon* had a long tail to help it balance. Most *Iguanodon* fossils have been found in sedimentary rocks in England and Europe.

HOW TO SPOT

Size: 30 feet (9.1 m) long

Identifying Features: A long skull with jaws that end in a beak-like shape, and heavy front limbs

Range: Europe, Asia, Africa, and North America

Habitat: Forests

An artist's depiction of what *Iguanodon* may have looked like

FUN FACT

Iguanodon was first discovered in 1822 by Mary Ann Mantell. She saw some strange rocks on the side of the road. The rocks contained *Iguanodon* teeth.

MAMMOTH *(MAMMUTHUS)*

Mammoths were large mammals, weighing about 6.6 to 11 tons (6 to 10 metric tons). They lived from the Pliocene to the Early Holocene epochs. Mammoths had thick, shaggy coats. They were plant eaters who grazed on grasses, low shrubs, roots, and small plants. Mammoths often foraged for these things by digging under the snow. Mammoths lived in the cold regions of the Arctic, Siberia, and Canada. Some intact mammoth bodies have been found frozen in the Arctic permafrost.

HOW TO SPOT

Size: Shoulder height of up to 11.5 feet (3.5 m); tusks are between 5 and 9 feet (1.5 and 2.7 m) long

Identifying Features: Skeleton resembles modern elephant bones, including tusks

Range: Europe, Asia, North America, and the Arctic

Habitat: Areas with low shrubs and grasses

FUN FACT

Scientists can estimate how old a mammoth was when it died by counting the growth rings in a section of its tusk.

MEGALOCEPHALUS

(MEGALOCEPHALUS)

Megalocephalus was a member of the baphetids amphibian group. It lived in the Late Carboniferous period. It was a fierce predator. *Megalocephalus* evolved to have toes and to lay its eggs on land. This means the amphibian could live out of the water.

HOW TO SPOT

Size: 6.5 feet (2 m) long
Identifying Features: Crocodile-like skull and keyhole-shaped eye sockets
Range: Europe and North America
Habitat: Near swamps

Megalocephalus **head**

NEANDERTHAL

(HOMO NEANDERTHALENSIS)

Neanderthals were mammals that lived during the Late Pleistocene epoch. They are the closest extinct relative that humans have. Neanderthals had heavy eyebrow ridges. They also had smaller foreheads and chins than modern humans. Neanderthals possessed larger noses and stockier bodies too. Neanderthals lived in both temperate and cold climates. Many of their fossils have been found in caves and quarries in Europe.

HOW TO SPOT

Size: 5.1 to 5.5 feet (1.6 to 1.7 m) tall; 119 to 143 pounds (54 to 65 kg)

Identifying Features: Prominent brow ridge and a small forehead and chin

Range: Europe and central to southwestern Asia

Habitat: Wide ranging, from cold, flat, unforested grasslands to warm woodlands

FUN FACT

Neanderthals created complex tools, made jewelry, and decorated caves with art.

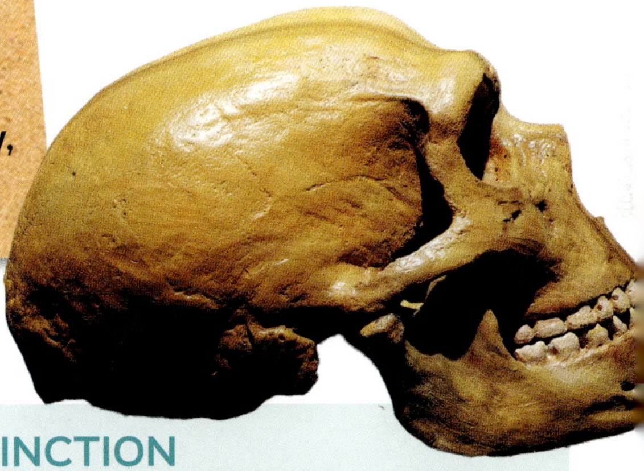

CAUSES OF EXTINCTION

Scientists aren't entirely sure why Neanderthals went extinct. Some think disease played a role. Others say the Neanderthal population was small near the end of the species' lifespan. Declining birth rates, inbreeding, and an unbalanced number of the sexes could have made the species go extinct.

SPINY SHARK *(CHEIRACANTHUS)*

The spiny shark lived during the Devonian period. It had a gaping jaw and teeth that grew in whorls. The spiny shark also had a blunt head and an upturned tail that made it a strong swimmer. It lived in freshwater lakes and rivers and swam at both mid-level and surface-level depths. Whole fossils have been found in Scotland. The fossils are often found in sandstone.

HOW TO SPOT

Size: 12 inches (30.5 cm) long

Identifying Features: One dorsal fin, three lower fins protected by spines, small scales, and an upturned tail

Range: Europe and Antarctica

Habitat: Freshwater lakes and rivers

STEREOSTERNUM (*STEREOSTERNUM*)

Stereosternum was part of a group of small, swimming reptiles that lived in the Early Permian period. This animal had fine, sharp teeth that may have been used to filter out small fish in the sea. It had webbed hands and feet and a flattened tail to help it move through the water. This animal most likely lived in shallow seawaters. Its fossils have been found in South America and South Africa.

HOW TO SPOT

Size: 12 inches (30.5 cm) long

Identifying Features: Long, needle-like teeth; an elongated head and body; short limbs; and a flattened tail

Range: South Africa and South America

Habitat: Shallow seawaters

THEROPOD TRACE FOSSIL

(THEROPOD)

Theropods were a group of dinosaurs that varied in size, from the massive *Tyrannosaurus rex* to the *Microraptor* that was the size of a crow. Trace fossils are imprints that animals left behind. They give people clues to animals' activities. Footprints are examples of trace fossils. Theropods had three-toed, bird-like tracks with claw marks and heel impressions. Fossils formed when theropods stepped in sand or mud and the sediments hardened, eventually turning into rocks and fossilizing the footprints.

FUN FACT

Trace fossils can take many forms. They can be footprints, burrows, nests, eggs, and even feces.

HOW TO SPOT

Size: Varies depending on the species

Identifying Features: Three toes and a V-shaped outline

Range: Worldwide

Habitat: Varies but includes coastal areas, floodplains, and forests

TYRANNOSAURUS REX

(TYRANNOSAURUS)

Tyrannosaurus rex lived during the Late Cretaceous period. Its name means "king of the tyrant lizards," and it was the largest dinosaur in its genus. The *Tyrannosaurus rex* walked on its hind legs and used its tail to balance its long body. This dinosaur was a fearsome predator. It had a large head, and its jaws were filled with serrated teeth that ripped into flesh.

HOW TO SPOT

Size: 40 feet (12 m) long; 11,000 to 15,000 pounds (4,990 to 6,800 kg)

Identifying Features: Massive body with a large head and sharp teeth

Range: Western North America

Habitat: Humid, semitropical areas with open forests, rivers, and coastal swamps

FUN FACT

Tyrannosaurus rex had two big holes in its skull. Scientists think the holes held blood vessels to help the animal control its temperature.

WHORL-TOOTHED SHARK

(HELICOPRION)

The whorl-toothed shark lived in the Early Permian period. It is related to modern sharks and skates. When a whorl-toothed shark died, its cartilage skeleton generally dissolved, leaving only its teeth and scales to be preserved in mud and fossilized in sedimentary rock. Most fossils have been found in the southwestern United States and in Russia's Ural Mountains. The whorl-toothed shark had distinctive teeth that were coiled and created a circular whorl. The shark kept its old teeth even after growing new ones.

HOW TO SPOT

Size: 18 feet (5.5 m) long

Identifying Features: Triangular teeth that grew in a spiral

Range: Worldwide

Habitat: Seas at mid-level depths

AMBER

Amber is fossilized tree resin. It can be found as a rounded pebble or lump, or even as a stalactite where a flow of sap has hardened. Amber formed when ancient conifer trees split open or were damaged. The trees produced resins to flow into and heal the damaged bark. Amber is found worldwide, and it comes in many yellow hues with shades of brown, orange, and sometimes red. Amber that appears milky white is known as bone amber.

HOW TO SPOT

Size: Varies from small drops to fist sizes

Identifying Features: Can be either smooth or spiky in shape; sometimes has air bubbles trapped inside

Range: Worldwide

Habitat: Pine forests

FUN FACT

Fossilized remains of insects or plants can sometimes be found inside amber.

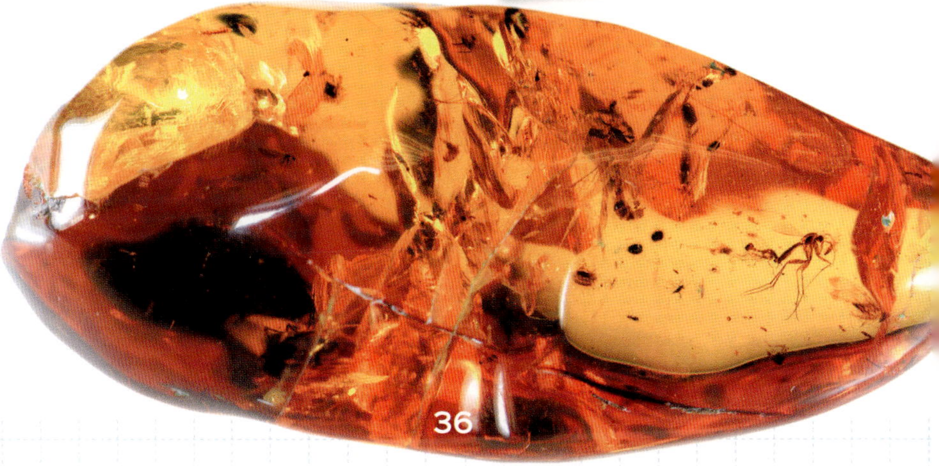

CORDAITES (*CORDAITES*)

Cordaites is a genus of extinct plants that grew during the Late Carboniferous to Early Permian periods. The genus included both trees and shrub-like plants. The plants thrived in both wet and dry areas. Their long stems or trunks were topped by crowns of leaves. *Cordaites* fossils have impressions of leaves, seeds, and petrified wood. These fossils have been found all over the world, including in North and South America, Europe, Asia, Australia, and Africa.

Illustration of what *Cordaites* may have looked like

HOW TO SPOT

Size: *Cordaites* grew 33 feet (10 m) tall on average

Identifying Features: Large, long leaves growing in tight spirals around stems

Range: Worldwide

Habitat: Hummocks and mangrove swamps

GIANT CLUB MOSS *(LEPIDODENDRON)*

The giant club moss is part of an extinct species of trees that existed during the Carboniferous period. The giant club moss had a tall, straight trunk covered in scale-like bark. The plant had grass-like leaves and cigar-shaped cones. The giant club moss thrived in swamps. Most giant club moss fossils are either imprints of leaves or sections of bark.

HOW TO SPOT

Size: The giant club moss grew 100 feet (30 m) tall on average

Identifying Features: Leaves that look like stems of grasses; bark with diamond-shaped scales

Range: Worldwide

Habitat: Hot, humid swamps

FUN FACT

The giant club moss grew quickly, but it lived only between ten and 15 years.

GINKGO *(GINKGO)*

Ginkgo trees date from the Late Triassic to the present day. They have fan-shaped leaves and nuts with a bad smell. Ginkgo trees prefer full sun. They do well in locations near well-drained water sources. The seeds and leaves of these trees are often preserved in sedimentary rocks, such as mudstone. The oldest ginkgo fossils have been found in Russia.

FUN FACT

Ginkgo trees are known as "living fossils" because they have changed very little over millions of years.

HOW TO SPOT

Size: Ginkgo trees grow 115 feet (35 m) tall on average

Identifying Features: Fan- or wedge-shaped leaves; spherical seeds

Range: Worldwide

Habitat: Near well-drained water sources in full sun

GREEN ALGA *(MASTOPORA)*

Green algae in the *Mastopora* genus lived between the Ordovician and Silurian periods. The algae had clusters of thalli, which are bodies that don't have distinct sections, such as leaves or stems. As a result, algae fossils have spherical structures that are typically around 3 inches (8 cm) long. The fossils have honeycombed patterns. Green algae can be found in saltwater seas, especially near coral reefs. The fossils are often found in deposits of limestone and mudstone.

HOW TO SPOT

Size: 3 inches (8 cm) long

Identifying Features: Dome-shaped structure covered with a honeycomb pattern

Range: Worldwide

Habitat: Saltwater seas near coral reefs

FUN FACT

Calcium chloride crystals fall off dead algae clusters. These crystals can help build coral reefs.

HORSETAIL *(EQUISETITES)*

Horsetails belonging to the *Equisetites* genus lived from the Late Carboniferous to Late Cretaceous periods. These horsetails preferred wetland conditions, such as swamps. They had ribbed stems. These plants also had small, scale-like leaves covering their bases. Horsetail fossils are usually stems and leaves preserved in sedimentary rocks.

Equisetites tubers

FUN FACT
People can see some horsetail fossils at Petrified Forest National Park in Arizona.

HOW TO SPOT

Size: 20 inches (51 cm) tall

Identifying Features: Ribbed, stemmed plants with jointed grass-like leaves growing in whorls; underground stems and tubers; small cones

Range: Worldwide

Habitat: Wetlands

MONKEY PUZZLE TREE

(ARAUCARIA)

The monkey puzzle tree has been around since the Jurassic period. Its distinctive leaves are leathery and needle-like. The tree produces nuts and has large, spiny cones. It grows in semitropical mountain forests. Fossilized remains of this tree can include leaves, cones, bark, and nuts.

HOW TO SPOT

Size: A monkey puzzle tree grows 100 feet (30 m) tall on average

Identifying Features: Small, needle-like leaves arranged in a spiral with large, spiny cones

Range: Worldwide

Habitat: Semitropical mountain forests

PALM TREE *(PALMOXYLON)*

Palm trees belonging to the extinct genus *Palmoxylon* are similar to today's palm trees. They lived in the Paleocene through Pliocene epochs. The plants grew from single-seed leaves. *Palmoxylon* lived in semitropical forests and woodlands. Some of their trunks became petrified wood fossils.

HOW TO SPOT

Size: This tree was 65 feet (20 m) tall on average

Identifying Features: Dark, round spots on light backgrounds that lack growth rings

Range: Worldwide

Habitat: Semitropical forests and woodlands

FUN FACT

Palmoxylon petrified wood is the official state fossil of Louisiana.

SIGILLARIA (*SIGILLARIA*)

Sigillaria is a genus of extinct trees that lived during the Carboniferous period. These trees had tall trunks covered in thick bark. The tops of the trees sprouted leaves. These long leaves grew in spirals, but the leaves only attached near the tips of the branches. Farther down on the branches, the leaves fell off and left polygonal scars. *Sigillaria* trees grew in river floodplains. Fossilized remains of these plants include trunks, leaves, and bark.

HOW TO SPOT

Size: Up to 98 feet (30 m) tall
Identifying Features: Long, thin leaves and thick trunk
Range: South Africa
Habitat: River floodplains

TREE FERN *(PECOPTERIS)*

Tree ferns that belonged to the *Pecopteris* genus grew during the Late Carboniferous and Early Permian periods. Tree ferns thrived in swamps. They had large fronds, but most broke down before they could be fossilized. Today, people often find only small fragments of a fossilized leaf, which juts out from a single long stem.

FUN FACT

During the Carboniferous period, the landscape was dominated by plants. These plants included both massive trees that grew 100 feet (30 m) tall and small shrubs.

HOW TO SPOT

Size: Tree ferns grew 13 feet (4 m) tall on average

Identifying Features: A long stem with fossilized leaves sticking out of it

Range: Worldwide

Habitat: Swamps

ANDESITE

Andesite is often found near volcanoes and lava flows in places where tectonic plates meet. The rock forms from the lava flows after an eruption from a stratovolcano. This type of cone-shaped volcano is made from layers of hardened ash and lava. Andesite may have white, gray, or black crystals. These are formed by rapidly cooling lava.

FUN FACT

Andesite gets its name from the Andes Mountains, which lie on the western edge of South America. This rock is commonly found there.

HOW TO SPOT

Color: Brown to dark gray

Identifying Features: Glassy white, gray, or black crystals

Mineral Composition: Plagioclase, pyroxene, hornblende, biotite, and magnetite

Range: Near volcanic areas

TECTONIC PLATES

The outer layer of Earth is made up of large slabs of strong rocks called tectonic plates. These plates glide over Earth's mantle and collide with each other, causing earthquakes. Convergent boundaries are where plates collide. A subduction zone is where one plate slips beneath another. Transform boundaries are where plates slip sideways past each other.

BASALT

Basalt forms when basaltic lava cools quickly. This process often happens underwater, when lava gets pushed from Earth's mantle onto the seafloor. Cold water presses down on it from all sides. This quickly cools the lava and creates basalt. If an ocean hotspot keeps producing lava, basalt rocks may eventually reach the ocean's surface and form islands.

FUN FACT

Basalt is the most prevalent type of rock on Earth's crust. Most of the ocean floor is covered with it.

HOW TO SPOT

Color: Often black, or black with a greenish tint

Identifying Features: Fine grained

Mineral Composition: Plagioclase and pyroxene, though the rock may have small amounts of olivine, magnetite, or quartz

Range: Worldwide

INTRUSIVE AND EXTRUSIVE

Igneous rocks can be either intrusive or extrusive. Intrusive igneous rocks are created when magma cools slowly under Earth's surface. These rocks include diabase, gabbro, and granite. Extrusive rocks form when lava and ash on Earth's surface cool and solidify quickly. Andesite and basalt are examples of extrusive igneous rocks.

DACITE

Dacite is often found above subduction zones. The lava flow that occurs in these areas can form dacite. The minerals found in a particular piece of dacite will determine its color. For example, plagioclase and quartz create a white to light gray rock. Hornblende and biotite create dacite that is light gray to light brown.

HOW TO SPOT

Color: Usually light colored, such as white, light gray, or light brown

Identifying Features: Fine grained

Mineral Composition: Plagioclase is the most abundant mineral in this rock, though other minerals may include quartz, biotite, hornblende, augite, and enstatite

Range: Europe, New Zealand, South America, western North America, and elsewhere

DIABASE

Diabase is often black to dark gray. It is a fine- or medium-grained rock. It forms when lava cools at a moderate rate. Diabase often has a lot of the mineral plagioclase in it. When polished, this mineral makes the rock look reflective. Because of this, some people use diabase as a stone for monuments or other architectural structures.

FUN FACT
The bluestone pillars that make up the Stonehenge monument are diabase.

HOW TO SPOT

Color: Dark gray, black, or greenish black; can weather to a rusty brown

Identifying Features: Fine- or medium-grained rock with large crystals

Mineral Composition: Plagioclase makes up approximately 40 to 70 percent of diabase. Pyroxene minerals are also found in the rock, and sometimes small amounts of hornblende, olivine, magnetite, and quartz will be there too.

Range: Widespread, including in Wales, Canada, and the United States

DIORITE

Diorite is often medium to dark gray with flecks of other colors, such as light gray and white. These coarse-grained rocks are often found in formations such as sills or dikes that form above places where ocean plates are forced below continental plates. The movement of the tectonic plates releases melted magma that mixes with the granite crust and forms crystals beneath the surface, creating diorite.

FUN FACT

The Inca and Maya civilizations of South America and many ancient civilizations in the Middle East used diorite to build their structures.

HOW TO SPOT

Color: Medium to dark gray with speckles of light gray, white, dark green, or black

Identifying Features: A salt-and-pepper appearance due to the flecks of mineral grains

Mineral Composition: Plagioclase with smaller amounts of hornblende, biotite, and pyroxene

Range: In areas that have a lot of silicon-rich rocks

GABBRO

Gabbro forms when magma below Earth's surface cools very slowly. The rock is exposed when uplift pushes it to the surface. This rock can also be seen in flood basalt formations, where large amounts of basalt erupted and spread over large areas. These are found in the Columbia River area of Washington, Idaho, and Oregon.

HOW TO SPOT

Color: Speckled with dark and light colors

Identifying Features: Medium or coarse grained, often with layers of darker and paler rock; layers can be less than 1 inch (2.5 cm) or as thick as several feet, depending on how the gabbro cooled

Mineral Composition: Plagioclase, pyroxene, and rarely quartz; sometimes olivine is also present, creating a rock called olivine gabbro

Range: In thick lava flows that have basalt compositions

FUN FACT

People sometimes call gabbro "black granite." It is often used for cemetery markers, signs, and polished stone counters and floors.

GRANITE

Granite has visible grains. This rock is paler than other igneous rocks and can be pink, reddish, and white. Sometimes it is dark gray flecked with black. Granite forms deep within Earth's crust, cooling very slowly over long periods of time. It reaches the surface through uplift and is often found in mountain ranges. People often use this rock as a building stone or for block paving.

HOW TO SPOT

Color: Pink, reddish, white, or darker gray with black specks

Identifying Features: Medium or coarse grained

Mineral Composition: Quartz and feldspar with small amounts of mica, amphiboles, and other minerals

Range: Most common in mountainous regions

FUN FACT

The Mount Rushmore monument in South Dakota is carved into a mountain made of granite.

OBSIDIAN

Obsidian can be black or dark green. Sometimes it has small white patches. This is known as snowflake obsidian. The rock can also be iridescent blue, red, orange, or yellow, which is called rainbow obsidian. When the rock has swirls of brown and black, it's known as mahogany obsidian. All obsidian has a glossy appearance. This rock forms when lava solidifies very rapidly.

FUN FACT
Ancient cultures, such as the Aztecs, used obsidian tools. When obsidian fractures, it gets a very sharp edge. This made it useful for hunting.

HOW TO SPOT

Color: Black; dark green; blue, red, orange, or yellow; brown and black; some have patches of white

Identifying Features: Very smooth, glassy texture; sometimes the rocks have visible flow patterns or sharp, broken edges

Mineral Composition: Volcanic glass, quartz, and magnetite

Range: Along the edges of recent lava flows or volcanic domes, or where lava contacts water or cools while airborne

Snowflake obsidian

PUMICE

Pumice is a porous rock that is used for polishing and cleaning. Pumice forms when frothy, gas-filled lava erupts either on land or in water. When the lava cools quickly, the bubbles of gas are trapped in it, creating the small cavities found in pumice. The lava does not have time to form crystals, making pumice a form of volcanic glass. A very large volcanic eruption can create a pumice block the size of a small house.

HOW TO SPOT

Color: White or gray

Identifying Features: Many small cavities or holes

Mineral Composition: Feldspar, ferromagnesian minerals, and glassy quartz

Range: Near lava flows and volcanic eruptions

FUN FACT

Due to the pockets of gas inside it, pumice is the only rock that can float on water.

RHYOLITE

Rhyolite forms from lava that has partially cooled in Earth's subsurface before erupting. The lava usually does not flow very far. Sometimes rhyolite solidifies as a plug in the volcano as the lava cools. Rhyolite sometimes has small cavities lined with mineral crystals.

HOW TO SPOT

Color: Very light gray to whitish, light brown, or pink

Identifying Features: Fine grains and small cavities

Mineral Composition: Quartz, plagioclase, and sanidine, with small amounts of hornblende and biotite

Range: Often found near continental volcanic eruptions or eruptions that take place near the edges of continents

FUN FACT

Some gemstones, including red beryl, topaz, agate, jasper, and opal, can form in rhyolite cavities.

BRECCIA

Breccia varies in color depending on the hues of its matrix and the fragments it contains. Breccia forms where small, broken fragments of rocks or minerals accumulate and cement together. Many different rocks and minerals can combine to form breccia, and the rock often has specific names to show what it is composed of, such as sandstone breccia, limestone breccia, and chert breccia.

HOW TO SPOT

Color: Varies

Identifying Features: Made up of large fragments of other rocks, cemented together by a mineral cement or matrix mixed with very small rock particles

Mineral Composition: Varies depending on the rock fragments it includes; the matrix often contains fine particles of silt, sand, quartz, or calcite

Range: Worldwide, at the base of slopes where weathering has taken place and created small rock fragments, or in stream deposits

SEDIMENTARY ROCK FORMATION

Ice, water, and wind chip away at rocks and break them into sediments. Over time, these sediments compact and cement together, forming sedimentary rocks. Sometimes organic materials, such as bones, shells, and plants, are embedded in these rocks too. Sedimentary rocks can also form when minerals precipitate from liquids.

CHALK

Chalk is a type of limestone, and it is often light gray or white and has fine grains. Chalk forms when tiny marine organisms die and their shells sink to the ocean floor to become a sediment called ooze. Over time, ooze becomes chalk. This rock is often powdery and can be easily broken.

HOW TO SPOT

Color: Light gray or white

Identifying Features: Very porous and soft

Mineral Composition: Calcite

Range: Worldwide

FUN FACT

In the 1800s, many fossils were found in western Kansas's chalk beds. These fossils were almost totally complete. Scientists were able to study the remains of mosasaurs, plesiosaurs, and pterosaurs.

CHERT

Chert has a glossy look and smooth texture. It can be various colors, including white, brown, gray, red, green, or black. The coloring depends on how much oxygen was in the sediment when it solidified into rock. For instance, if there is a lot of oxygen, the chert may turn red. If there is not a lot of oxygen, the chert can turn black or green. This rock can be broken into smooth, sharp pieces. Because of this, throughout history many people have used chert as part of their tools or weapons.

FUN FACT

Black chert is often called flint. Striking flint against steel produces sparks, and people can use these materials to start fires.

HOW TO SPOT

Color: Red, green, black, white, brown, or gray

Identifying Features: Glossy, smooth, very hard, and fractures into pieces with sharp edges

Mineral Composition: Cryptocrystalline or microcrystalline quartz

Range: In limestone and chalk formations, or where there have been deep deposits of marine sediments

COAL

Coal is composed of plant matter that once grew in or near swamps in humid, warm areas. The plant matter underwent pressure and heat. Around 10 feet (3 m) of plant matter can compress down into just 1 foot (0.3 m) of coal. People burn coal for fuel. In 2020, around 10 percent of the United States' energy consumption came from coal.

HOW TO SPOT

Color: Brown or black

Identifying Features: Shiny or dull, banded in layers, some crumbling possible

Mineral Composition: Carbonaceous plant materials, some silt and clay

Range: Worldwide, though the largest deposits are found in the United States, Russia, China, Australia, and India

CONGLOMERATE

Conglomerate is a sedimentary rock that is made up of round, often smooth fragments bigger than 0.08 inches (0.2 cm) wide. The matrix cements these fragments together. If the matrix is soft, people may crush the conglomerate to use in construction materials. If the matrix is hard, people may polish and cut the rock to use as a floor or wall decoration.

HOW TO SPOT

Color: Varies depending on the rock fragments included

Identifying Features: Chunks or grains of rock fragments that are held together by a matrix

Mineral Composition: Fragments may have particles of quartz, feldspar, or even other rocks

Range: Areas that once had flowing water or glaciers

FUN FACT

In September 2012, NASA's rover *Curiosity* was traveling across the surface of Mars. It found an area of conglomerate. Scientists believe this is evidence that water once flowed on Mars.

LIMESTONE

Limestone forms when shells, corals, algae, feces, and other organic debris accumulate. It can also form when calcium carbonate dissolves and is taken out of lakes or oceans. Limestone is a relatively soft rock. Due to that, the rock can experience weathering, and pieces of it may break off. This can create formations such as limestone cliffs and caves.

HOW TO SPOT

Color: White, tan, gray, yellow, blue, green, pink, brown, red, or black

Identifying Features: Varies, but sometimes fossils are found in limestone

Mineral Composition: Calcite

Range: Worldwide, originating in warm, shallow, and clear ocean waters

ROCK SALT

Rock salt can appear pink or red if iron oxide is present, gray if certain mineral impurities are present, and colorless or white if pure. The rock forms in large volumes of seawater or salty lake water. The salty water evaporates, leaving behind rock salt residue.

HOW TO SPOT

Color: Pink, red, gray, white, or colorless

Identifying Features: Forms a cube-like crystal shape; tastes like salt

Mineral Composition: Halite (sodium chloride) and sometimes impurities such as clay minerals, quartz, and silt

Range: In and around salt springs, salt lakes, and oceans; can also be found in underground salt domes, where heavy layers of sediment pressed down and forced salt to flow upward

FUN FACT

Salt used to be so valuable that ancient Roman soldiers were paid with it. This monthly allowance was known as *salarium*. The term evolved into the English word "salary," meaning pay.

SANDSTONE

Sandstone's color depends on its composition, but it can be white, brown, red, yellow, or green. This rock is made when particles of sand collect, compress, and get cemented together. The sand consists of minerals, rocks, or organic materials that have become smaller because of weathering. Sandstone is one of the most common sedimentary rocks.

HOW TO SPOT

Color: White, brown, red, yellow, or green

Identifying Features: Medium to fine grained; some may contain fossils

Mineral Composition: Quartz, feldspar, mica, and sometimes silt or clay, depending on the type

Range: In ancient basins where sand collected

SHALE

Shale can be black, dark gray, dark green, brown, or even red. Typically, the more organic material it has inside, the darker the shale will be. This rock is made from compacted layers of clay mud and sometimes contains fossils. Shale is often seen in large sheets. It splits into narrow layers.

HOW TO SPOT

Color: Black, dark gray, dark green, brown, or red

Identifying Features: Easily splits into long, thin-layered pieces

Mineral Composition: Quartz, mica, feldspar, clay minerals, and sometimes pyrite, calcite, and iron oxide

Range: In areas of Earth's crust where sediments accumulate

FUN FACT

Shale can be used in creating pottery, tiles, and bricks. It's also used in some cements.

TURBIDITE

Turbidites can be gray, brown, or black. These rocks form due to underwater landslides. Sediments are deposited in heavy layers on underwater slopes, and eventually sediments slide down those slopes and create sedimentary structures. Earthquakes often trigger landslides that create turbidites.

HOW TO SPOT

Color: Gray, brown, or black

Identifying Features: Layers of sediment with ripples and waves

Mineral Composition: Volcanic glass, pumice, and shells of single-celled organisms

Range: Originating in lakes and oceans, either deep in the water or near the surface if there is a steep slope present

AMPHIBOLITE

Amphibolite can be green, brown, or black. This rock forms where convergent tectonic plates trigger extreme temperatures and pressures. This process changes igneous rocks, such as basalt or gabbro, or sedimentary rocks, such as marl or graywacke, into amphibolite.

FUN FACT

Amphibolite sometimes contains garnet. This gives the rock dots of dark red coloring.

HOW TO SPOT

Color: Green, brown, or black

Identifying Features: Heavy with coarse grains; may be speckled or streaked with other minerals

Mineral Composition: Feldspar and hornblende; can also include small amounts of biotite, epidote, garnet, wollastonite, andalusite, staurolite, kyanite, sillimanite, quartz, magnetite, and calcite

Range: Worldwide

ECLOGITE

Eclogite can be light to dark gray. Sometimes it's speckled with red garnet and green pyroxene. Eclogite forms from igneous or metamorphic rocks that have high mafic mineral contents. When these rocks undergo incredibly high pressures and moderate to high temperatures, eclogite is formed.

HOW TO SPOT

Color: Light to dark gray, speckled with red and green

Identifying Features: Coarse grained, speckled with garnet and pyroxene; does not show layers

Mineral Composition: Pyroxene and garnet; can also contain disthene, quartz, and actinolite

Range: Areas near current or ancient subduction zones

TYPES OF METAMORPHISM

Metamorphic rocks can form in three ways: through regional, contact, or dynamic metamorphism. Regional metamorphism happens over a large area and through processes such as mountain formation. Contact metamorphism happens when magma makes contact with an existing rock. In dynamic metamorphism, strong forces of heat and pressure cause the rocks to bend or fold, or to get crushed, flattened, or sheared.

GNEISS

Gneiss has parallel but irregular banding on its surface. The bands are often a result of different amounts of minerals in those sections or various mineral grain sizes in the rock. Gneiss forms at plate boundaries, where heat enlarges the mineral grains. Other rocks can transform into gneiss. For instance, metamorphism changes shale into slate, then the slate can turn into phyllite, then schist, and then finally gneiss.

HOW TO SPOT

Color: Light to dark gray, brown, or lighter colors; the rock is streaked with additional colors

Identifying Features: Medium to coarse grained, light and dark areas that can be streaked or folded, and many thin layers

Mineral Composition: Feldspar, quartz, muscovite, and biotite, with smaller amounts of garnet, cordierite, sillimanite, and hornblende

Range: Lower parts of Earth's crust

MARBLE

Marble forms when limestone is exposed to high temperatures and pressures. Marble is white in its pure form. When it has other minerals inside it, the rock's color can turn to pink, gray, brown, green, yellow, blue, or black. It can also have streaks or patches of various colors. Marble has a sparkling, almost sugary appearance. This rock has many uses, such as building foundations, sculptures, and monuments.

HOW TO SPOT

Color: White, pink, gray, brown, green, yellow, blue, black, or a combination of colors, depending on the rock's minerals

Identifying Features: Medium grained and gritty

Mineral Composition: Calcite, clay minerals, mica, quartz, pyrite, iron oxide, and graphite

Range: Worldwide at convergent plate boundaries with high temperatures and pressures

FUN FACT

Sometimes colored veins appear in marble. This happens when Earth's movement cuts open the rock, creating fissures. These openings are then filled with minerals that bring more color to the rock and create a veiny appearance.

A FAMOUS MARBLE MONUMENT

The Washington Monument in Washington, DC, is made from marble. It took more than 30 years to finish the monument, and the marble came from three different places. Each quarry produced a slightly different color, so there are three shades of white in the monument.

MIGMATITE

Migmatite typically forms when lava heats up an existing metamorphic rock and melts it. The liquid rock forms a light color. The minerals within the rock stay solid and are often dark. When the new rock eventually cools, it appears dark with pale streaks.

HOW TO SPOT

Color: Dark with pale streaks

Identifying Features: Coarse with a grainy texture

Mineral Composition: Amphibole, pyroxene, and biotite mica in darker sections; feldspar, quartz, and mica in paler areas

Range: Usually found in areas where there is strong tectonic plate activity and sections of crust have been affected by high temperatures and pressures

QUARTZITE

Quartzite is usually white to gray, but minerals can color the rock red, pink, yellow, green, blue, and orange. This rock has a sandpapery feel, but people can polish the rock into a glossy shine. Quartzite forms when sandstone or chert, which are high in quartz, are exposed to extreme heat and pressure.

HOW TO SPOT

Color: White, gray, red, pink, yellow, green, blue, and orange

Identifying Features: Extremely hard material, sugary appearance, glassy shine, breaks into flat pieces

Mineral Composition: Quartz and sometimes mica

Range: Found in many mountain ranges around the world, including the Baraboo Range in Wisconsin, the Wasatch Range in Utah, the La Cloche Mountains in Canada, and Monte Binga in Mozambique

FUN FACT

Quartzite is so hard that even a metal blade can't scratch it.

SCHIST

Schist is created when compression, heat, and chemical activity turn shale into slate, then into phyllite, and finally into schist. Schist's thin layers can be split apart. This rock is grouped by what minerals are inside it. For instance, talc schist holds a lot of the mineral talc. Mica schist contains muscovite mica.

HOW TO SPOT

Color: Dark gray, green, brown, tan, or black

Identifying Features: Large grains of minerals that can be easily seen

Mineral Composition: Muscovite, chlorite, sericite, talc, graphite, and biotite

Range: Near convergent plate boundaries

SERPENTINITE

Serpentinite typically has a veiny appearance. This rock forms as a result of serpentinization. This process converts certain minerals into other minerals by pushing hot water through tiny pores and fractures in the rock. This dissolves some of the silica inside it. The silica water causes a chemical reaction that creates serpentine minerals, which make up the majority of this rock.

HOW TO SPOT

Color: Gray green, yellow green, dark green, or brown
Identifying Features: Coarse grained, flaky, and dense
Mineral Composition: Serpentine minerals
Range: Worldwide; mined in California, Arizona, New Jersey, and New York

FUN FACT
Serpentinite has a slippery feel, like snakeskin.

SKARN

Skarn can have pale or dark coloring with patches of gray, black, brown, and green. This rock is not defined by the types of minerals it has. Instead, it is defined by the process that altered it: metasomatism. This process occurs when magma heats fluids, such as water, which then interact directly with rocks such as limestones or dolostones. This morphs the original rock's structure. The resulting skarn is a coarse-grained, hard rock.

HOW TO SPOT

Color: Varies from pale to dark with additional patches of color

Identifying Features: Coarse grained and hard

Mineral Composition: Often includes calcium, iron, and magnesium

Range: Typically around the edges of magma fields

SLATE

Slate is a fine-grained rock that easily breaks into thin layers. The rock's color is determined by what mineral is in it. For instance, iron oxide produces purple or red slate. Green slate is caused by chlorite. Slate is formed from sedimentary rocks, such as shale or mudstone, that have been changed by pressure and heat.

HOW TO SPOT

Color: Black, gray, blue, purple, green, or red

Identifying Features: Smooth to the touch and breaks into sheets

Mineral Composition: Clay minerals, small amounts of quartz, mica, calcite, and feldspar; may also contain fossils

Range: Found as layers between sedimentary rocks, usually in saltwater deposits, but sometimes where lakes existed during previous ice ages

FUN FACT

Since slate breaks into sheets or slabs, it is often used for roof tiles and flooring.

ANORTHITE

The mineral anorthite has glassy, brittle, white or gray crystals. The crystals can also be green, yellow, or a range of pink to red. Anorthite is often found in igneous and metamorphic rocks. People use this mineral to manufacture ceramics and glass.

HOW TO SPOT

Color: White, gray, green, yellow, pink, or red

Streak Color: White

Hardness: 6 to 6.5

Crystal System: Triclinic

Luster: Vitreous

Range: Major deposits are found in India, Sweden, Japan, Italy, and New Jersey in the United States

CRYSTAL SYSTEMS

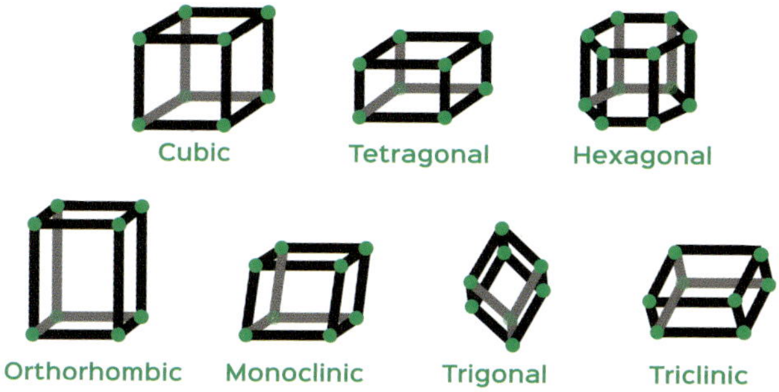

Minerals are classified by what crystal system their shapes belong to. The shape is determined by the symmetry of a mineral's crystals.

WHAT IS LUSTER?

Luster refers to how reflective a mineral's surface is. A vitreous luster looks like regular window glass. Metallic looks like polished metal. Silky may look similar to the way light shimmers on silk. A pitchy luster looks tar-like. A greasy luster looks like grease stains on paper. Adamantine appears like cut diamonds or lead crystal glass. A pearly luster looks like the inside of a shell.

ARSENIC

Arsenic looks like a mass of blackish-gray lumps. It has a metallic sheen when freshly mined, but after a few hours it turns dark and dull. Arsenic is found in Earth's crust. It is mostly mined in China and Morocco.

FUN FACT
Arsenic is a poison that can be used for pesticides. People also use it to keep wood from rotting.

HOW TO SPOT

Color: Blackish gray
Streak Color: Black
Hardness: 3 to 4
Crystal System: Trigonal
Luster: Metallic to dull
Range: Found in small quantities in rock, soil, water, and air

MINERAL HARDNESS

Testing the hardness of a mineral can help identify it. The Mohs Hardness Scale measures a mineral's hardness based on its resistance to being scratched. The scale ranges from one to ten, with one being soft and ten being hard. For instance, talc is a one on the scale. It can be scratched with a fingernail. A diamond is a ten. Not many things can scratch a diamond.

BARITE

Barite can look like fan-shaped masses of crystals, or it can form as a series of rosette shapes. Some of its colors might be luminescent. Barite is often found in veins of ore, in sedimentary or igneous rocks, and in clay or marine deposits. Barite is mined in many countries, including India, China, Morocco, Iran, and the United States. The mineral can be used in the creation of cements, paints, and other materials.

FUN FACT

Barite made from sand is brown. It may have crystals that resemble flowers. These are known as barite desert roses.

HOW TO SPOT

Color: White, gray, orange, red, pink, purple, brown, blue, green, black, or colorless

Streak Color: White

Hardness: 3 to 3.5

Crystal System: Orthorhombic

Luster: Vitreous, pearly

Range: Worldwide, in sedimentary rock layers and ore veins

STREAK COLOR

Streak colors can help classify minerals. They are found by drawing lines with the minerals, usually by scraping the minerals on rough surfaces. The line colors are characteristic of certain types of minerals. Some minerals come in a variety of colors. But the streak color for a certain mineral will always be the same. For example, barite can be many different colors. But its streak color will always be white.

CALCITE

Calcite is a common mineral that can be white or colorless when pure, or almost any other color when impure. Calcite is soft and can be easily scratched by a knife. Most calcite is found in limestone. When limestone undergoes metamorphism, the calcite often recrystallizes and turns the rock into a calcite marble. Calcite and the rocks it is found in can have various uses. For instance, limestone helps make cement. Marble is used for carvings and statues.

FUN FACT

One of the most useful ways scientists can identify calcite is by putting hydrochloric acid on it. Calcite will fizz when the acid touches it.

HOW TO SPOT

Color: White, colorless, red, yellow, pink, blue, green, black, brown, or lavender

Streak Color: White

Hardness: 3

Crystal System: Trigonal

Luster: Vitreous

Range: Many countries in the world, including Mexico, the United States, India, and Germany

CALCITE IN NATURE

One type of calcite forms from calcium-rich waters inside caverns or on limestone cliffs, creating stalagmites, stalactites, and strange globular growths. These growths constantly accumulate, creating layers. They often trap organic matter such as leaves, twigs, and mosses. These things make the calcite impure.

CARNALLITE

Carnallite dissolves in cold water. It has a bitter, salty taste. If carnallite is placed in a flame, it melts easily and makes the flame purple. Carnallite can be found in the upper sections of marine salt deposits. This mineral serves as a source of potassium used in fertilizers.

HOW TO SPOT

Color: Blue, yellow, red, white, or colorless
Streak Color: White
Hardness: 2.5
Crystal System: Orthorhombic
Luster: Greasy, and transparent to translucent
Range: Northern Germany, Spain, Tunisia, and the southwestern United States

CHROMITE

Chromite is brownish black to greenish black. It is usually found as grains or crystals embedded in rocks, much like chocolate chips in cookies. Chromite has chromium in it. People extract this element and use it to create steel.

FUN FACT

Many gemstone colors occur because they contain small amounts of chromium. Red rubies, pink sapphires, and green emeralds get their colors from this element.

HOW TO SPOT

Color: Brownish black to greenish black

Streak Color: Dark brown

Hardness: 5.5

Crystal System: Cubic

Luster: Metallic to greasy

Range: Russia, India, Kazakhstan, the Philippines, New Caledonia, Kosovo, Zimbabwe, Turkey, Brazil, and Cuba

CINNABAR

Cinnabar is known for its rich red color. It is often found as a crystal on a rock's surface. Cinnabar can be found around volcanic vents and hot springs, and as mineral veins in locations with volcanic activity.

HOW TO SPOT

Color: Bright red to brownish red; sometimes gray
Streak Color: Red
Hardness: 2 to 2.5
Crystal System: Trigonal
Luster: Either adamantine or a flat matte without a glossy finish
Range: Worldwide

FUN FACT

Cinnabar is a mineral ore of mercury. That means cinnabar is extremely toxic. It was once used as a red pigment for paint, but it has now been replaced with safer pigments.

COPPER

Copper has a reddish, metallic sheen. It is only found in small quantities throughout the world. Copper is found in basaltic volcanic rocks or as a compound with other minerals. Copper has been used by humans for thousands of years. Around 5500 BCE, people began using copper to make tools. Today, copper can be used in wiring, plumbing, machines, car parts, and more.

HOW TO SPOT

Color: Reddish
Streak Color: Copper red
Hardness: 2.5 to 3
Crystal System: Cubic
Luster: Metallic
Range: Large copper ore mines exist in the United States, Canada, Bolivia, Mexico, Chile, Australia, Botswana, and Uganda

FUN FACT
When exposed to air for a long time, copper can form a thin, green coating.

NATIVE ELEMENTS

Native elements are minerals made up of chemical elements that exist alone. They are not combined with other chemical elements to form compounds. Examples of native elements include copper, gold, antimony, arsenic, sulfur, and carbon.

CROCOITE

Crocoite is a bright, orangish-red mineral. It forms where deposits containing lead and chromium have been weathered and oxidized. Crocoite is rare because lead and chromium normally do not exist together. Crocoite melts when exposed to a flame, and it dissolves only in a strong acid. This mineral has a vitreous to adamantine luster that grows dull when exposed to sunlight.

FUN FACT

Due to crocoite's colorful crystals, this mineral is popular with collectors. Crocoite was also once used as a paint pigment.

HOW TO SPOT

Color: Orange red
Streak Color: Yellow orange
Hardness: 2.5 to 3
Crystal System: Monoclinic
Luster: Vitreous to adamantine
Range: Tasmania, Brazil, southwestern United States, and Russia

DOLOMITE

The term *dolomite* can describe both the mineral in its pure form and a type of limestone that is primarily made up of dolomite. The crystals in this mineral can be white, colorless, blue, dark to light gray, or tan. Dolomite is often found in rocks that were formed from calcium carbonate mud that was then altered by water rich in magnesium. Dolomite is often used to make cement.

HOW TO SPOT

Color: White, colorless, blue, dark to light gray, or tan
Streak Color: White
Hardness: 3.5 to 4
Crystal System: Trigonal
Luster: Vitreous or pearly
Range: The most famous quarries are located in the midwestern United States; Ontario, Canada; Switzerland; Pamplona, Spain; and Mexico

ENARGITE

The crystals in enargite are metallic gray and heavy. Sometimes the crystals are coated with thin layers of pyrite, giving them more of a yellow color. Enargite crystals are sometimes clearly arranged in long, thin, parallel streaks. Enargite is found in veins of copper ore that are rich in arsenic.

FUN FACT

Enargite is a sulfosalt, which is a type of mineral that has both sulfur and metal.

HOW TO SPOT

Color: Grayish black to black

Streak Color: Black to dark gray

Hardness: 3.5

Crystal System: Orthorhombic

Luster: Metallic

Range: Deposits are found in Montana in the United States, and in Italy, Chile, the Balkans, and Peru

FLUORITE

Fluorite is popular with collectors because of its beautiful, varied colors. This mineral is found in hydrothermal veins of heated water in Earth's crust, such as hot springs, and especially in those containing lead and zinc. Fluorite is used in steel manufacturing.

HOW TO SPOT

Color: Purple, golden yellow, green, colorless, blue, pink, champagne, or brown

Streak Color: White

Hardness: 4

Crystal System: Cubic

Luster: Vitreous

Range: Worldwide

FUN FACT

Fluorite glows under ultraviolet light. This mineral's name is the origin of the word *fluorescent*.

GARNET

Garnet is a group of minerals. Most form at plate boundaries where shale is metamorphosed by heat and pressure. Garnets begin as tiny grains that slowly grow over time and displace or replace the rock materials around them. Garnets are usually red, but they can be orange, green, yellow, purple, black, or brown. Blue garnets are extremely rare. Garnets are used as gemstones.

HOW TO SPOT

Color: Typically red
Streak Color: Colorless
Hardness: 6.5 to 7.5
Crystal System: Cubic
Luster: Vitreous
Range: Mined around the world, including in Australia, the United States, India, China, and more

GEMSTONES

Gemstones are minerals that are used in jewelry. Gemstones with beautiful colors are polished so that they shine and sparkle. This is especially important because some minerals in their natural states, such as diamonds, are colorless and uninteresting.

GOLD

Gold is one of the most well-known minerals. In its natural mineral form, gold almost always contains traces of silver. For instance, a gold nugget is usually 70 to 95 percent gold and the remainder is mostly silver. It may also have traces of copper and iron.

HOW TO SPOT

Color: Golden yellow, but has a lighter color when it contains silver

Streak Color: Yellow

Hardness: 2.5 to 3

Crystal System: Cubic

Luster: Metallic

Range: Mined in South Africa, Russia, Australia, Canada, and Nevada and Alaska in the United States

FUN FACT

Gold is a precious metal. In 2019, people mined about 3,892 tons (3,531 metric tons) of gold. People have used this mineral for thousands of years to create decorative objects and jewelry.

GYPSUM

Gypsum is best known for its use in making plaster. This mineral forms in deposits of evaporated water, usually where marine seas or inland lakes have dried out. It can also occur near hot springs. Gypsum crystals with sand trapped inside become brown, gray, or opaque, and the crystals may form rosettes in a desert rose flower shape.

FUN FACT

The largest gypsum crystal ever found was in Chile. It was more than 10 feet (3 m) long and 1.5 feet (0.46 m) wide.

HOW TO SPOT

Color: Colorless, white, gray, yellow, red, or brown

Streak Color: White

Hardness: 2

Crystal System: Monoclinic

Luster: Pearly

Range: Deposits located in Spain, Thailand, the United States, Turkey, and Russia

HALITE

Halite is rock salt that occurs naturally. It forms in places where salt water has evaporated, such as marine lagoons or inland salt lakes. Halite can also occur near volcanic vents. It forms when volcanic solids become gases in a process called sublimation. Halite is found on every continent. Sometimes halite beds are only about 9 to 10 feet (2.7 to 3 m) thick. Other times they are more than 1,000 feet (305 m) thick.

HOW TO SPOT

Color: Colorless, white, red, orange, yellow, purple, or blue
Streak Color: White
Hardness: 2
Crystal System: Cubic
Luster: Vitreous
Range: Large deposits are found in Russia, France, India, Ontario, and the United States

FUN FACT

In some underground halite deposits, the mineral is pushed upward by either tectonic or gravitational forces. It pops out through soft ground and forms an arched structure known as a salt dome.

HEMATITE

Hematite is found in sedimentary, metamorphic, and igneous rocks. It is the most valuable ore in iron. Hematite sometimes has enough magnetite in it to attract a common magnet. Hematite can be black or red. Some samples have steel-gray crystals with a metallic luster. Others are soft with fine grains.

FUN FACT

Hematite is one of the most common minerals found on Earth's surface and in the planet's crust.

HOW TO SPOT

Color: Black, red, or steel-gray crystals
Streak Color: Red or reddish brown
Hardness: 6.5
Crystal System: Trigonal
Luster: Metallic to dull
Range: Most often mined in China, Australia, Brazil, India, Russia, Ukraine, South Africa, Canada, Venezuela, and the United States

LAZULITE

Lazulite is popular for its range of blue colors. This mineral forms in many different geological environments, especially in veins of quartz, igneous rocks, and quartzites. It is often seen as either grains or glassy crystals. Lazulite embedded in white quartz is often cut into slabs and polished for collectors. When heated, lazulite breaks into small pieces but does not melt.

FUN FACT

Lazulite comes from the German word *lazurstein*, which means "blue stone."

HOW TO SPOT

Color: Deep azure blue, pale blue, or bluish green

Streak Color: White

Hardness: 5 to 6

Crystal System: Monoclinic

Luster: Vitreous to dull, or translucent to opaque; can be transparent in rare cases

Range: Austria, Sweden, California, and Brazil

MAGNETITE

Magnetite is the only mineral that is naturally magnetic. It can sometimes be found with small iron filings stuck to its surface. Magnetite frequently forms in rocks that come from magma and in mineral veins that contain large amounts of sulphates. Magnetite develops a reddish-brown rust when it gets wet.

HOW TO SPOT

Color: Black
Streak Color: Black
Hardness: 6 to 6.5
Crystal System: Cubic
Luster: Dull metallic
Range: Various places around the world, such as in Hong Kong, California, and the west coast of New Zealand's North Island

FUN FACT

The first magnetic compasses were made by hanging magnetite from strings. They were used in China as early as 300 BCE. When freely hanging from strings, small pieces of magnetite will align themselves with Earth's magnetic field.

NITRATINE

Nitratine is found in arid environments where it hardly ever rains. This mineral is efflorescent, meaning it loses water from its crystal structure and develops a white, powdery surface. Nitratine is used in the manufacturing of fertilizer, and it has also been used to create gunpowder.

HOW TO SPOT

Color: Colorless, white, light yellow, light gray, or light brown
Streak Color: White
Hardness: 1.5 to 2
Crystal System: Hexagonal
Luster: Vitreous
Range: Arid environments

OLIVINE

Olivine is a name for a group of minerals. One mineral in this group is forsterite. It is also known as white olivine. It has a lot of magnesium. Another mineral in this group is fayalite. It is rich in iron. The gem variety of olivine is called peridot. Olivine minerals are mostly found at Earth's surface in dark colored igneous rocks.

FUN FACT

Olivine has been identified on the Moon and Mars. It's also seen in meteorites and in a comet called Wild 2.

HOW TO SPOT

Color: Green, greenish yellow, yellow, yellowish brown, brown, white, or colorless

Streak Color: Colorless

Hardness: 6.5 to 7

Crystal System: Orthorhombic

Luster: Vitreous and slightly greasy

Range: Myanmar, Pakistan, Russia, Mexico, Brazil, Australia, Germany, Norway, Sweden, Ethiopia, China, and the United States

PYRITE

Pyrite is extremely common. It can form in both high and low temperatures and is found in igneous, metamorphic, and sedimentary rocks all over the world. Its name comes from the Greek word for fire, *pyr*. That's because pyrite gives off sparks when struck with something made of metal.

Pyrite can be confused with gold. That's because, to the untrained eye, the two seem similar in color and shape. This has led to pyrite's nickname, "fool's gold."

HOW TO SPOT

Color: Brassy yellow

Streak Color: Greenish to brownish black

Hardness: 6 to 6.5

Crystal System: Cubic

Luster: Metallic

Range: Italy, Spain, Kazakhstan, Peru, and the United States

QUARTZ

Quartz is a common mineral that forms in igneous, sedimentary, and metamorphic rocks. It is very resistant to weathering. That makes it the dominant mineral of mountaintops and the primary part of beach, river, and desert sands. Quartz can be a wide variety of colors. This mineral is used for many things, including the creation of glass, fire bricks, rubber, and paint.

HOW TO SPOT

Color: Colorless, white, gray, yellow, green, purple, pink, red, brown, or black

Streak Color: Colorless

Hardness: 7

Crystal System: Trigonal

Luster: Vitreous to greasy

Range: Worldwide, especially the Alps, Brazil, Madagascar, Japan, and the United States

FUN FACT

Well-shaped quartz crystals in the United States have been found in Hot Springs, Arkansas, and Little Falls and Ellenville, New York.

SCHEELITE

Scheelite is brown, yellow, white, or green. This mineral is found in hydrothermal, or heated, water veins and coarse-grained igneous rocks. It is also found in rocks altered by contact metamorphism. Under ultraviolet light, scheelite gives off white or bluish-white fluorescence.

HOW TO SPOT

Color: Brown, yellow, white, or green

Streak Color: White

Hardness: 4.5 to 5

Crystal System: Tetragonal

Luster: Greasy

Range: England, Bolivia, New Zealand, New South Wales, Switzerland, France, Siberia, and the United States

SILVER

Silver is a well-known mineral that is often used to make jewelry. Silver can be found in a pure state, but it is usually mixed with small amounts of gold, arsenic, and antimony. Silver is found in volcanic basalt rocks and in water veins with hot or moderate temperatures. It may also form by the breakdown of sulfur from lead or zinc deposits.

FUN FACT

Silver has many unique physical properties that give it a special status. For instance, it is a good conductor of electricity. It is also easy to either hammer silver out or stretch it into a thin wire.

HOW TO SPOT

Color: Whitish silver; tarnishes when exposed to air

Streak Color: Silvery white

Hardness: 2.5 to 3

Crystal System: Cubic

Luster: Metallic, opaque

Range: Mined in many different countries, such as the United States, Canada, Mexico, Peru, and Bolivia

SPERRYLITE

Sperrylite is often found in rocks that have been changed through contact metamorphism. Since sperrylite is very resistant to weathering, it is also found in the sand and gravel of rivers. This mineral is prized by collectors. As an ore of platinum, sperrylite is valuable as a metal ore mineral.

FUN FACT

Sperrylite is named after Francis Louis Sperry. He was a chemist who discovered this mineral in 1889.

HOW TO SPOT

Color: Gray
Streak Color: Black to dark gray
Hardness: 6 to 7
Crystal System: Cubic
Luster: Metallic
Range: Canada, Russia, South Africa, and North Carolina in the United States

SYLVANITE

Sylvanite has both gold and silver in its chemical formula. It is valued by collectors because it is rare and because it contains gold. Sylvanite forms in hydrothermal veins. It often forms with gold, quartz, fluorite, pyrite, and other sulphates. Sylvanite is often a silvery white color but can also be yellow.

HOW TO SPOT

Color: Silvery white, gray; sometimes yellowish

Streak Color: Black to dark gray

Hardness: 1.5 to 2

Crystal System: Monoclinic

Luster: Metallic

Range: Hungary, Australia, Canada, and the western United States

TOPAZ

Topaz is a mineral gemstone that can be used in jewelry. Most topaz grows as crystals within igneous rocks. Topaz in its pure form is colorless. In other cases, the mineral can be different shades of brown, blue, or yellow. In rare cases, the mineral can be red. However, the colors can change over time. For instance, brown topaz may get bleached by sunlight.

FUN FACT
When exposed to heat, yellow topaz turns pink.

HOW TO SPOT

Color: Colorless, brown, blue, yellow, pink, or red
Streak Color: Colorless
Hardness: 8
Crystal System: Orthorhombic
Luster: Vitreous, transparent to translucent
Range: Brazil, the United States, Madagascar, Burma, Namibia, Zimbabwe, Mexico, Sri Lanka, Pakistan, Russia, and China

TORBERNITE

Torbernite forms in coarse granite or in other igneous rocks. It may also appear as a secondary mineral when the highly radioactive mineral uraninite is formed. Torbernite itself is radioactive and gives off small amounts of toxic radon gas. It is occasionally found coating the walls of crevices in rocks.

HOW TO SPOT

Color: Various shades of green
Streak Color: Pale green
Hardness: 2 to 2.5
Crystal System: Tetragonal
Luster: Sub-adamantine, vitreous, waxy, pearly
Range: England, Germany, Czech Republic, and many other places where uraninite minerals exist

FUN FACT

Torbernite is radioactive because it contains uranium. For this reason, it has to be handled carefully. Torbernite should not be kept where people live. Always wash your hands after touching this mineral. It should be stored in containers with X-ray shielding.

TURQUOISE

Turquoise is a popular mineral used in jewelry. It forms in arid climates in altered and weathered volcanic rocks. Its color can vary from greenish to blue. Sky-blue turquoise is a popular gemstone color. Some turquoise has part of its host rock in it. This looks like black patches or spider webbing. Turquoise has been prized by people for centuries. For instance, the ancient Egyptians used it to make beads and amulets.

HOW TO SPOT

Color: Greenish to blue
Streak Color: Greenish to bluish white
Hardness: 6
Crystal System: Triclinic
Luster: Waxy to dull
Range: Most come from the southwestern United States, China, Chile, Egypt, Iran, and Mexico

FUN FACT

Turquoise has been used as an ornament by Native American cultures since 200 BCE. Those making turquoise ornaments today include the Navajo, Hopi, and Zuni peoples. The ornaments are used for ceremonies, art, jewelry, and more.

URANINITE

Uraninite is often black, brown, or gray. However, it can also turn yellow, orange red, or greenish yellow. Uraninite can occur in granite. It is also found in sedimentary rocks. Uranium is the major element in uraninite. Uranium is a chemical element known for being radioactive.

FUN FACT

Uraninite is an important radioactive mineral, but it was once thought to be worthless. When its uranium content was discovered, it became valuable. Scientist Marie Curie studied radioactivity by looking at samples of uraninite.

HOW TO SPOT

Color: Black, brown, gray, yellow, orange red, or greenish yellow

Streak Color: Black, brownish black, gray, or greenish

Hardness: 5 to 6

Crystal System: Cubic

Luster: Submetallic or greasy

Range: Deposits have been found in the United States, Canada, Australia, Austria, the Czech Republic, England, Germany, Hungary, Namibia, Norway, Rwanda, and South Africa

VANADINITE

Vanadinite usually forms where lead minerals are oxidized, or chemically combined with oxygen. This often happens in areas with arid climates. Vanadinite is often a red, orange, or brown color. Many people like vanadinite for its bright colors and large crystals.

HOW TO SPOT

Color: Red, orange, or brown

Streak Color: Yellowish brown to pale yellow

Hardness: 3

Crystal System: Hexagonal

Luster: Greasy to adamantine

Range: Morocco, Namibia, Argentina, Australia, and the United States

GLOSSARY

crystal
A piece of a solid material that has molecules fitting together in a repeating pattern.

dorsal
Located near or on the back, especially of an animal.

genus
A group of related animals or plants that is narrower than a family but broader than a species.

hummocks
Rounded mounds of earth.

invertebrate
An animal that does not have a backbone.

luminescent
Emitting light that is not caused by heat.

mafic
A group of minerals that are rich in iron and magnesium.

magma
Melted rock that comes from deep inside Earth's crust and is called lava when it erupts onto the surface.

matrix
Substances such as silt and clay that hold fragments together in sedimentary rocks.

petrified
Has become hard like stone over a long period of time.

quarry
A large, deep pit where stones or other materials are extracted.

vertebrate
An animal with a backbone.

weathering
The process by which rocks or other materials are worn down by things such as water, wind, or climate.

whorl
A pattern of spirals or concentric circles.

TO LEARN MORE

FURTHER READINGS

Eboch, Chris. *Rocks and Minerals: Get the Dirt on Geology*. Nomad Press, 2020.

Swanson, Jennifer. *Rock, Fossil, and Shell Hunting.* Odd Dot, 2021.

Wang, Yinan. *The 50 State Fossils: A Guidebook for Aspiring Paleontologists*. Schiffer, 2018.

ONLINE RESOURCES

Booklinks
NONFICTION NETWORK
FREE! ONLINE NONFICTION RESOURCES

To learn more about fossils, rocks, and minerals, please visit **abdobooklinks.com** or scan this QR code. These links are routinely monitored and updated to provide the most current information available.

PHOTO CREDITS

Cover Photos: iStockphoto, front (conglomerate), front (amber), front (mahogany obsidian), front (calcite), back (rock salt); Minakryn Ruslan/iStockphoto, front (chert), back (fluorite); Julia Reschke/Shutterstock Images, front (gold); Albert Russ/Shutterstock Images, front (barite); Shutterstock Images, front (fluorite), front (serpentinite), back (Ichthyosaur); Sebastian Janicki/Shutterstock Images, front (quartz); Andriy Kananovych/Shutterstock Images, front (trilobite); Fokin Oleg/Shutterstock Images, back (granite); Minakryn Ruslan/Shutterstock Images, back (garnet)

Interior Photos: iStockphoto, 1 (top left), 1 (center), 7 (right), 15 (right), 20 (bottom), 24 (top), 27 (bottom), 30, 33, 34 (top), 36 (top), 36 (bottom), 44, 53 (bottom), 54 (top), 56 (top), 56 (bottom), 59 (top), 59 (bottom), 60 (top), 60 (bottom), 61 (top), 64 (top), 68 (top), 68 (bottom), 75 (top), 75 (bottom), 79, 81, 82 (top), 82 (bottom), 87 (top), 88, 89 (top), 90 (top), 90 (bottom), 92, 93, 96 (bottom), 97 (top), 97 (bottom), 98 (bottom), 100, 103, 104 (top), 107 (top), 112 (top left), 112 (top right), 112 (bottom left); Colin Keates/Dorling Kindersley/Science Source, 1 (top right), 8, 10, 16, 17, 19, 42; Daniel V. Fung/iStockphoto, 1 (bottom left), 62; Shutterstock Images, 1 (bottom right), 9 (left), 9 (right), 22 (right), 26 (bottom), 38, 45, 49, 52 (top), 52 (bottom), 58, 64 (top), 65, 71, 73, 76 (crystals), 85, 91; Minakryn Ruslan/iStockphoto, 4 (left), 5 (copper), 74, 83, 99 (top), 99 (bottom), 107 (bottom); Guillermo Guerao Serra/Shutterstock Images, 4 (middle), 6 (bottom), 14 (bottom); Igor Sokalski/iStockphoto, 4 (right), 105; Red Line Editorial, 5 (infographic); Bjoern Wylezich/Shutterstock Images, 5 (Diplomystus), 24 (bottom); Studio Empreinte/iStockphoto, 5 (obsidian), 53 (top); Krim Kate/iStockphoto, 5 (eclogite), 46, 51 (top), 51 (bottom), 54 (bottom), 57 (top), 66, 67; Bruce Block/iStockphoto, 87 (bottom); Ibe van Oort/Shutterstock Images, 6 (top), 14 (top); S. Leggio/Shutterstock Images, 7 (left), 15 (left); The Natural History Museum, London/Alamy, 11;

The Natural History Museum, London/Science Source, 12, 32, 40; Millard H. Sharp/Science Source, 13; Andriy Kananovych/Shutterstock Images, 18, 80; Natalia van D/Shutterstock Images, 20 (top); Colin Keates/Dorling Kindersley/Natural History Museum, London/Science Source, 21, 29, 37 (right), 41, 43; Martin Shields/Science Source, 22 (left); Nick Fox/Shutterstock Images, 23; Jirik V./Shutterstock Images, 25; Joaquin Corbalan/iStockphoto, 26 (top); Danny Ye/Shutterstock Images, 27 (top); Akkharat Jarusilawong/Shutterstock Images, 28 (top); Arpad Benedek/iStockphoto, 28 (bottom); Science Stock Photography/Science Source, 31; David H. Coder/iStockphoto, 34 (bottom); Bob Cranston/Blue Planet Archive, 35; Corey Ford/iStockphoto, 37 (left); Gerald Corsi/iStockphoto, 39; Evan Austen/iStockphoto, 47; Brack P. Kent/Shutterstock Images, 48; Selahattin Volkan Kuru/iStockphoto, 50; Iseo Yang/iStockphoto, 55; Andreas Nesslinger/iStockphoto, 57 (bottom); A. Pobedimskiy/iStockphoto, 61 (bottom); Warunee Chanopas/Shutterstock Images, 63 (top); Daria Ga/Shutterstock Images, 63 (bottom); Shaun L./iStockphoto, 64 (bottom); Aleksandr Pobedimskiy/Shutterstock Images, 69 (top); Tyler Boyes/Shutterstock Images, 69 (bottom), 112 (top center); Dr. Lars Hansen, 70; Moha El-Jaw/iStockphoto, 72 (top), 112 (bottom right); Liudmila Shevaga/iStockphoto, 72 (bottom); Dirk Wiersma/Science Source, 76 (top), 86, 102; Andreas Kermann/iStockphoto, 77, 94; Michel Viard/iStockphoto, 78, 84 (top); Dan Olsen/iStockphoto, 84 (bottom), 104 (bottom); Studio Casper/iStockphoto, 89 (bottom); Harry Taylor/Dorling Kindersley/Science Source, 95, 106; Joel Papalini/iStockphoto, 96 (top); Peter Hermes Furian/iStockphoto, 98 (top); Albert Russ/Shutterstock Images, 101

ABDOBOOKS.COM
Published by Abdo Publishing, a division of ABDO, PO Box 398166, Minneapolis, Minnesota 55439.

102021
012022

THIS BOOK CONTAINS
RECYCLED MATERIALS

Editor: Alyssa Sorenson
Series Designer: Colleen McLaren
Content Consultant: Lars Hansen, PhD, Associate Professor, Department of Earth and Environmental Sciences, University of Minnesota

Library of Congress Control Number: 2021941709

Publisher's Cataloging-in-Publication Data
Names: Lusted, Marcia Amidon, author.
Title: Fossils, rocks, and minerals / by Marcia Amidon Lusted
Description: Minneapolis, Minnesota : Abdo Publishing, 2022 | Series: Field guides | Includes online resources and index.
Identifiers: ISBN 9781532196966 (lib. bdg.) | ISBN 9781098218775 (ebook)
Subjects: LCSH: Fossils--Juvenile literature. | Rocks--Juvenile literature. | Mineralogy--Juvenile literature. | Geology--Juvenile literature. | Field guides--Juvenile literature.
Classification: DDC 550--dc23

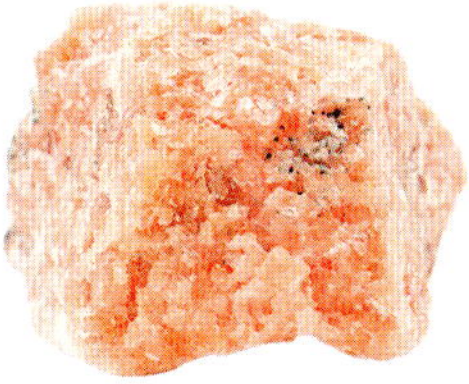

FIELD GUIDES

FLOWERS AND PLANTS

Andrea Debbink

Abdo Reference

An Imprint of Abdo Publishing | abdobooks.com

CONTENTS

Garden Flowers and Herbs

Vines

Berries and Shrubs

Carnivorous Plants

Ferns

Mosses

Liverworts

WHAT ARE FLOWERS AND PLANTS?

A plant is a living thing that makes its own food using photosynthesis. The plant kingdom is incredibly diverse. Plants may have tall trunks or many sturdy stems. Some plants produce flowers while others don't have flowers or seeds at all. Plants can live in nearly every habitat and climate on Earth. Some plants are edible and others are poisonous. Even edible plants can have poisonous look-alikes.

There are many differences between plant species. People categorize plants based on these differences. The two most common groupings are flowering plants and nonflowering plants.

FLOWERING PLANTS

Flowering plants are also called angiosperms. These plants produce flowers that turn into fruits, which contain seeds. Flowers can be colorful and showy, or so small that they're hardly visible. Fruits can be large or fleshy, like apples. Or they can be small and dry, like grains from bread wheat. There are two main types of flowering plants: monocots and eudicots.

- A monocot is a flowering plant that has one cotyledon, the part of the seed that becomes a plant's leaf. Examples of monocots are grasses, rushes, sedges, some freshwater aquatic plants, and bromeliads.

- A eudicot is a flowering plant that has two cotyledons. Examples of eudicots are succulents, wildflowers, garden flowers, herbs, vines, berries, shrubs, and carnivorous plants.

NONFLOWERING PLANTS

Nonflowering plants don't produce flowers or fruits. They reproduce by releasing spores or undergoing vegetative propagation. Vegetative propagation is when new plants grow from parts of parent plants, or when they grow from reproductive structures, such as rhizomes. Some types of nonflowering plants include ferns, mosses, and liverworts.

FLOWER AND PLANT IDENTIFICATION

People can use the following characteristics to help them identify plants:

- Height: Most plants have average heights.
- Stem: Most plants have either woody or herbaceous stems, but some plants don't have stems at all. Woody stems are rigid. They can live for several years and add new growths each year. Herbaceous stems are soft. They last for only one growing season.
- Leaves: The sizes, shapes, colors, and arrangements of leaves can help identify plants.
- Flowers, fruits, and seeds: Plants may produce flowers, fruits, and seeds depending on the seasons. However, not all plants have these things.
- Range: A plant's range is where it is found in the world. Sometimes plants are introduced into non-native areas. They can become invasive.
- Habitat: A plant's habitat is the type of environment it grows in.
- Bloom period: Most plants bloom during specific seasons. They may bloom a few times a year, once a year, or even less frequently than that.

HOW TO USE THIS BOOK

Tab shows the plant category.

OTHER FRESHWATER AQUATIC PLANTS

SACRED LOTUS *(NELUMBO NUCIFERA)*

The sacred lotus is an aquatic plant known for its large, showy flower and its long history with people. These plants ...ical freshwater habitats such as lagoons and ... but they're also popular garden plants. The ... has large, green leaves and a large flower that ...ite in color. The flower rises above the water's ...he plant's stem.

HOW TO SPOT

Height: Aquatic
Stem: Herbaceous
Leaves: Rounded, waxy leaves; up to 2 feet (0.6 m) wide
Flowers: Pink or white flowers with yellow centers; 8 to 12 inches (20 to 30 cm) wide
Range: Asia, A... North America
Habitat: Fresh... ...ltas, lagoons, and slow-mov...
Bloom Perio...

RELIGION AND THE LOTUS

The sacred lotus is important to the Buddhist and Hindu religions. It's seen as a symbol of beauty, purity, and divinity.

26

The plant's common name appears here.

Images show the plant.

Sidebars provide additional information about the topic.

The plant's scientific name appears here.

WATER SHIELD *(BRASENIA SCHREBERI)*

The water shield is a common aquatic plant. It is known for spreading its small, oval-shaped leaves across the surfaces of ponds and lakes. The water shield has a small, compact flower. A thick slime coats the plant's underwater stem and the undersides of its leaves. This slime may protect the water shield from drought and animals.

This paragraph provides information about the plant.

How to Spot boxes give information on how to identify the plant.

HOW TO SPOT

Height: Aquatic
Stem: Herbaceous
Leaves: Floating, oval-shaped leaves; 1 to 4.5 inches (2.5 to 11 cm) long
Flowers: Small, maroon flowers; 1 inch (2.5 cm) long
Range: Africa, Asia, Australia, North America, Central America, South America, and the Caribbean
Habitat: Ponds, lakes, and slow-moving streams
Bloom Period: Summer

FUN FACT
The water shield is a food source for waterfowl.

Fun Facts give interesting information related to the plant.

27

BIG BLUESTEM

(ANDROPOGON GERARDII)

Big bluestems are tall perennial grasses. They once dominated in North American prairies. These grasses can still be found in prairie habitats, and they are also used as ornamental plants in landscaping. They thrive in full sun, and their complex root systems help them survive droughts. Big bluestems are bunchgrasses. That means they grow in large clumps.

HOW TO SPOT

Height: 4 to 6 feet (1.2 to 1.8 m)

Stem: Herbaceous

Leaves: Clusters of flattened leaves; up to 2 inches (5 cm) long and 3.8 inches (9.7 cm) wide

Flowers: Purplish flower clusters; up to 4 inches (10 cm) long

Range: North America

Habitat: Prairies or fields in full sun

Bloom Period: Fall and winter

GRASSES

There are more than 10,000 grass species, and they can grow in many habitats. Grasses are flowering plants. They have hollow, round stems that are jointed, or broken into segments. They also have far-reaching root systems and can have long, blade-like leaves.

BREAD WHEAT *(TRITICUM AESTIVUM)*

Bread wheat is an annual domesticated grass that is grown for its fruit, or grain. The grains are either ground or used whole to make foods such as flour, breakfast cereals, and pasta noodles. Bread wheat is a bunchgrass with a hollow stem. Long, thin leaves grow around the stem in a whorl.

HOW TO SPOT

Height: Up to 4 feet (1.2 m)
Stem: Herbaceous
Leaves: Narrow leaves; 7 to 15 inches (18 to 38 cm) long and 0.5 inches (1.3 cm) wide
Flowers: Overlapping spikelets; 2 to 4 inches (5 to 10 cm) long
Range: Worldwide
Habitat: Sunny fields in temperate climates
Bloom Period: Fall and winter

FUN FACT
Bread wheat is also known as common wheat. It's one of the most important food crops in the world.

COMMON BAMBOO

(BAMBUSA VULGARIS)

There are more than 1,000 species of bamboo. Common bamboo is among the largest and fastest growing. These tree-like grasses grow in clumps of tall, hollow shoots. The plants produce green compound leaves with thin leaflets. The smooth, above-ground stems are divided into segments. They sprout from an underground stem called a rhizome. Common bamboos rarely produce flowers.

HOW TO SPOT

Height: Up to 65 feet (20 m)
Stem: Woody
Leaves: Compound leaves with several narrow leaflets; up to 12 inches (30 cm) long
Flowers: Uncommon
Range: Asia, Africa, Australia, North America, and South America
Habitat: Moist, tropical forests
Bloom Period: Rare

BAMBOO'S USES

Bamboo is an incredibly useful plant. Its young shoots are edible, and parts of the plant can be used for medicinal purposes. Bamboo is also used worldwide as a building material for things such as flooring, tool handles, fences, and furniture. It can even be used to make clothing.

COMMON MEADOW GRASS

(POA PRATENSIS)

Common meadow grass is native to most of Europe and northern Asia, and it's found throughout North America. Also known as Kentucky bluegrass, it's one of the most popular lawn grasses in the United States. That's because common meadow grass is a turfgrass. That means its many green blades form a dense, thick mat.

HOW TO SPOT

Height: 1 to 4 inches (2.5 to 10 cm) on lawns; up to 3 feet (0.9 m) in the wild

Stem: Herbaceous

Leaves: Long, narrow leaves; up to 8 inches (20 cm) long and 0.2 inches (0.5 cm) wide

Flowers: Clusters of spikelets that are light to purplish green; 2 to 8 inches (5 to 20 cm) long

Range: Europe, northern Asia, and North America

Habitat: Fields and lawns in cool, temperate climates

Bloom Period: Late spring to early summer

FUN FACT

When common meadow grass grows to its natural height of 3 feet (0.9 m), it produces colorful spikelet clusters.

COMMON RICE *(ORYZA SATIVA)*

Common rice is sometimes called Asian rice, and it's one of the most popular rice species. While it's no longer found in the wild, people grow it in fields and hillsides as a food crop. Common rice, like all rice varieties, produces long, spike-like clusters of flowers that eventually become grains. These grains are the rice that people eat.

FUN FACT

There are three main categories of rice: long, medium, and short.

HOW TO SPOT

Height: Up to 4 feet (1.2 m)
Stem: Herbaceous
Leaves: Long, flat leaves
Flowers: Long spikelets of tiny flowers
Range: Africa, Asia, Australia, Europe, North America, and South America
Habitat: Cultivated fields in the tropics and subtropics
Bloom Period: Variable

AN ANCIENT, IMPORTANT CROP

Rice is an ancient crop. There's archaeological evidence that people grew it in China between 7000 and 5000 BCE. Today, rice is the main food source for half the world's population.

ELEPHANT GRASS

(PENNISETUM PURPUREUM)

Elephant grass is a tall, perennial plant that's also known as Napier grass. Elephant grasses grow in clumps of thin, upright stems. They have very long, narrow leaves. Elephant grasses produce cylindrical-shaped clusters made of many tiny flowers. The flower clusters are greenish tan and have feathery and bristly appearances.

HOW TO SPOT

Height: Up to 15 feet (4.6 m)
Stem: Herbaceous
Leaves: Flat, strap-like leaves that are several feet long
Flowers: Greenish-tan, cylindrical-shaped clusters with tiny flower spikelets; 5 to 12 inches (12.7 to 30 cm) long
Range: Asia, Africa, Australia, Europe, North America, and South America
Habitat: Swamps and lowlands
Bloom Period: Fall

EUROPEAN BEACHGRASS

(AMMOPHILA ARENARIA)

European beachgrass is a tall perennial grass. It grows along sandy beaches throughout the world, but it is native to Europe and western Asia. As a bunchgrass, it grows in a large clump that can be nearly 4 feet (1.2 m) tall. European beachgrasses grow from rhizomes. These are large, underground plant stems that anchor the grasses into the sand.

HOW TO SPOT

Height: Nearly 4 feet (1.2 m)
Stem: Herbaceous
Leaves: Clusters of flattened leaves; up to 2 feet (0.6 m) long and 3.8 inches (9.7 cm) wide
Flowers: Whitish flower clusters; up to 1 foot (0.3 m) long
Range: Asia, Europe, and North America
Habitat: Sand dunes
Bloom Period: Spring and summer

NATIVE, NON-NATIVE, AND INVASIVE

Plants are often described as being native, non-native, or invasive. A native plant originated in the location being described. A non-native plant was introduced to a specific location, usually by people. An invasive plant can be native or non-native. It causes harm to the ecosystem where it lives. For example, European beachgrass is a native plant in Europe but an invasive species in North America, where it crowds out native plants.

PAMPAS GRASS

(CORTADERIA SELLOANA)

Pampas grass is originally from South America. Today, people have pampas grasses in lawns and gardens throughout the world. These plants grow in dense clumps, and their leaves and flowers give them dramatic appearances. Their thin, serrated leaves bend in graceful arches. In the fall, the plants produce flowers that look like feathery plumes.

FUN FACT

Pampas is the name for the South American grasslands east of the Andes Mountains.

HOW TO SPOT

Height: Up to 9 feet (2.7 m)
Stem: Herbaceous
Leaves: Sharp-edged, narrow leaves; 6 to 8 feet (1.8 to 2.4 m) long
Flowers: Silver-white, feathery plumes; 1 to 3 feet (0.3 to 0.9 m) long
Range: Africa, Australia, Europe, North America, and South America
Habitat: Fields, lawns, and gardens
Bloom Period: Early fall to winter

ARCTIC RUSH *(JUNCUS ARCTICUS)*

Rushes look like grasses, but they have round, solid stems instead of hollow stems like grasses. Arctic rush plants produce several dark-green stems that grow straight and tall. Arctic rushes don't have leaves, but they do have brownish-purple flowers that grow directly from the stems. This plant is also known as Baltic rush.

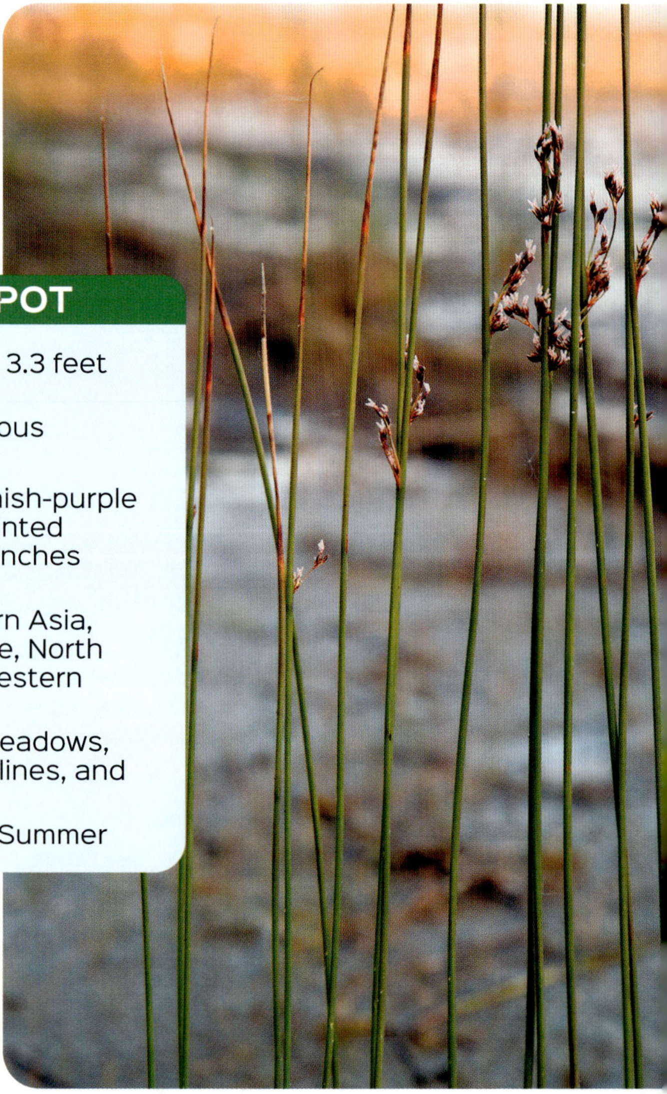

HOW TO SPOT

Height: 0.67 to 3.3 feet (0.2 to 1 m)

Stem: Herbaceous

Leaves: None

Flowers: Brownish-purple flowers with pointed petals; up to 6 inches (15 cm) long

Range: Northern Asia, northern Europe, North America, and western South America

Habitat: Wet meadows, marshes, shorelines, and roadsides

Bloom Period: Summer

COMMON RUSH *(JUNCUS EFFUSUS)*

Common rushes are grass-like plants that grow in clumps of thin, leafless stems. The stems are green and smooth. Although they look stiff, they're soft to the touch. After the plant's flowers die and produce seeds in the fall, the common rush turns yellow, then brown.

HOW TO SPOT

Height: Up to 4 feet (1.2 m)
Stem: Herbaceous
Leaves: None
Flowers: Loose clusters of tiny, yellowish-green or pale-brown flowers; flowers are less than 1 inch (2.5 cm) wide
Range: Asia, Australia, Europe, and North America
Habitat: Swamps, marshes, riverbanks, shorelines, and wet pastures
Bloom Period: Summer

HARD RUSH *(JUNCUS INFLEXUS)*

Hard rushes thrive in moist soils and freshwater habitats. These plants can grow in standing water that's up to 3 feet (0.9 m) deep. The rhizomes of hard rushes sprout cylindrical, blue-green stems that grow upright and tall. In the late spring, some of the stems produce flower clusters.

HOW TO SPOT

Height: Up to around 3 feet (0.9 m)

Stem: Herbaceous

Leaves: None

Flowers: Loose clusters of tiny, reddish-brown flowers

Range: Asia, northern Africa, Europe, and North America

Habitat: Wet meadows, marshes, and shorelines

Bloom Period: Late spring to summer

SPREADING RUSH *(JUNCUS PATENS)*

The spreading rush is also called the California gray rush. These plants grow in dense clumps of cylindrical stems. The stems are gray green and leafless. From spring through fall, some of the stems produce golden-brown flowers. Although the spreading rush is native to North America and can be found in the wild, it's also often grown as a garden plant.

FUN FACT

Spreading rushes are also called wire grasses because of their thin, leafless stems.

HOW TO SPOT

Height: Up to 2 feet (0.6 m)
Stem: Herbaceous
Leaves: None
Flowers: Loose clusters of small, golden-brown flowers
Range: North America
Habitat: Shaded gardens, fields, and shorelines
Bloom Period: Spring and fall

PAPYRUS SEDGE *(CYPERUS PAPYRUS)*

Papyrus sedges thrive in water. They grow in dense clumps spread along the ground. Like all plants in this family, papyrus sedges have solid, triangular stems. They don't have leaves, but the tops of the stems produce growths that looks like feather dusters. Flowers bloom at the ends of these thread-like stems.

FUN FACT

People in ancient Egypt used papyrus sedge stems to make an early form of paper called papyrus.

HOW TO SPOT

Height: Up to 15 feet (4.6 m)
Stem: Herbaceous
Leaves: None
Flowers: Tiny, greenish-brown flowers
Range: Africa, Europe, and North America
Habitat: Marshes, riverbanks, and shorelines
Bloom Period: Summer and fall

SAW GRASS *(CLADIUM JAMAICENSE)*

Despite having *grass* in its name, saw grass is a species of sedge. Saw grasses are usually found in wet habitats, such as tropical marshes and swamps, but they can also grow in drier soils. The plant gets its name from its sharp-edged leaves.

HOW TO SPOT

Height: 7 feet (2 m)
Stem: Herbaceous
Leaves: Stiff, narrow leaves with serrated edges; up to 3 feet (0.9 m) long
Flowers: Large, drooping clusters of brown spikelets; 12 to 20 inches (30 to 50 cm) long
Range: North America, Central America, and South America
Habitat: Freshwater and brackish wetlands and shorelines
Bloom Period: Spring and summer

SEDGES, GRASSES, AND RUSHES

Sedges are grass-like plants that are easy to mistake for grasses or rushes. One way to tell if a plant is a sedge is to feel its stem. The cross section of a sedge stem is usually triangular and has edges that can be felt when rolled between the fingers, unlike a grass or rush. Sedges also tend to have branches and solid stems rather than hollow ones.

TUSSOCK COTTONGRASS

(ERIOPHORUM VAGINATUM)

Tussock cottongrasses are common sedges found in the northern parts of the northern hemisphere, especially in wet habitats such as swamps and bogs. These plants grow in dense clumps of triangular stems. The clumps are called tussocks. They are made up of cottongrass roots and old stems that have died. At the top of each stem is a feathery flower cluster. It looks like a rabbit's tail, which is why tussock cottongrass is sometimes called hare's-tail cottongrass.

HOW TO SPOT

Height: Up to 2 feet (0.6 m)
Stem: Herbaceous
Leaves: None
Flowers: Dense clusters of feathery flowers; up to 2 inches (5 cm) long
Range: Asia, Europe, North America, and the Arctic
Habitat: Wet meadows, swamps, and tundra
Bloom Period: Summer

WATER CHESTNUT

(ELEOCHARIS DULCIS)

Water chestnuts grow in shallow waters and along swamps, ponds, and lakes. They're known for producing edible underground vegetables that are also called water chestnuts. These plants have thin, leafless stems and can have yellow-brown flower spikelets.

HOW TO SPOT

Height: Up to 3 feet (0.9 m)
Stem: Herbaceous
Leaves: None
Flowers: Cylindrical, yellow-brown flower spikelets; up to 2 inches (5 cm) long
Range: Asia, Australia, and North America
Habitat: In or along ponds, swamps, and lakes
Bloom Period: Summer and fall

FUN FACT

A water chestnut vegetable can be eaten raw or cooked. It has a slightly sweet flavor and a crunchy texture.

BROADLEAF CATTAIL

(TYPHA LATIFOLIA)

The broadleaf cattail is also known as the common cattail. These plants are found in freshwater wetlands throughout the world. Broadleaf cattails grow along the edges of swamps and marshes in shallow waters up to 1 foot (0.3 m) deep. The upper part of the cattail's flower pollinates the lower half. When these seeds mature, they become soft fruits that are shaped like hot dogs.

HOW TO SPOT

Height: 4 to 6 feet (1.2 to 1.8 m)
Stem: Herbaceous
Leaves: Narrow, sword-like leaves; 7 inches (18 cm) long
Flowers: Dense, cylinder-shaped spikes; 6 to 10 inches (15 to 25 cm) long
Range: Northern Africa, northern and central Asia, Europe, and North America
Habitat: Wetlands
Bloom Period: Summer

COMMON DUCKWEED *(LEMNA MINOR)*

Common duckweed often looks like a bright-green, carpet-like growth on the surface of ponds or lakes. The growth is made up of hundreds of common duckweed plants. Each plant has just one small leaf that floats on the water's surface while a small root hangs below. Duckweeds have microscopic flowers, yet pollinators such as bees are still able to find them.

FUN FACT

Duckweeds are the smallest known flowering plants. They're a popular food among many aquatic animals, including ducks, which give the plants their name.

HOW TO SPOT

Height: Aquatic
Stem: Herbaceous
Leaves: Single oval leaf; up to 0.25 inches (0.64 cm) long
Flowers: Microscopic
Range: Africa, Asia, Europe, and North America
Habitat: Freshwater ponds and lakes
Bloom Period: Summer

SACRED LOTUS *(NELUMBO NUCIFERA)*

The sacred lotus is an aquatic plant known for its large, showy flower and its long history with people. These plants grow in tropical freshwater habitats such as lagoons and river deltas, but they're also popular garden plants. The sacred lotus has large, green leaves and a large flower that is pink or white in color. The flower rises above the water's surface on the plant's stem.

HOW TO SPOT

Height: Aquatic
Stem: Herbaceous
Leaves: Rounded, waxy leaves; up to 2 feet (0.6 m) wide
Flowers: Pink or white flowers with yellow centers; 8 to 12 inches (20 to 30 cm) wide
Range: Asia, Australia, and North America
Habitat: Freshwater ponds, lakes, river deltas, lagoons, and slow-moving streams
Bloom Period: Summer

RELIGION AND THE LOTUS

The sacred lotus is important to the Buddhist and Hindu religions. It's seen as a symbol of beauty, purity, and divinity.

WATER SHIELD *(BRASENIA SCHREBERI)*

The water shield is a common aquatic plant. It is known for spreading its small, oval-shaped leaves across the surfaces of ponds and lakes. The water shield has a small, compact flower. A thick slime coats the plant's underwater stem and the undersides of its leaves. This slime may protect the water shield from drought and animals.

HOW TO SPOT

Height: Aquatic
Stem: Herbaceous
Leaves: Floating, oval-shaped leaves; 1 to 4.5 inches (2.5 to 11 cm) long
Flowers: Small, maroon flowers; 1 inch (2.5 cm) long
Range: Africa, Asia, Australia, North America, Central America, South America, and the Caribbean
Habitat: Ponds, lakes, and slow-moving streams
Bloom Period: Summer

FUN FACT
The water shield is a food source for waterfowl.

WHITE WATER LILY

(NYMPHAEA ODORATA)

White water lilies are aquatic plants that float on the surfaces of still ponds and lakes. Sometimes they're found in slow-moving streams. The plant's stem is rooted in mud at the bottom of the body of water. The lily's leaves are sometimes called lily pads. The leaves are large, shiny, and green. The plant's cup-like flower is white with many pointed petals and a yellow center.

HOW TO SPOT

Height: Aquatic
Stem: Herbaceous
Leaves: Smooth leaves that are round or heart-shaped; 6 to 12 inches (15 to 30 cm) wide
Flowers: White flowers with pointed petals and yellow centers; 3 to 6 inches (7.6 to 15 cm) wide
Range: North America
Habitat: Freshwater ponds, lakes, and streams
Bloom Period: Summer

YELLOW POND LILY *(NUPHAR LUTEA)*

Like other water lilies, yellow pond lilies have leaves and flowers that float on the water's surface. They also have underwater stems that grow up from the mud below. However, the yellow pond lily can grow in deeper water than other lily species. That's because the yellow lily's stem can grow up to 6 feet (1.8 m) tall. In the summer, yellow pond lilies have rounded, cup-shaped, yellow flowers that open in the morning and close at night.

FUN FACT
There are more than 50 water lily species.

HOW TO SPOT

Height: Aquatic
Stem: Herbaceous
Leaves: Smooth leaves that are round or heart-shaped; 3 to 8 inches (7.6 to 20 cm) long
Flowers: Yellow, cup-shaped flowers; 2 inches (5 cm) wide
Range: Africa, Asia, Europe, North America, and the Caribbean
Habitat: Freshwater ponds and lakes
Bloom Period: Summer and fall

PINEAPPLE *(ANANAS COMOSUS)*

Pineapples have pointed succulent leaves that grow in rosettes. These plants produce clusters of purple or burgundy flowers that grow on long stalks. A cluster will eventually become the plant's fruit, a pineapple. A single pineapple plant only produces one pineapple. Before it dies, the plant creates other pineapple plants by spreading its small shoots, called suckers.

HOW TO SPOT

Height: 3 to 4 feet (0.9 to 1.2 m)

Stem: Herbaceous

Leaves: Pointed, spiny-edged leaves; 3 feet (0.9 m) long or more

Flowers: Clusters of purple or burgundy flowers on long stalks; flowers are less than 1 inch (2.5 cm) long

Fruits: Rough, oval-shaped fruits; up to 1 foot (0.3 m) long

Range: South America, South Africa, Asia, Hawaii, and southern Florida

Habitat: Cultivated fields and gardens

Bloom Period: Seasonal

FUN FACT

It is possible to grow a pineapple indoors, but the fruit doesn't get as large or taste as sweet as a pineapple grown outside.

QUEEN OF THE ANDES

(PUYA RAIMONDII)

The queen of the Andes is the largest bromeliad in the world, growing up to 30 feet (9 m) tall. It's also very rare, living only in the Andes Mountains and in some botanical gardens. The queen of the Andes has long, spike-like leaves that grow in a spherical pattern. After living for decades, the plant produces a single tall stalk that has thousands of white flowers.

HOW TO SPOT

Height: Up to 30 feet (9 m)

Stem: Herbaceous

Leaves: Long, spike-like leaves; 9 to 13 feet (2.7 to 4 m) long

Flowers: Thousands of white flowers on a tall central stalk

Range: South America

Habitat: Mountains

Bloom Period: Once in the plant's lifetime

SKY PLANT *(TILLANDSIA IONANTHA)*

The sky plant is a type of air plant—a species that doesn't need to be in soil to grow. Instead, it gets its moisture and nutrients from the rain and air. In the wild, air plants often grow on other plants, including trees. Sky plants have succulent leaves that usually grow in rosettes. The inner leaves often turn red before sky plants produce bluish-purple, spike-like flowers.

HOW TO SPOT

Height: 6 to 12 inches (15 to 30 cm)
Stem: Herbaceous
Leaves: Narrow, blade-shaped leaves; 1 to 3 inches (2.5 to 7.6 cm) long
Flowers: Bluish-purple, spike-like flowers; 1 inch (2.5 cm) wide
Range: North America, Central America, and South America
Habitat: Tropical and subtropical areas
Bloom Period: Each season

WHAT ARE BROMELIADS?

Air plants are a type of bromeliad. Bromeliads are a group of evergreen perennial plants that usually have succulent-like leaves growing in spirals. Some bromeliads, such as air plants, are epiphytes. That means they grow on other plants and get their nutrients from the air. Other bromeliads, such as pineapples, are terrestrial. That means they grow in the ground.

SPANISH MOSS

(TILLANDSIA USNEOIDES)

Spanish moss is not actually a type of moss but a species of bromeliad. As an air plant, Spanish moss doesn't have roots. It grows by attaching itself to a tree and sometimes to a human-made structure, such as a fence. These plants appear in dense, drooping clumps of tiny, greenish-gray evergreen leaves.

HOW TO SPOT

Height: 3 to 20 feet (0.9 to 6 m)
Stem: Woody
Leaves: Needle-like evergreen leaves; 1 to 3 inches (2.5 to 7.6 cm) long
Flowers: A single blue-green, spike-like flower; less than 1 inch (2.5 cm) long
Range: North America and South America
Habitat: Trees in humid environments that are near water
Bloom Period: Summer and fall

FUN FACT
Because of its appearance, Spanish moss is sometimes called old man's beard.

ALOE VERA *(ALOE BARBADENSIS)*

Aloe vera is an evergreen succulent. These popular garden plants are best known for the juices inside their leaves, also called aloe. Aloe vera plants grow in large clumps of long, fleshy leaves that form rosettes. The leaves are light green and have sharp, spiny edges and pointed tips. In winter, aloe vera can produce a reddish flower that blooms on a stalk in the center of the plant.

FUN FACT

The juices inside aloe vera leaves have long been used to treat skin conditions such as sunburns.

HOW TO SPOT

Height: 1 to 2 feet (0.3 to 0.6 m)
Stem: Succulent
Leaves: Fleshy, spiny-edged leaves with pointed ends; 1.5 to 3 feet (0.45 to 0.9 m) long
Flowers: Reddish flowers; up to 3 inches (7.6 cm) long
Range: Africa, Asia, Australia, Europe, North America, and the Middle East
Habitat: Dry forests, shrublands, and gardens
Bloom Period: Winter

BEAVERTAIL CACTUS

(OPUNTIA BASILARIS)

The beavertail cactus is a species of prickly pear cactus. A single plant can be made up of hundreds of flat, fleshy stem segments that are shaped like beaver tails. The beavertail cactus doesn't have long spines, but it does have many short, sharp bristles. In spring, the cactus produces bright magenta flowers.

HOW TO SPOT

Height: 6 to 12 inches (15 to 30 cm)

Stem: Succulent

Leaves: None

Flowers: Magenta flowers; 2 to 3 inches (5 to 7.6 cm) wide

Range: Mexico and the southwestern United States

Habitat: Deserts

Bloom Period: Spring

BURRO'S TAIL *(SEDUM MORGANIANUM)*

Burro's tail is an evergreen succulent that's native to Mexico and Central America, though it's a popular houseplant throughout the world. These plants have long, trailing stems covered in many small, fragile, bean-shaped leaves that can be easily broken off. In the summer, burro's tails produce clusters of red or pink flowers at the ends of their stems.

HOW TO SPOT

Height: 2 feet (0.6 m)
Stem: Succulent
Leaves: Fleshy, bean-shaped leaves; less than 1 inch (2.5 cm) long
Flowers: Clusters of red or pink flowers; less than 1 inch (2.5 cm) long
Range: North America and Central America
Habitat: Dry environments
Bloom Period: Summer

CALIFORNIA BARREL CACTUS

(FEROCACTUS CYLINDRACEUS)

The California barrel cactus grows in a rounded, cylindrical shape that looks like a barrel. Its shape can also be spherical. When these cacti are young, they're covered in long red spines. The spines turn gray as the plants age. California barrel cacti produce yellow flowers with red or yellow centers.

FUN FACT
The California barrel cactus can live to be 100 years old.

HOW TO SPOT

Height: 6.6 to 10 feet (2 to 3 m)
Stem: Succulent
Leaves: None
Flowers: Cup-shaped, yellow flowers with red or yellow centers; up to 2.3 inches (6 cm) wide
Range: North America
Habitat: Deserts and rocky and sandy soils
Bloom Period: Spring

COMMON HOUSELEEK

(SEMPERVIVUM TECTORUM)

The common houseleek is a compact succulent. It's native to southern Europe, where it grows in sandy or rocky soil. Houseleeks have fleshy, light-green, pointed leaves that form several layers of rosettes. One common houseleek can produce many rosettes, forming a mat along the ground. It's a popular house and garden plant.

FUN FACT

The common houseleek is also called hens and chicks. That's because each mature plant, known as the hen, can produce offshoots that grow new plants known as chicks.

HOW TO SPOT

Height: 6 to 12 inches (15 to 30 cm)
Stem: Succulent
Leaves: Rosettes can be up to 4 inches (10 cm) wide with 50 to 60 fleshy leaves
Flowers: Reddish-purple flower clusters on stems that can grow 12 inches (30 cm) tall
Range: Europe and North America
Habitat: Mountains and gardens
Bloom Period: Summer

EASTERN PRICKLY PEAR

(OPUNTIA HUMIFUSA)

Eastern prickly pears are flowering cacti known for their beautiful, yellowish-orange flowers. These plants are divided into several fleshy green segments and are covered in short bristles and long spikes. Eastern prickly pears can grow along the ground or become upright shrubs.

HOW TO SPOT

Height: 2 feet (0.6 m)
Stem: Succulent
Leaves: None
Flowers: Multiple yellowish-orange flowers; 2 to 3 inches (5 to 7.6 cm) wide
Range: North America
Habitat: Sandy and rocky soils
Bloom Period: Spring and summer

BLACK-EYED SUSAN

(RUDBECKIA HIRTA)

A black-eyed Susan can have several stems, and each stem has a single flower. The flower's yellow petals radiate from its center. The cone-shaped center of this prairie wildflower appears black or brown from a distance, but it's actually a very dark purple.

HOW TO SPOT

Height: 1 to 3 feet (0.3 to 0.9 m)
Stem: Herbaceous
Leaves: Narrow, smooth-edged leaves with hairy surfaces; 2 to 7 inches (5 to 18 cm) long
Flowers: Yellow, disk-shaped flowers with dark-purple centers; 2 to 3 inches (5 to 7.6 cm) wide
Range: North America
Habitat: Prairies, fields, and deciduous forests
Bloom Period: Summer and fall

BLOODROOT *(SANGUINARIA CANADENSIS)*

Bloodroot is a woodland flower that blooms in early spring. Each plant has several large, lobed leaves and a single flower. The flower is usually white, but it can also be pink. It has several pointed petals radiating from a yellow center. The flower opens in the morning and closes at night.

FUN FACT

Bloodroots have leaves and roots that contain red-orange juices. That's how the plant got its name.

HOW TO SPOT

Height: 4 to 8 inches (10 to 20 cm)

Stem: Herbaceous

Leaves: Large, rounded leaves with five to nine lobes; 4 to 7 inches (10 to 18 cm) wide

Flowers: White or pink flowers with eight or more petals and yellow centers; 2 inches (5 cm) wide

Range: North America

Habitat: Deciduous woods

Bloom Period: Spring

BLUEBELL *(CAMPANULA ROTUNDIFOLIA)*

Bluebells can grow in challenging environments, such as on mountainsides or along rivers or streams. The flowers can be blue or purple, and they are shaped like tiny bells. They droop from thin stalks. Each bell is made up of five petals that are connected along their sides. These wildflowers grow in small patches.

HOW TO SPOT

Height: 6 to 20 inches (15 to 51 cm)

Stem: Herbaceous

Leaves: Thin, grass-like leaves; 3 inches (7.6 cm) long

Flowers: Pale blue or purple bell-shaped flowers; 0.75 inches (1.9 cm) long

Range: Europe and North America

Habitat: Rocky slopes, riverbanks, and meadows

Bloom Period: Summer

BULL THISTLE *(CIRSIUM VULGARE)*

The bull thistle is the largest species in the thistle family. Thistles are a group of flowering plants that have sharp spines. The bull thistle has the most spines of any thistle. The stems, leaves, and blossoms are all covered by spines. Despite their spiky appearance, these plants have reddish-purple flowers that attract many pollinators, such as bees.

HOW TO SPOT

Height: 2 to 6 feet (0.6 to 1.8 m)

Stem: Herbaceous

Leaves: Narrow, lobed leaves; up to 7 inches (18 cm) long

Flowers: Reddish-purple flowers on spiky green bases; 1.5 to 2 inches (3.8 to 5 cm) wide

Range: Western Asia, northwestern Africa, Europe, and North America

Habitat: Fields, pastures, and roadsides

Bloom Period: Summer and fall

FUN FACT

The bull thistle is an invasive species in North America. It spreads easily, and it quickly grows to a large size. It can outcompete native plants for resources.

BUTTERFLY WEED

(ASCLEPIAS TUBEROSA)

The butterfly weed is a cousin to the common milkweed. In fact, another name for the butterfly weed is orange milkweed. Butterfly weeds grow in clumps on prairies and disturbed areas such as roadsides and railroad tracks. People also plant butterfly weeds in their gardens to attract butterflies. The bright-orange flowers grow in clusters at the tops of the plants. They become seedpods in the fall.

HOW TO SPOT

Height: 1 to 3 feet (0.3 to 0.9 m)
Stem: Herbaceous
Leaves: Long, pointed leaves with wide bases; 2 to 6 inches (5 to 15 cm) long
Flowers: Flat clusters of small, orange flowers; 2 inches (5 cm) wide
Range: North America
Habitat: Prairies and meadows with sandy soils
Bloom Period: Spring and summer

FUN FACT

Butterfly weed is a species of milkweed. It is one of the host plants for monarch butterfly caterpillars.

CHICORY *(CICHORIUM INTYBUS)*

Chicories are wildflowers that thrive in disturbed areas, such as along roadsides or cultivated fields. Chicories have several small, violet-blue flowers along their stems. The flower petals have fringed ends.

HOW TO SPOT

Height: 2 to 6 feet (0.6 to 1.8 m)
Stem: Herbaceous
Leaves: Long, toothed leaves; 3 to 6 inches (7.6 to 15 cm) long
Flowers: Disk-shaped flowers with violet-blue petals; 1.5 inches (3.8 cm) wide
Range: Asia, Australia, Europe, and North America
Habitat: Sunny fields and roadsides
Bloom Period: Summer and fall

THE CHICORY ROOT

The chicory has a long main root called a taproot. It reaches deep into the ground and can be harvested for cooking purposes. The root can be roasted and ground up. Some people add it to coffee. Others brew it to make a bitter drink similar to coffee.

COMMON MILKWEED

(ASCLEPIAS SYRIACA)

Common milkweeds grow in fields and along roadsides. In the summer, milkweeds have clusters of pinkish-purple flowers. They also have large, oval-shaped leaves with fuzzy undersides. In the fall, the plants have bumpy seedpods. These open and release many brown seeds attached to fluffy, white hairs.

HOW TO SPOT

Height: 2 to 6 feet (0.6 to 1.8 m)
Stem: Herbaceous
Leaves: Large, smooth, oval leaves; 6 to 8 inches (15 to 20 cm) long
Flowers: Round clusters of pinkish-purple flowers; 2 inches (5 cm) wide
Range: North America
Habitat: Prairies, fields, and roadsides
Bloom Period: Summer

COMMON MILKWEEDS AND BUTTERFLIES

Common milkweeds are food sources for more than 450 insects. This includes North America's monarch butterflies. Monarch butterfly caterpillars eat only milkweed plants.

COMMON MULLEIN

(VERBASCUM THAPSUS)

Common mulleins are biennial plants. That means they only bloom about every two years. In their first year, these plants have rosettes of leaves that grow close to the ground. By their second year, mulleins are tall, narrow plants. They have large leaves that point upward and spike-shaped clusters of small flowers.

HOW TO SPOT

Height: 2 to 7 feet (0.6 to 2 m)
Stem: Herbaceous
Leaves: Large leaves covered in soft hairs; 6 to 15 inches (15 to 38 cm) long
Flowers: Spike-shaped clusters that are 1.6 feet (0.48 m) long and consist of many small, yellow flowers
Range: Asia, Europe, and North America
Habitat: Dry fields and meadows with stony soils
Bloom Period: Summer and fall

FUN FACT

Another name for the common mullein is the flannel plant. That's due to its very soft leaves. They feel like flannel fabric.

COMMON YELLOW WOOD SORREL *(OXALIS STRICTA)*

The common yellow wood sorrel has a long taproot that grows deep into the ground. Above ground, wood sorrels produce many stems that can grow upright or spread along the ground. Yellow flowers usually bloom from spring to fall. However, in some parts of the common yellow wood sorrels' range, their flowers bloom year-round.

FUN FACT

The common yellow wood sorrel's compound, heart-shaped leaf is also known as a shamrock.

HOW TO SPOT

Height: Up to 9 inches (23 cm)
Stem: Herbaceous
Leaves: Compound leaves with three heart-shaped leaflets; 0.75 to 1 inch (1.9 to 2.5 cm) wide
Flowers: Small, yellow flowers with five distinct petals; 0.4 inches (1 cm) wide
Range: North America
Habitat: Open forests, fields, lawns, and gardens
Bloom Period: Spring and fall or year-round

DANDELION *(TARAXACUM OFFICINALE)*

Today, many people view dandelions as weeds. These adaptable flowers were first brought to the Americas as food plants and were a common sight in eastern North America by the mid-1600s. Their familiar yellow flowers start blooming in early spring and soon transform into fuzzy, globe-shaped seed heads. Dandelions can bloom several times throughout a growing season.

HOW TO SPOT

Height: 8 to 12 inches (20 to 30 cm)
Stem: Herbaceous
Leaves: Toothed and lobed leaves; 3 to 6 inches (7.6 to 15 cm) long
Flowers: Yellow, disk-shaped flowers; 1 to 3 inches (2.5 to 7.6 cm) wide
Range: Southern Africa, Asia, Europe, North America, and South America
Habitat: Sunny fields and lawns
Bloom Period: Spring

THE LION'S TOOTH

Dandelions are named for lions, but not because of their golden, mane-like blooms. The French called the plant *dent-de-lion*, meaning "lion's tooth." That's because the leaves have jagged edges that slightly resemble sharp teeth.

LARGE-FLOWERED TRILLIUM

(TRILLIUM GRANDIFLORUM)

Large-flowered trilliums are woodland-loving wildflowers. They have the largest blooms in the trillium family. Each plant has three broad leaves and produces a single flower. The flower has three wavy-edged petals that start off white but slowly turn pale pink as the flower ages. In the fall, each plant produces a single red berry.

HOW TO SPOT

Height: 8 to 18 inches (20 to 46 cm)

Stem: Herbaceous

Leaves: Three broad, pointed leaves; 3 to 6 inches (7.6 to 15 cm) long

Flowers: White flowers with three triangle-shaped petals; 2 to 4 inches (5 to 10 cm) long

Range: North America

Habitat: Moist, deciduous forests

Bloom Period: Spring

FUN FACT

The large-flowered trillium is also known as the wood lily.

OXEYE DAISY

(LEUCANTHEMUM VULGARE)

Also called the common daisy, the oxeye daisy originated in Europe. Bright-white petals radiate from yellow centers. The daisy's stem holds leaves that get smaller the closer they are to the flower. Because they grow so quickly and overtake other plants, some places in the world see oxeye daises as harmful weeds.

HOW TO SPOT

Height: 1 to 3 feet (0.3 to 0.9 m)
Stem: Herbaceous
Leaves: Lobed, narrow leaves; up to 5 inches (12.7 cm) long
Flowers: White, disk-shaped flowers with yellow centers; up to 2 inches (5 cm) wide
Range: Asia, Australia, Europe, and North America
Habitat: Fields, pastures, and roadsides
Bloom Period: Summer

DAY'S EYES TO DAISY

The daisy was originally called day's eye. That's because of the way the flower opens in the morning and closes in the evening.

PASQUEFLOWER *(PULSATILLA PATENS)*

The pasqueflower is an early spring wildflower. It lives in the northern parts of the northern hemisphere, sometimes blooming while there's still snow on the ground. The pasqueflower has fern-like leaves. The entire plant—even the bell-shaped flower—is covered in a layer of soft, silky hair. The flowers can be pale lavender, purple, or blue.

HOW TO SPOT

Height: 8 to 12 inches (20 to 30 cm)
Stem: Herbaceous
Leaves: Lobed, basal leaves with long stalks
Flowers: Bell-shaped flowers; 1.5 to 2 inches (3.8 to 5 cm) wide
Range: Europe, North America, and northern Russia
Habitat: Prairies, meadows, and mountain slopes
Bloom Period: Spring and summer

FUN FACT

In old French, *pasque* refers to Easter. That's why this plant is called pasqueflower—it blooms in early spring, right around the Easter holiday.

PURPLE CONEFLOWER

(ECHINACEA PURPUREA)

The purple coneflower is a common wildflower in North America. Because of its adaptability to various growing conditions, it thrives in meadows, fields, and ditches. It can also be planted in gardens. Its narrow petals radiate from an orange center and drop downward. Its leaves and stem are covered in fine, stiff hairs. This gives the plant a rough texture.

HOW TO SPOT

Height: 2 to 5 feet (0.6 to 1.5 m)

Stem: Herbaceous

Leaves: Toothed, three-veined leaves; up to 8 inches (20 cm) long

Flowers: Disk-shaped flowers with orange centers; 3 to 6 inches (7.6 to 15 cm) wide

Range: North America

Habitat: Dry, sunny meadows, fields, or ditches

Bloom Period: Summer to mid-fall

QUEEN ANNE'S LACE

(DAUCUS CAROTA)

Queen Anne's lace is a tall meadow flower. These plants develop many umbrella-shaped clusters of tiny, white flowers. In the fall, the dried flower clusters curl up and resemble small birds' nests. Queen Anne's lace is considered an invasive weed throughout most of its range. The fast-spreading plant crowds out native plant species.

HOW TO SPOT

Height: 2 to 4 feet (0.6 to 1.2 m)
Stem: Herbaceous
Leaves: Thin, fern-like leaves; 5 inches (12.7 cm) long
Flowers: Umbrella-shaped clusters of tiny, white flowers; 3 to 6 inches (7.6 to 15 cm) wide
Range: Southwest Asia, Australia, Europe, and North America
Habitat: Fields and roadsides
Bloom Period: Summer and fall

RED COLUMBINE

(AQUILEGIA CANADENSIS)

The red columbine is a delicate-looking wildflower. It grows best in part shade to full sun, which is why it is often found in forests. Red columbines have three-lobed compound leaves. They also have red-and-yellow, bell-shaped flowers that hang down from thin stems.

FUN FACT

The red columbine's shape makes it difficult for most pollinators to reach its nectar. But hummingbirds and long-tongued moths have ideal mouthparts to reach into these flowers.

HOW TO SPOT

Height: 1 to 3 feet (0.3 to 0.9 m)

Stem: Herbaceous

Leaves: Three-lobed compound leaves; 1 to 3 inches (2.5 to 7.6 cm) long

Flowers: Red-and-yellow, bell-shaped flowers with pointed tips; 1 to 2 inches (2.5 to 5 cm) long

Range: North America

Habitat: Forests, hillsides, and roadsides

Bloom Period: Summer

STARFLOWER *(TRIENTALIS BOREALIS)*

Starflowers have white, star-shaped blooms that can have between five and nine pointed petals radiating from the centers. These flowers grow in moist environments, such as forests, and they're often found alongside mosses. Starflowers' leaves are large, pointed ovals that are usually a glossy green.

FUN FACT

Starflowers attract flies and bees. These insects feed on and collect pollen. Starflowers also attract chipmunks, who consume the plants' seeds.

HOW TO SPOT

Height: 4 to 8 inches (10 to 20 cm)
Stem: Herbaceous
Leaves: Pointed, oval leaves; 4 inches (10 cm) long
Flowers: White, star-shaped flowers with five to nine petals; 0.5 inches (1.3 cm) wide
Range: North America
Habitat: Conifer and deciduous forests
Bloom Period: Spring and summer

WHITE CLOVER *(TRIFOLIUM REPENS)*

The white clover is native to Europe. Today, these flowers are found throughout North America, where they are a common sight in lawns. White clovers are low, creeping plants with many compound leaves that have three leaflets. Each leaflet is green with two lighter green stripes. White clovers also produce small clusters of white flowers that can have pink edges.

HOW TO SPOT

Height: 4 inches (10 cm)
Stem: Herbaceous
Leaves: Compound leaves with three round leaflets; 1.5 inches (3.8 cm) wide
Flowers: Small, round clusters of white-and-pink flowers; 0.5 inches (1.3 cm) wide
Range: Asia, Europe, and North America
Habitat: Fields and lawns
Bloom Period: Spring and summer

FOUR-LEAF CLOVERS

White clovers' leaflets usually have only three leaves. However, these plants sometimes produce leaflets with four leaves that are known as lucky four-leaf clovers.

WILD LEEK *(ALLIUM TRICOCCUM)*

Wild leeks are spring wildflowers found in North American forests. They have long, green leaves that are reddish at the bases and produce small clusters of greenish-white flowers. Wild leeks are edible. They're part of the onion family. Their leaves and flowers have an onion scent, and the leaves and white bulbs can be used in recipes that call for onions.

FUN FACT

Wild leeks have several common names, including ramps, ramsons, and spring onions.

HOW TO SPOT

Height: Up to 9 inches (23 cm)
Stem: Herbaceous
Leaves: Two to three long, narrow leaves; 6 to 12 inches (15 to 30 cm) long
Flowers: Small clusters of greenish-white flowers; 0.25 inches (0.64 cm) long
Range: North America
Habitat: Shady, moist forests
Bloom Period: Summer

YELLOW GENTIAN *(GENTIANA ALBA)*

The yellow gentian is one of many species of gentians, a plant family known for its trumpet-shaped flowers. This species is native to North American prairies, but it is also grown in gardens. Yellow gentians have flowers that grow in clusters, and they can be white or white with a yellow or green tint. Like other species in the gentian family, yellow gentian flowers are tube-shaped. But unlike other gentians, yellow gentian flowers are closed at the ends rather than open like trumpets.

HOW TO SPOT

Height: 1 to 3 feet (0.3 to 0.9 m)

Stem: Herbaceous

Leaves: Smooth, pointed leaves; 5 inches (12.7 cm) long

Flowers: Round clusters of flowers that are closed at the ends; 1.5 to 2 inches (3.8 to 5 cm) long

Range: Central North America

Habitat: Prairies and fields

Bloom Period: Fall

COMMON LILAC *(SYRINGA VULGARIS)*

Common lilacs are native to Europe but are now grown in other places for their fragrant spring flowers. Lilacs have many small stems. They also have green, heart-shaped leaves and produce cone-shaped clusters of tiny, purple flowers in the spring. Other lilac species can have pink or white flowers.

FUN FACT
All lilac species are members of the olive family.

HOW TO SPOT

Height: 8 to 15 feet (2.4 to 4.6 m)
Stem: Woody
Leaves: Heart-shaped leaves; 3 to 6 inches (7.6 to 15 cm) long
Flowers: Cone-shaped clusters of tiny, purple flowers; up to 8 inches (20 cm) long
Range: Europe and North America
Habitat: Open woodlands, rocky hillsides, and gardens
Bloom Period: Spring

COMMON PEONY

(PAEONIA OFFICINALIS)

Peonies are flowering shrubs. They are known for their large, showy flowers that bloom in the spring. The common peony is one of 30 peony species. These flowers have bright-green leaves and produce large, red-pink flowers that have yellow centers. Like most peonies, the flowers of common peonies have strong, sweet fragrances. Peony flowers often attract ants, but these insects don't harm the plants.

HOW TO SPOT

Height: 1.5 to 3 feet (0.45 to 0.9 m)

Stem: Herbaceous

Leaves: Divided, compound leaves

Flowers: Cup-shaped flowers with yellow centers; up to 5 inches (12.7 cm) wide

Range: Europe and North America

Habitat: Open woodlands and gardens

Bloom Period: Spring

COMMON SUNFLOWER

(HELIANTHUS ANNUUS)

Many of the large sunflowers grown in gardens are cultivars of the common sunflower. Common sunflowers have tall, upright stems. They also have large, sandpaper-like leaves and multiple branching stems at the tops. Each plant produces several large, yellow flowers that bloom in the summer and produce many edible seeds in the fall.

FUN FACT

Sunflowers got their name because their blooms follow the sun's path as it crosses the sky.

HOW TO SPOT

Height: 3 to 10 feet (0.9 to 3 m)
Stem: Herbaceous
Leaves: Triangular or heart-shaped leaves with coarse-toothed edges; up to 12 inches (30 cm) long
Flowers: Saucer-shaped flowers with yellow petals surrounding dark-brown centers; 3 to 6 inches (7.6 to 15 cm) wide
Range: North America
Habitat: Moist forests, fields, roadsides, and gardens
Bloom Period: Summer and fall

DILL *(ANETHUM GRAVEOLENS)*

Dill is a perennial herb grown for its appearance and for cooking purposes. Its stem sprouts branches of lacy, fern-like leaves and umbrella-shaped flower clusters. In the fall, dill seeds can be harvested and used in cooking.

HOW TO SPOT

Height: 2 to 3 feet (0.6 to 0.9 m)
Stem: Herbaceous
Leaves: Fern-like leaves
Flowers: Umbrella-like clusters of yellow flowers; 1 to 3.5 inches (2.5 to 9 cm) wide
Range: Asia, Europe, and North America
Habitat: Gardens
Bloom Period: Summer and fall

ENGLISH LAVENDER

(LAVANDULA ANGUSTIFOLIA)

English lavender is not actually from England. It's a perennial herb from the Mediterranean region. English lavender grows in clumps of dense, straight stems that have tiny, gray-green leaves. In the summer, lavender has many spike-like clusters of small, purple flowers.

HOW TO SPOT

Height: 2 to 3 feet (0.6 to 0.9 m)
Stem: Semiwoody
Leaves: Narrow, gray-green leaves; up to 2.5 inches (6.3 cm) long
Flowers: Spike-like clusters of purple flowers; 0.7 to 3 inches (1.7 to 7.6 cm) long
Range: Europe and North America
Habitat: Dry, sunny fields and gardens
Bloom Period: Late spring to summer

FUN FACT

Lavender leaves and flowers are used in cooking. These plants also have oils that people use to create essential oils and perfumes.

FRENCH MARIGOLD

(TAGETES PATULA)

The French marigold is one of about 50 marigold species. It comes from Mexico and Guatemala. It became popular in France in the 1500s. French marigolds are bushy, low-growing annuals that have fern-like compound leaves and bright, compact flowers. The flowers are saucer-shaped. They can be shades of orange, red, yellow, or a combination of these colors.

HOW TO SPOT

Height: 6 to 12 inches (15 to 30 cm)
Stem: Herbaceous
Leaves: Compound leaves of toothed leaflets; up to 6 inches (15 cm) long
Flowers: Small, saucer-shaped flowers with layers of petals; 1 to 2 inches (2.5 to 5 cm) wide
Range: Native to Mexico and Guatemala
Habitat: Gardens
Bloom Period: Spring and fall

HYBRID TEA ROSE *(ROSA)*

The *Rosa* genus has more than 100 species of roses and thousands of cultivars. The most popular roses among gardeners today are hybrid tea roses. These roses have thorny stems and compound leaves. They produce a single rose per stem. The flowers can be a variety of colors, depending on the specific cultivar.

FUN FACT

All of today's hybrid tea rose cultivars can be traced back to one rose called La France that was developed in 1867. The botanical names for hybrid tea roses are created by using *Rosa* followed by their cultivar name. For example, the flower developed in 1867 is called *Rosa* "La France."

HOW TO SPOT

Height: 3 to 8 feet (0.9 to 2.4 m)
Stem: Herbaceous
Leaves: Compound leaves
Flowers: Cup-shaped blooms; up to 7 inches (18 cm) wide
Range: Worldwide, usually in temperate climates
Habitat: Gardens
Bloom Period: Summer

IMPATIENS *(IMPATIENS WALLERIANA)*

Impatiens are flowers that thrive in cool shade. They first grew in African rain forests. Today, they're one of the most popular garden plants in the United States. Impatiens have thick succulent stems. They grow into large mounds of dense leaves and colorful flowers that bloom all summer. Depending on the cultivar, impatiens can be a variety of colors, including shades of pink, red, orange, purple, and white.

HOW TO SPOT

Height: 6 to 24 inches (15 to 61 cm)

Stem: Herbaceous

Leaves: Pointed, oval leaves; up to 3 inches (7.6 cm) long

Flowers: Five-petaled flowers; 1 to 3 inches (2.5 to 7.6 cm) wide

Range: Native to Africa

Habitat: Shady gardens and containers

Bloom Period: Summer and fall

LILY OF THE VALLEY

(CONVALLARIA MAJALIS)

The lily of the valley grows in forests and is commonly planted in gardens throughout the world. In the spring, each plant sprouts two to three long leaves and an arching stem that has several white, bell-shaped flowers. The flowers have a strong, sweet scent, but the plant is poisonous if eaten.

HOW TO SPOT

Height: 6 to 12 inches (15 to 30 cm)
Stem: Herbaceous
Leaves: Two to three large, pointed, oval leaves; 5 to 10 inches (12.7 to 25 cm) long
Flowers: Arching stem of five to ten white, bell-shaped flowers; flowers are less than 1 inch (2.5 cm) long
Range: Worldwide
Habitat: Forests and gardens
Bloom Period: Spring

SPEARMINT *(MENTHA SPICATA)*

There are many plant species in the mint family, including those that grow in the wild, but spearmint is the most popular mint grown in gardens. This perennial herb spreads quickly. Its flexible stem is full of small, fragrant leaves. People can eat the leaves fresh, or they can dry the leaves and use them in cooking. In the summer, spearmints produce clusters of tiny flowers.

HOW TO SPOT

Height: 1 to 2 feet (0.3 to 0.6 m)
Stem: Herbaceous
Leaves: Pointed, oval leaves with toothed edges; 1 to 3 inches (2.5 to 7.6 cm) long
Flowers: Dense spikes of small, pinkish-white flowers; 1 to 6 inches (2.5 to 15 cm) long
Range: Europe and North America
Habitat: Gardens and moist forests
Bloom Period: Summer

FUN FACT
Spearmint leaves are used to flavor teas, candies, sauces, beverages, and syrups.

BOUGAINVILLEA

(BOUGAINVILLEA GLABRA)

The bougainvillea, sometimes called the lesser bougainvillea, is a flowering vine from South America. Lesser bougainvilleas have woody vines, green leaves, and tiny, tube-shaped flowers. The flowers are surrounded by colorful bracts (or specialized leaves) that, depending on the species, can be yellow, pink, purple, red, or white. These bracts are often mistaken for flower petals.

HOW TO SPOT

Height: 10 to 20 feet (3 to 6 m)
Stem: Woody
Leaves: Pointed, oval leaves; 3 to 6 inches (7.6 to 15 cm) long
Flowers: Clusters of tiny, tube-shaped flowers surrounded by colorful bracts
Range: South America
Habitat: Gardens and subtropical and tropical woods
Bloom Period: Spring and summer

EUROPEAN IVY *(HEDERA HELIX)*

European ivy is a fast-growing perennial vine that's native to Europe and Asia. This shrub-like plant either spreads along the ground or climbs trees and structures such as walls and buildings. European ivies have flexible stems covered with three- to five-lobed green leaves. In some places, this ivy is considered an invasive species in the wild. It can harm native plants and habitats.

FUN FACT

European ivy is also known as common ivy. It has long been a popular houseplant.

HOW TO SPOT

Height: 20 to 80 feet (6 to 24 m)
Stem: Woody
Leaves: Pointed leaves with three to five lobes; 4 inches (10 cm) long
Flowers: Umbrella-shaped clusters of small, greenish-white flowers; flowers are less than 1 inch (2.5 cm) long
Range: Native to Europe and Asia
Habitat: Deciduous forests, urban forests, and shrublands
Bloom Period: Summer and fall

GRAPE HONEYSUCKLE

(LONICERA RETICULATA)

Grape honeysuckle is a woody vine. It belongs to the honeysuckle family, a group of plants that has 180 species of shrubs and vines. Grape honeysuckle is native to North America and usually grows in moist forests and thickets. If there isn't a tree or structure nearby to climb, the plant will sometimes appear as a leafy mound or shrub. Grape honeysuckles have rounded green leaves. In the summer, these plants have clusters of yellow, tube-shaped flowers.

HOW TO SPOT

Height: 10 to 15 feet (3 to 4.6 m)
Stem: Woody
Leaves: Rounded leaves; 1.5 to 3.5 inches (3.8 to 9 cm) long
Flowers: Clusters of yellow, tube-shaped flowers with long stamens; up to 1 inch (2.5 cm) long
Fruits: Round, red berries; up to 0.5 inches (1.3 cm) long
Range: North America
Habitat: Moist forests and riverbanks
Bloom Period: Spring and summer

JAPANESE WISTERIA

(WISTERIA FLORIBUNDA)

The Japanese wisteria is known for its fragrance and abundant flowers. This climbing vine is native to Japan. People brought it to other countries as a garden plant. Today, it is often grown on fences, trellises, and buildings. In the spring, it has large, drooping clusters of pinkish-purple flowers. In some parts of the world, wisteria species are aggressive, invasive plants that crowd out native plants in the wild.

HOW TO SPOT

Height: 10 to 25 feet (3 to 7.6 m)

Stem: Woody

Leaves: Compound leaves with 15 to 19 leaflets; 1 to 1.3 feet (0.3 to 0.4 m) long

Flowers: Drooping clusters of pinkish-purple flowers; 1 to 1.5 feet (0.3 to 0.45 m) long

Range: Asia, Europe, and North America

Habitat: Forests and gardens

Bloom Period: Spring

FUN FACT

Bark from the Japanese wisteria can be used to make rope.

MORNING GLORY

(IPOMOEA PURPUREA)

Morning glory is a popular garden plant that's often grown on a trellis or wall. It's a fast-growing, climbing vine. These plants have green, heart-shaped leaves. They also have purple, trumpet-shaped flowers that open in the morning and close in the afternoon. That's why the plant's common name is morning glory.

HOW TO SPOT

Height: 6 to 10 feet (1.8 to 3 m)
Stem: Herbaceous
Leaves: Heart-shaped leaves; up to 4 inches (10 cm) long
Flowers: Purple, trumpet-shaped flowers; up to 2.5 inches (6.3 cm) wide
Range: North America, Central America, and South America
Habitat: Open forests and gardens
Bloom Period: Summer and fall

PASSION FRUIT *(PASSIFLORA EDULIS)*

Passion fruit is a climbing vine that's native to South America. It's now grown in tropical and subtropical locations around the world. Passion fruits are known for both their showy flowers and their fruits. Their large, bowl-shaped flowers have purple centers and white edges. The plant produces a deep-purple, rounded fruit known as passion fruit.

FUN FACT

Passion fruit can be eaten raw or used to make food products such as beverages, jellies, and sherbets.

HOW TO SPOT

Height: 10 to 15 feet (3 to 4.6 m)
Stem: Woody
Leaves: Three-lobed leaves with toothed edges; 3 to 8 inches (7.6 to 20 cm) long
Flowers: Bowl-shaped, purple-and-white flowers; up to 3 inches (7.6 cm) wide
Fruits: Oval-shaped, purple fruits; up to 2 inches (5 cm) wide
Range: Worldwide
Habitat: Tropical and subtropical areas
Bloom Period: Seasonal

STAR JASMINE

(TRACHELOSPERMUM JASMINOIDES)

Star jasmine is a perennial vine with fragrant, star-shaped, white flowers that bloom in the spring. It can appear as a shrub, a ground cover, or a climbing vine. Depending on its location and environment, the star jasmine's glossy, green leaves may turn red or drop off the plant in the fall.

HOW TO SPOT

Height: 3 to 6 feet (0.9 to 1.8 m)

Stem: Woody

Leaves: Oval leaves; 3.5 inches (9 cm) long

Flowers: Clusters of white, star-shaped flowers; up to 1 inch (2.5 cm) wide

Range: Asia, Europe, and North America

Habitat: Sunny gardens or containers

Bloom Period: Spring

VIRGINIA CREEPER

(PARTHENOCISSUS QUINQUEFOLIA)

As its name suggests, the Virginia creeper is a plant known for either creeping along the ground or climbing structures. Virginia creepers have small, sucker-like discs that grow along the vines and help them attach to trees and other surfaces. In the spring, Virginia creepers produce clusters of white flowers. In the fall, their green compound leaves turn shades of purple and red.

HOW TO SPOT

Height: Up to 90 feet (27 m)
Stem: Woody
Leaves: Compound leaves with four to five leaflets; up to 6 inches (15 cm) long
Flowers: Branching clusters of white flowers; 3 to 6 inches (7.6 to 15 cm) long
Range: North America
Habitat: Deciduous forests and bluffs
Bloom Period: Summer

FUN FACT

People sometimes grow Virginia creepers outside their homes. However, if allowed to run wild, these vines can damage window shutters, gutters, and even electrical wiring.

AMERICAN CRANBERRY

(VACCINIUM MACROCARPON)

The American cranberry is native to North America. Cranberries are grown for their tart fruits that can be made into juices, sauces, and other products. American cranberries grow as either vines or small shrubs, and they have small, glossy leaves. In the fall, their pink-and-white flowers become oval-shaped, red fruits called cranberries.

HOW TO SPOT

Height: 9 to 12 inches (23 to 30 cm)
Stem: Woody
Leaves: Oval leaves; less than 1 inch (2.5 cm) long
Flowers: Clusters of drooping pink-and-white flowers; less than 1 inch (2.5 cm) long
Range: North America
Habitat: Bogs, swamps, and shorelines
Bloom Period: Spring and summer

BLACK RASPBERRY

(RUBUS OCCIDENTALIS)

Black raspberry plants are known for their small, edible fruits and thorny stems. These plants have compound leaves with three to five leaflets per leaf. The leaflets also have toothed edges and fuzzy undersides. In the spring, black raspberry plants produce white flowers that eventually turn into fruits. The fruits start out red, then turn a very dark purple—nearly black—when they're ripe.

HOW TO SPOT

Height: 3 to 5 feet (0.9 to 1.5 m)

Stem: Woody

Leaves: Compound leaves with three to five leaflets; 2 to 4 inches (5 to 10 cm) long

Flowers: White flowers with five petals; up to 0.5 inches (1.3 cm) wide

Fruits: Dark-purple raspberries; 0.5 inches (1.3 cm) long

Range: North America

Habitat: Deciduous forests, roadsides, and disturbed areas

Bloom Period: Spring

BOXWOOD *(BUXUS SEMPERVIRENS)*

Boxwoods are dense evergreen shrubs that keep their small, glossy, green leaves year-round. Boxwoods have many short branches, but under certain conditions they can also look like small trees. In the spring, boxwoods produce clusters of small, yellowish-green flowers.

FUN FACT

Boxwoods are often used as hedges. People may also make topiaries or wreaths out of them. Topiaries are plants that people have shaped into art.

HOW TO SPOT

Height: 5 to 15 feet (1.5 to 4.6 m)
Stem: Woody
Leaves: Small, oval leaves; 0.5 to 1.5 inches (1.3 to 3.8 cm) long
Flowers: Small clusters of greenish-yellow flowers; flowers are less than 1 inch (2.5 cm) long
Range: Africa, Asia, Europe, and North America
Habitat: Open forests and rocky hillsides
Bloom Period: Spring

BUNCHBERRY *(CORNUS CANADENSIS)*

The bunchberry is a very small deciduous shrub. It thrives in shady forests in northern climates. It grows low to the ground and is known for its ability to spread quickly. Bunchberries have glossy, green leaves. Their flowers bloom in tiny clusters. Each cluster is surrounded by four white bracts that look like flower petals. In the fall, bunchberries have clusters of small, red berries.

HOW TO SPOT

Height: Up to 9 inches (23 cm)

Stem: Woody

Leaves: Pointed, oval leaves in clusters of four to six leaves; 1 to 2 inches (2.5 to 5 cm) long

Flowers: Clusters of tiny flowers surrounded by four white bracts; up to 1 inch (2.5 cm) wide

Fruits: Round, red berries; 0.25 inches (0.64 cm) wide

Range: Asia, Greenland, and North America

Habitat: Forests

Bloom Period: Early summer

CACAO TREE *(THEOBROMA CACAO)*

The cacao tree is also called the cocoa tree, and it's best known for being the source of chocolate. These plants have spindly branches and large, oval leaves that are green year-round. Cacao trees have clusters of tiny flowers that eventually grow into large, egg-shaped fruits called cocoa pods. Each pod contains 30 to 40 seeds known as cocoa beans.

HOW TO SPOT

Height: Up to 26 feet (8 m)
Stem: Woody
Leaves: Large, oval leaves; 15 inches (38 cm) long
Flowers: Clusters of small, pink flowers
Fruits: Yellowish-orange, oval pods; 6 to 10 inches (15 to 25 cm) long
Range: North America, Central America, and South America
Habitat: Moist forests
Bloom Period: Year-round

COCOA BEANS

The seeds from cacao trees are the most important ingredient in chocolate. People cut through cocoa pods with sharp knives to reveal clusters of wet seeds inside. Then they scrape the seeds out and dry them. Dried seeds are used to make both cocoa butter and cocoa powder, which can then be made into chocolate.

CLOUDBERRY *(RUBUS CHAMAEMORUS)*

Cloudberry plants thrive in moist soils and cool temperatures. They are native to the Arctic, where they grow in bogs and on the tundra. These low-growing plants spread across the ground and have green, leathery leaves. In the summer, the white flowers turn into cloudberries, which are yellowish-orange fruits that look a bit like raspberries.

HOW TO SPOT

Height: 8 to 12 inches (20 to 30 cm)

Stem: Woody

Leaves: Simple leaves with three to seven rounded lobes; 1.5 to 4.25 inches (3.8 to 10.7 cm) long

Flowers: White flowers with four or five rounded petals; up to 1.25 inches (3 cm) wide

Fruits: Yellow-orange, raspberry-like fruits; up to 0.75 inches (1.9 cm) wide

Range: Arctic and subarctic regions

Habitat: Boreal forests, bogs, and tundra

Bloom Period: Summer

FUN FACT

Cloudberries are a circumpolar species. This means they are found in the regions around the North Pole.

ENGLISH HOLLY *(ILEX AQUIFOLIUM)*

English holly is an evergreen plant that can appear as a shrub or be used as a hedge in gardens or fields. The English holly's glossy leaves have sharp spines along their edges and stay green throughout the year. In the fall and winter, the plant produces tiny berries that are usually red but can also be orange or yellow.

HOW TO SPOT

Height: 30 to 50 feet (9 to 15 m)
Stem: Woody
Leaves: Glossy, sharp-edged leaves; 1 to 3 inches (2.5 to 7.6 cm) long
Flowers: Small, greenish-white flowers; less than 1 inch (2.5 cm) wide
Fruits: Small, red berries; 0.25 inches (0.64 cm) wide
Range: Africa, Asia, Europe, and North America
Habitat: Forests and gardens
Bloom Period: Spring

FUN FACT

English holly's evergreen leaves and red berries have made it a popular Christmas decoration.

EUROPEAN ELDER *(SAMBUCUS NIGRA)*

European elders are shrubs with many stems. During the growing seasons, European elders are recognized by their delicate, umbrella-shaped clusters of white flowers. Later, the flowers become clusters of round, black fruits called elderberries. People use both the flowers and berries in cooking.

HOW TO SPOT

Height: 8 to 20 feet (2.4 to 6 m)
Stem: Woody
Leaves: Compound leaves of three to seven leaflets; up to 5 inches (12.7 cm) long
Flowers: Umbrella-shaped clusters of tiny, white flowers; up to 10 inches (25 cm) wide
Fruits: Clusters of black elderberries; fruits are less than 1 inch (2.5 cm) long
Range: Africa, Asia, and Europe
Habitat: Open forests and gardens
Bloom Period: Summer

FUN FACT
The European elder's bark, leaves, and raw berries are poisonous.

JAPANESE CAMELLIA

(CAMELLIA JAPONICA)

The Japanese camellia is an evergreen shrub. It's native to Japan but has become popular worldwide as a garden plant. These plants have thick, glossy leaves that are dark green. They also have clusters of round flowers. The flowers are often pruned after they first appear so that a larger single flower grows in the place of each cluster. Like other camellia species, Japanese camellia flowers can be a range of colors, including white, pink, red, yellow, and lavender.

HOW TO SPOT

Height: 7 to 12 feet (2 to 3.6 m)
Stem: Woody
Leaves: Oval, leathery leaves; 3 to 4 inches (7.6 to 10 cm) long
Flowers: Clusters of round flowers with many petals; 3 to 5 inches (7.6 to 12.7 cm) wide
Range: Worldwide
Habitat: Gardens
Bloom Period: Spring or winter, depending on the climate

FUN FACT
People sometimes call the Japanese camellia the rose of winter.

LOWBUSH BLUEBERRY

(VACCINIUM ANGUSTIFOLIUM)

The lowbush blueberry is a low-growing deciduous shrub that is both wild and cultivated. These plants are common in the northern conifer forests of North America, where they are important food sources for black bears, deer, and moose. Lowbush blueberry plants have many woody stems and green leaves with finely toothed edges. In the spring, these plants grow clusters of bell-shaped flowers that later mature into blueberries.

HOW TO SPOT

Height: 12 to 20 inches (30 to 51 cm)

Stem: Woody

Leaves: Pointed, oval leaves with finely serrated edges; 0.75 to 1.5 inches (1.9 to 3.8 cm) long

Flowers: Clusters of small, white, bell-shaped flowers; 0.25 inches (0.64 cm) long

Fruits: Round blueberries; up to 0.3 inches (0.7 cm) wide

Range: Northern North America

Habitat: Open conifer woods and fields

Bloom Period: Summer

FUN FACT

Lowbush blueberries are small and sweet, so they're often used in making jams. Another species, highbush blueberries, are typically sold whole in stores.

SAND CHERRY *(PRUNUS PUMILA)*

The sand cherry is a deciduous shrub that produces large fruits. These fruits can be reddish-purple to almost black and have one hard seed inside. Sand cherries usually grow in sandy soils in prairies, savannas, or dunes. They have shiny green leaves and produce clusters of white flowers in the spring.

HOW TO SPOT

Height: 1 to 6 feet (0.3 to 1.8 m)

Stem: Woody

Leaves: Pointed, oval leaves; 1.5 to 2.5 inches (3.8 to 6.3 cm) long

Flowers: Clusters of white flowers with five petals; 0.5 inches (1.3 cm) wide

Fruits: Round, reddish-purple to black fruits; up to 0.5 inches (1.3 cm) wide

Range: North America

Habitat: Prairies, savannas, and dunes

Bloom Period: Summer

STAGHORN SUMAC *(RHUS TYPHINA)*

The staghorn sumac is the largest of all sumac species. Although it's technically a shrub, it can often look like a small tree. Staghorn sumacs have many branches coated with layers of fine hairs. This gives the branches a soft texture similar to the velvet on young deer antlers. Staghorn sumacs have large, green, compound leaves. In the fall, these leaves turn red. Staghorn sumacs produce many spike-shaped clusters of reddish-brown fruits.

HOW TO SPOT

Height: 15 to 25 feet (4.5 to 7.6 m)
Stem: Woody
Leaves: Compound leaves of nine to 27 leaflets; up to 1.5 feet (0.45 m) long
Flowers: Pointed clusters of tiny, greenish-yellow flowers; up to 8 inches (20 cm) long
Fruits: Pointed clusters of red, berry-like fruits; up to 8 inches (20 cm) long
Range: North America
Habitat: Forests, stream banks, and roadsides
Bloom Period: Summer

FUN FACT

Staghorn sumac fruits can be ground into powders and used as seasonings.

TEA PLANT *(CAMELLIA SINENSIS)*

The most widely grown camellia species in the world is the tea plant. These plants are slow-growing, dense evergreen shrubs with dark leaves and fragrant white flowers. Tea plants' leaves are harvested and dried to make tea, a drink that's consumed all over the world. The tea plant is also grown as a decorative plant or hedge.

HOW TO SPOT

Height: 6 to 15 feet (1.8 to 4.6 m)
Stem: Woody
Leaves: Oval-shaped leaves with serrated edges; 3 to 6 inches (7.6 to 15 cm) long
Flowers: White flowers; 1 to 3 inches (2.5 to 7.6 cm) wide
Range: Africa, Asia, and South America
Habitat: Cultivated fields and gardens
Bloom Period: Fall and winter

BLACK AND GREEN TEA

Black tea and green tea are both made from tea plant leaves. For green tea, the leaves are picked and then steamed to prevent them from losing their green color. This process also gives green tea a different flavor than black tea. To make black tea, the leaves are picked and rolled. Then they are exposed to air so they darken.

TRUE INDIGO *(INDIGOFERA TINCTORIA)*

True indigo is a tropical shrub. It was once widely used to create a dark-blue dye called indigo. The plant itself is not blue at all. It has compound leaves of several green leaflets. In the summer, these plants have clusters of pink or violet flowers. After blooming, true indigo produces seed pods that can be up to 2 inches (5 cm) long.

HOW TO SPOT

Height: 2 to 3 feet (0.6 to 0.9 m)

Stem: Woody

Leaves: Compound leaves with three to seven leaflet pairs

Flowers: Spike-like clusters of small pink or violet flowers

Range: Asia

Habitat: Tropical or subtropical fields or gardens

Bloom Period: Summer

FUN FACT

Making dye from the true indigo plant is a complicated process with several steps. Indigo leaves must undergo fermentation (a chemical change) in order to produce the dye's blue color. Most indigo-colored dye used today is not made from plants.

WILD BLACK CURRANT

(RIBES AMERICANUM)

There are more than 100 species of currants. This is a family of shrubs that produces round berries—called currants—that are used in jams, jellies, and flavorings. Wild black currants grow in cool, moist habitats in the northern parts of North America. Wild black currants have smooth, thornless stems and coarse, lobed leaves. Currants grow in clusters. The fruits turn black when ripe.

HOW TO SPOT

Height: 2 to 5 feet (0.6 to 1.5 m)

Stem: Woody

Leaves: Wide leaves with three to five lobes and toothed edges; 1 to 2 inches (2.5 to 5 cm) long

Flowers: Dangling clusters of six to 20 pale-yellow, bell-shaped flowers; flowers are 0.5 inches (1.3 cm) long

Fruits: Smooth, round, black berries; up to 0.3 inches (0.8 cm) wide

Range: North America

Habitat: Open forests, swamps, and stream banks

Bloom Period: Spring and summer

WILD STRAWBERRY

(FRAGARIA VESCA)

The wild strawberry is one of many strawberry species, and it can be found growing in the wild or in gardens. Wild strawberries have horizontal stems that help these plants spread along the ground. Wild strawberries are everbearing, which means they continue to produce flowers and fruits throughout the growing season and will often have fruits and flowers on them at the same time.

HOW TO SPOT

Height: 4 to 8 inches (10 to 20 cm)
Stem: Herbaceous
Leaves: Compound leaves with three toothed leaflets; up to 1 inch (2.5 cm) long
Flowers: Small, white flowers with five petals and yellow centers; 0.5 inches (1.3 cm) wide
Fruits: Bright-red strawberries; 0.5 inches (1.3 cm) long
Range: Asia, Europe, and North America
Habitat: Open forests and gardens
Bloom Period: Spring and summer

FUN FACT
Since wild strawberries are bright red and small, they're often grown in gardens or containers for decoration rather than for eating.

COMMON BLADDERWORT

(UTRICULARIA VULGARIS)

Common bladderworts don't have any roots. Instead, these carnivorous plants float on the water's surface in freshwater habitats, such as lakes, ponds, and wetlands. Common bladderworts have many stems and needle-like leaves. These plants have small sacs called bladders that are used to catch tiny, aquatic organisms for food.

HOW TO SPOT

Height: 1 to 3 feet (0.3 to 0.9 m)
Stem: Herbaceous
Leaves: Many needle-like leaves along multibranched stems; 0.75 to 2 inches (1.9 to 5 cm) long
Flowers: Small clusters of yellow flowers; 0.5 to 0.75 inches (1.3 to 1.9 cm) wide
Range: Throughout the northern hemisphere
Habitat: Lakes, wetlands, ponds, and streams
Bloom Period: Summer

FUN FACT

The tiny sacs on common bladderworts have hairs. When small organisms brush against these hairs, the sacs spring open and suck in the organisms.

COMMON SUNDEW

(DROSERA ROTUNDIFOLIA)

There are more than 150 species of sundews, and each of them is carnivorous. The term *sundew* comes from the drops of nectar the plants use to attract insects. Sundew plants look like they're covered with dew. Low-growing common sundews have round, paddle-shaped leaves that are covered with red hairs. Insects get stuck when they land on the sticky substance that coats the common sundews' leaves.

HOW TO SPOT

Height: 2 to 10 inches (5 to 25 cm)

Stem: Herbaceous

Leaves: Round, sticky leaves with red hairs; 0.75 inches (1.9 cm) wide

Flowers: Small clusters of white flowers on long, leafless stems; 0.25 inches (0.64 cm) wide

Range: Asia, Europe, and North America

Habitat: Bogs and wetlands

Bloom Period: Summer

CARNIVOROUS PLANTS

Most plants get their nutrients through the soil and photosynthesis. Carnivorous plants get some or all of their nutrients from consuming animals, such as insects or even frogs. These plants tend to attract prey with nectar. Then they trap the prey with a sticky or slippery substance that makes it impossible for the prey to escape. Some plants, like Venus flytraps, can close on prey, trapping them inside.

VENUS FLYTRAP *(DIONAEA MUSCIPULA)*

Venus flytraps are endangered carnivorous plants that get most of their necessary nutrients from consuming insects. At the end of each leaf, the Venus flytrap has a clam-shaped growth with spines along the edges and trigger hairs inside. If an insect lands on the plant and touches two trigger hairs, the trap quickly closes. The plant then produces enzymes that break down and digest the insect.

FUN FACT

Carnivorous plants such as the Venus flytrap might look dangerous, but they can't actually harm humans.

HOW TO SPOT

Height: 6 to 12 inches (15 to 30 cm)
Stem: Herbaceous
Leaves: Rosettes of up to eight blade-shaped leaves with hinged traps on the ends; 2 to 5 inches (5 to 12.7 cm) long
Flowers: Cluster of white, cup-shaped flowers on long stems; less than 1 inch (2.5 cm) long
Range: North America
Habitat: Marshes, wet grasslands, and savannas
Bloom Period: Summer

YELLOW PITCHER PLANT

(SARRACENIA FLAVA)

Yellow pitcher plants lure in nearby insects with nectar. Then the plants trap the insects. These plants have yellowish-green leaves that grow straight from the ground and look like trumpets. These are called pitchers. The insides of the pitchers are coated with slippery, ultrafine hairs. Once insects are inside, they can't escape.

HOW TO SPOT

Height: 1.5 to 3 feet (0.45 to 0.9 m)

Stem: None

Leaves: Tall, yellowish-green, trumpet-shaped leaves with horizontal lids; 1.6 to 3 feet (0.48 to 0.9 m) tall

Flowers: Yellow flowers with five petals; up to 2 inches (5 cm) wide

Range: North America

Habitat: Sandy bogs and savannas

Bloom Period: Spring

BIRD'S-NEST FERN *(ASPLENIUM NIDUS)*

Bird's-nest ferns are tropical evergreen plants with large, leathery leaves. The leaves grow in rosette arrangements and can be up to 5 feet (1.5 m) long. When inner fronds die, they turn brown and curl up into the center of the plant, resembling a bird's nest.

HOW TO SPOT

Height: 3 to 5 feet (0.9 to 1.5 m)
Stem: Herbaceous
Leaves: Smooth, wavy-edged leaves that grow in rosettes; 4 to 5 feet (1.2 to 1.5 m) long
Range: Southeast Asia, Australia, Hawaii, Madagascar, North America, and Polynesia
Habitat: Rain forests and gardens

WHAT ARE FERNS?

Ferns are plants that don't have flowers or seeds. Instead, they reproduce through cells called spores. Before they are released, spores are contained in capsules. These usually appear as tiny bumps on the undersides of ferns' leaves.

LADY FERN *(ATHYRIUM FILIX-FEMINA)*

Lady ferns are green plants with tall, lacy leaves called fronds that sprout from the ground, usually in upright clumps. The undersides of the leaves are covered in tiny dots called spores that lady ferns use to reproduce. Lady ferns are perennial, so their leaves drop in the fall. New ones grow in the spring.

HOW TO SPOT

Height: 2 to 5 feet (0.6 to 1.5 m)
Stem: Herbaceous
Leaves: Lacy fronds; up to 1 foot (0.3 m) wide and 3 feet (0.9 m) long
Range: North America
Habitat: Moist forests, meadows, and swamps

FUN FACT

Many fern species do well in low light, which is one of the reasons they're popular houseplants.

OSTRICH FERN

(MATTEUCCIA STRUTHIOPTERIS)

With their long, feather-like fronds, it's easy to see how ostrich ferns got their name. In the spring, ostrich ferns first appear as small, curled sprouts. They gradually grow and uncurl into large, green fronds. In midsummer, the ostrich fern produces at least one woody, dark-brown frond in its center. This frond contains the spores that allow the fern to reproduce.

HOW TO SPOT

Height: 3 to 6 feet (0.9 to 1.8 m)
Stem: Herbaceous
Leaves: Feather-like fronds; up to 4 feet (1.2 m) long
Range: Eastern Asia, Europe, and North America
Habitat: Moist, shady forests

FUN FACT

The ostrich fern's first sprouts are called fiddleheads. These are edible, but they must be washed and cooked very carefully in order to be eaten safely.

ROYAL FERN *(OSMUNDA REGALIS)*

Since royal ferns have double compound leaves instead of feathery fronds, it's easy to mistake them for shrubs rather than ferns. Royal ferns have spores that look like flower clusters. These grow on tassel-like stalks. Like other fern species, royal ferns thrive in cool, moist environments and are often found in shaded areas near water.

HOW TO SPOT

Height: 2 to 3 feet (0.6 to 0.9 m)

Stem: Herbaceous

Leaves: Double compound leaves of several leaflets; up to 3 feet (0.9 m) long

Range: North America

Habitat: Swamps, wet forests, stream banks, and bluffs

BONFIRE MOSS

(FUNARIA HYGROMETRICA)

Bonfire moss can grow in many places with moist soil, but it's commonly found in areas that have been recently burned. Like all mosses, the stems and leaves of bonfire mosses are very small. Up close, the leaves look like tiny, green threads with beads on the ends. Those beads are spore capsules, which bonfire mosses use to reproduce.

HOW TO SPOT

Height: 0.15 to 0.4 inches (0.38 to 1 cm)

Stem: Herbaceous

Leaves: Thread-like leaves with spore capsules on the ends; 0.07 to 0.1 inches (0.17 to 0.25 cm) long

Range: Asia, Australia, Europe, and North America

Habitat: Fields, forests, roadsides, and stream banks

FUN FACT

Another common name for bonfire moss is Cinderella moss.

COMMON HAIRCAP MOSS

(POLYTRICHUM COMMUNE)

The common haircap moss is a dark-green moss species that grows in moist, coniferous forests. It's a low-growing plant that spreads along the ground, forming a green, carpet-like growth. The moss's stems look like tiny bottlebrushes because they're covered in short, needle-like leaves.

HOW TO SPOT

Height: 1.5 to 6 inches (4 to 15 cm)
Stem: Herbaceous
Leaves: Tiny, spine-like leaves; 0.25 to 0.4 inches (0.6 to 1 cm) long
Range: Asia, Australia, Europe, and North America
Habitat: Moist, coniferous forests

WHAT ARE MOSSES?

Mosses are tiny plants that can look like green carpets growing across forest floors or over rocks. Mosses are land plants that reproduce using spores instead of seeds. They don't have roots, but they do have stems and leaves. There are at least 12,000 moss species.

PINCUSHION MOSS

(LEUCOBRYUM GLAUCUM)

Pincushion moss is an evergreen moss that grows throughout North America and Europe. As an evergreen moss, it remains green year-round. It resembles the object its name suggests: a pincushion. The moss grows in a dense, green mound in shady areas of forests, bluffs, and even city parks. Pincushion mosses are made up of tiny stems and blade-shaped leaves. The moss ranges in color from gray-green to bright yellowish green.

HOW TO SPOT

Height: 0.5 to 5 inches (1.3 to 12.7 cm)
Stem: Herbaceous
Leaves: Tiny, blade-shaped leaves; 0.1 to 0.3 inches (0.25 to 0.76 cm) long
Range: Europe and North America
Habitat: Rocky forests, wooded bluffs, roadsides, and urban parks

SPLENDID FEATHER MOSS

(HYLOCOMIUM SPLENDENS)

The splendid feather moss is a common moss species in the northern parts of the northern hemisphere—it even grows in the Arctic. Splendid feather mosses look like ferns because their branches and tiny leaves appear frond- or feather-like. These plants grow in large patches and can form dense mats on the ground.

FUN FACT

In the United Kingdom, splendid feather moss is called glittering wood moss.

HOW TO SPOT

Height: 4 to 6 inches (10 to 15 cm)

Stem: Herbaceous

Leaves: Small frond- or feather-like leaves; 0.07 to 0.11 inches (0.17 to 0.27 cm) long

Range: Africa, Asia, Australia, Europe, New Zealand, North America, and the Caribbean

Habitat: Forests and tundra

FLOATING CRYSTALWORT

(RICCIA FLUITANS)

The floating crystalwort is a type of liverwort. Instead of stems or leaves, floating crystalworts are made up of plant tissues called thalli. The thalli look like green stems with many Y-shaped branches. Floating crystalworts can form large colonies that float in freshwater habitats with still water, such as ponds and lakes. They may also survive underwater. Floating crystalworts don't produce flowers or seeds.

HOW TO SPOT

Stem: None
Leaves: None
Range: Europe, Asia, and North America
Habitat: Ponds, lakes, swamps, and ditches

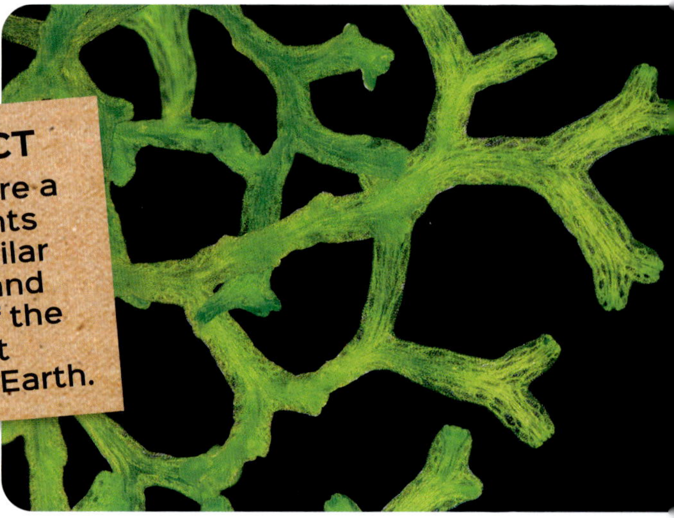

FUN FACT

Liverworts are a class of plants that are similar to mosses and are some of the oldest plant species on Earth.

UMBRELLA LIVERWORT

(MARCHANTIA POLYMORPHA)

Umbrella liverworts are commonly found clinging to wet rocks or forming large, green mats on the ground. Like other liverworts, these plants don't have stems or leaves. Instead, umbrella liverworts are made up of rosette-shaped thalli. Sometimes umbrella liverworts sprout growths that look like tiny umbrellas or palm trees. These growths are how liverworts reproduce.

HOW TO SPOT

Stem: None

Leaves: None

Range: Worldwide, from the Arctic to tropical climates

Habitat: Freshwater habitats and on wet rocks

GLOSSARY

basal
Leaves that grow from the base of a plant, often growing in a circle.

brackish
Water that is slightly salty, such as when seawater and river water mix.

compound leaf
A leaf that has many different leaflets attached to one stem.

conifer
A tree with cones and needle-like leaves; often an evergreen.

cultivar
A specific variety of plant developed by people.

deciduous
Trees that drop their leaves at least once a year, often in fall or winter.

disturbed area
A place where the topsoil has been removed or the natural habitat has been dramatically changed.

invasive
A species that is introduced to a new area and causes damage to the habitat.

leaflet
A smaller leaf that's a part of a larger compound leaf.

perennial
A plant that lives for several years.

photosynthesis
The process used by plants to convert sunlight into usable energy.

rosette
A cluster of leaves or petals that grow in a circle.

serrated
Having a jagged, saw-like edge.

spikelet
One of the small, spike-shaped flowers that make up a larger spike-shaped flower cluster.

stamen
The male, pollen-producing part of a flower.

temperate climate
A moderate climate that doesn't have temperature extremes.

TO LEARN MORE

FURTHER READINGS

Debbink, Andrea. *Trees*. Abdo, 2021.

Jose, Sarah. *Trees, Leaves, Flowers & Seeds: A Visual Encyclopedia of the Plant Kingdom*. DK, 2019.

Romero, Libby. *Wildflowers*. National Geographic, 2018.

ONLINE RESOURCES

Booklinks
NONFICTION NETWORK
FREE! ONLINE NONFICTION RESOURCES

To learn more about flowers and plants, please visit **abdobooklinks.com** or scan this QR code. These links are routinely monitored and updated to provide the most current information available.

PHOTO CREDITS

Cover Photos: iStockphoto, front (aloe vera), front (wisteria), front (cloudberries), front (sacred lotus), front (wild strawberries), back (purple coneflower), back (passion fruit); Shutterstock Images, front (bread wheat), back (black-eyed Susan); Valentyn Volkov/iStockphoto, front (chicory); Wulan Rohmawati/Shutterstock Images, front (white water lily); Nedim Bajramovic/Shutterstock Images, front (common houseleek); Deanna Oliva Kelly/Shutterstock Images, front (Venus flytrap)

Interior Photos: iStockphoto, 1 (black-eyed Susan), 1 (common lilac), 5 (bottom right), 8, 9 (bottom), 13, 14 (left), 17 (bottom), 19, 22 (left), 29 (bottom), 30, 33, 34, 40 (top), 40 (bottom), 41, 44, 45 (right), 46 (top), 52, 53 (top), 57 (top), 60 (bottom), 63 (bottom), 67 (top), 67 (bottom), 68 (top), 69, 73, 76 (top), 76 (bottom), 77, 78 (top), 81 (bottom), 82 (left), 82 (right), 84, 85 (top), 86, 90, 92 (top), 94 (top), 99 (bottom), 106 (bottom), 112 (American cranberry); Shutterstock Images, 1 (common mullein), 4 (right), 5 (top left), 5 (bottom left), 6, 7, 10, 11, 20 (top), 23, 24 (top), 26 (left), 27 (bottom), 35 (bottom), 39 (top), 42 (bottom), 43, 45 (left), 47 (bottom), 54 (top), 57 (bottom), 61 (top), 61 (bottom), 62, 64, 65 (top), 65 (bottom), 71, 74 (top), 74 (bottom), 75 (right), 78 (bottom), 83 (top), 91, 96, 97 (top), 98, 101 (bottom), 102 (top), 103, 112 (morning glory), 112 (yellow pitcher plant); Le Do/Shutterstock Images, 1 (lily of the valley), 68 (bottom); Mark Brandon/Shutterstock Images, 1 (sky plant), 32; Avalon Studio/iStockphoto, 4 (left), 5 (top right), 9 (top), 49; Nick Kurzenko/iStockphoto, 4 (middle), 50 (top); Iurii Garmash/iStockphoto, 5 (top middle), 70 (top); Alvin E. Staffan/Science Source, 6–7 (top), 27 (top); Lotus Images/Shutterstock Images, 6–7 (bottom), 26 (right), 112 (sacred lotus); Hariani Rahayu/Shutterstock Images, 12; Andrea Meling/iStockphoto, 14 (right); Peter Turner Photography/Shutterstock Images, 15; Bob Gibbons/Alamy, 16; Floral Images/Alamy, 17 (top); Ian Redding/iStockphoto, 18 (left); Victoria Tucholka/Shutterstock Images, 18 (right); Ruki Media/Shutterstock Images, 20 (bottom); Holly Guerrio/Shutterstock Images, 21; James Elkington/iStockphoto, 22 (right); Gabriele Grassl/iStockphoto, 24 (bottom); Esa Hiltula/iStockphoto, 25; Holly Guerrio/iStockphoto, 28 (top); Gerry Bishop/Shutterstock Images,

28 (bottom); Christian Ader/iStockphoto, 29 (top); Jaroslava V./Shutterstock Images, 31 (top); Christian Vinces/Shutterstock Images, 31 (bottom); Dominic Gentilcore PhD/Shutterstock Images, 35 (top); N. Nehring/iStockphoto, 36 (top); Bozhena Melnyk/Shutterstock Images, 36 (bottom); Gary Kavanagh/iStockphoto, 37; Nedim Bajramovic/Shutterstock Images, 38; Svetlana Klaise/Shutterstock Images, 39 (bottom); Milan Vachal/Shutterstock Images, 42 (top); Ksenia Lada/Shutterstock Images, 46 (bottom); Martin Fowler/Shutterstock Images, 47 (top); Waldemar Seehagen/iStockphoto, 48 (top); Artesia Wells/iStockphoto, 48 (bottom); SHS Photography/iStockphoto, 50 (bottom); Martin Wahlborg/iStockphoto, 51; Meindert van der Haven/iStockphoto, 53 (bottom); Sergey Kohl/Shutterstock Images, 54 (bottom); Picture This Images/Shutterstock Images, 55; Oscar Cadejo/iStockphoto, 56; Nancy J. Ondra/Shutterstock Images, 58; Mark Baldwin/Shutterstock Images, 59; Viktor Kitaykin/iStockphoto, 60 (top); Andrei Sitnikov/iStockphoto, 63 (top); Jane McIlroy/Shutterstock Images, 66; Khlong Wang Chao/iStockphoto, 70 (bottom); Steffen Hauser/botanikfoto/Alamy, 72; Picture Partners/Shutterstock Images, 75 (left); Vadym Zaitsev/Shutterstock Images, 79; Alexander Denisenko/iStockphoto, 80; Yves Dery/iStockphoto, 81 (top); Grigorii Pisotckii/iStockphoto, 83 (bottom); Ralf Blechschmidt/iStockphoto, 85 (bottom); Gail Jankus/Science Source, 87 (top); Nadya So/iStockphoto, 87 (bottom); Jonathan O'Rourke/Alamy, 88; Zeljko VranjkovicShutterstock Images, 89; Paul Bein/iStockphoto, 92 (bottom); Kuttelvaserova Stuchelova/Shutterstock Images, 93; Liudmyla Liudmyla/iStockphoto, 94 (bottom); Miroslav Hlavko/Shutterstock Images, 95; Gardens by Design/Shutterstock Images, 97 (bottom); Przemyslaw Muszynsk/Shutterstock Images, 99 (top), 107 (top); Manfred Ruckszio/Shutterstock Images, 100; Mark Heighes/Shutterstock Images, 101 (top); Henri Koskinen/Shutterstock Images, 102 (bottom); Ihor Hvozdetskyi/Shutterstock Images, 104; Duncan Shaw/Science Source, 105; Chonlasub Woravichan/Shutterstock Images, 106 (top); Ian Redding/Shutterstock Images, 107 (bottom)

ABDOBOOKS.COM
Published by Abdo Publishing, a division of ABDO, PO Box 398166, Minneapolis, Minnesota 55439.

102021
012022

THIS BOOK CONTAINS
RECYCLED MATERIALS

Editor: Alyssa Sorenson
Series Designer: Colleen McLaren
Content Consultant: Sarah Chamberlain, MS, Curator, The Pennsylvania State University Herbarium

Library of Congress Control Number: 2021941714
Publisher's Cataloging-in-Publication Data
Names: Debbink, Andrea, author.
Title: Flowers and plants / by Andrea Debbink
Description: Minneapolis, Minnesota : Abdo Publishing, 2022 | Series: Field guides | Includes online resources and index.
Identifiers: ISBN 9781532196959 (lib. bdg.) | ISBN 9781098218768 (ebook)
Subjects: LCSH: Flowers--Juvenile literature. | Plants--Juvenile literature. | Vegetation--Juvenile literature. | Field guides--Juvenile literature.
Classification: DDC 582--dc23